A Peace Corps Martyr

The Story of Nancy Coutu

A Peace Corps Martyr

The Story of Nancy Coutu

by

Connie Coutu

Table of Contents

"Mom, it's a fashion statement. I'm a University of New Hampshire Wildlife Graduate!"

Endorsements

"Nancy is an amazing person-so simply selfless, always cheerful, always giving. I am thankful for every day I spent with her.
—Joe Shaeffer
Returned Peace Corps Volunteer
Andriamanero, Madagascar

Students come and go, but after 16 years of teaching, there are few that I will always remember. Nancy was one of those special students who make teaching a delight. Nancy had an exceptional way with people and her enjoyment of life was contagious. It was sometime during her senior year that Nancy asked for a letter of recommendation to support her application to the Peace Corps. While filling out the questionnaire, I realized that Nancy was making a hard choice, but one that seemed right for her. She was the right person to take on such an adventure. Some time after she arrived in Madagascar, I received a Christmas card from her. In it, she described some of the exciting times that she had, and her plans to work with the people in the small village of Bereketa. She was having the time of her life. This book describes some of those adventures and gives the reader a glimpse of who Nancy was, a very special person.

—John A. Litvaitis
Professor of Wildlife Ecology
Department of Natural Resources
University of New Hampshire

"The Madagascar Government recognized something that we knew all along-that Nancy was a lady. Read to discover why they called her "Lady Nancy". It is a story of a courageous young American that you will not soon forget."
—State Representative Loren Jean
Vice-Chairman of the Judiciary

Acknowledgements

I wish to thank my whole family, special friends, Peace Corps Volunteers and their parents and most of the villagers of Madagascar.

Nancy Coutu

Introduction

I'm sorry I only know Nancy Coutu from her diary and her letters. As a reader, on all too rare occasions you encounter a person whose words and deeds touch your soul. Nancy Coutu is that kind of person.

She's not trying to impress you. In her writing there's much unvarnished honesty, a willingness to examine and confront herself, to speak truths, to wrestle with her own desires.

Nancy Coutu's letters and diary from her Peace Corps posting in Madagascar are an unforgettable portrait of a young woman who represents the best of our American instincts and character. She is the kind of person we would want as a friend, a co-worker, or a wife.

She is forthright, honest, engaged, committed, energetic, and self-examining. Her words are at turns entertaining, moving, and enlightening.

She writes early in her stay:

Ranohira, the "big tourist" town. I laughed long and hard. I thought, "If this is the big tourist town what the heck am I living in, an ant hill?"

The town was probably a twentieth the size of Hudson, New Hampshire. It was quite civilized though, with a couple hotels, a school, small and big houses. But then, we drove 20 km. down a dirt road on the edge of the beautiful mountains of Isalo. We passed no one, not any villages at all. We arrived at a small village with about 13 huts, small ones. Many people came out; adults and children...about 50 people. The headman wore a striped shirt ripped down the front, ripped on the sleeve. The other people's clothes were the same: ripped dresses, pants. The children had dirty faces and messy, braided hair. I looked around and as I stood by Joe who was very scared I said, "No crap, Joe, we're in the Peace Corps!"

She embraces the exotic:

I have the biggest cockroach I've ever seen in my life! He's in my hut now! It's the size of a small mouse and it just flew at me 'cause the candle is next to me! He has a tusk coming out of his head!

So far I've learned how to mandesa (piler rice), and mehola rice (get the husks and rocks out), I learned how to plant peanuts, I know how to make "mofo gasy" (rice bread) and godro godro mofo gasy (made with bananas and as good as banana bread). It's amazing, Dan; you don't need flour to make bread. The dry rice is put in water to soak for about five minutes, and then the water is drained out. After pilering it, sifting it, and pilering the stuff again that didn't sift, it's like flour.

And soon she notes, "I have to admit I'm incredibly happy here."

She writes to her sister:

Kids don't fight here, Denise. There's no maliciousness…people just take care of each other. The people, the family, I live with, are constantly giving me food and helping me work on my hut, (mudding two rooms and painting).

But Nancy Coutu's time in Madagascar is not just an exotic working idyll and journey of self-discovery. It's also a tragedy. Perhaps it was a tragedy foreshadowed by her being suddenly stabbed with a needle when walking down a city street, or returning to her village and finding her hut pilfered, her possessions stolen. Perhaps her death was the fate that can effect audacious young women alone in any place in the world at the hands of malicious thugs.

She writes: Sometimes I feel at one with the villagers, and feel like they accept me and take me at face value. Yet, sometimes I feel like I'm being laughed at, like they just want me here to get what they can from me.

She is left alone and unprotected by the Peace Corps, without companion or radio, and forced to rely upon her, usually, own good instincts:

Narie (a villager) said he loves me and I tried to explain the difference between like a lot and love, but he said he knows the difference and he's liked me for 4 months watching me bike in, and he's sure he loves me.

Her transportation is by bicycle along deserted roads and it is one early morning, near the end of her posting, on a long distance ride to beat the heat of the day that leads her to her fatal encounter with men ready to ambush her.

Politically, the lesson of this book is that due care need be taken to protect the best of our young men and women placed potentially in harm's way. They should at least work in pairs, be equipped with communication, and cognizant of the threats that they may face.

But this book is not about lessons. It's about the life and spirit of Nancy Coutu, her adventures, her keen eye, her sense of humor, and her honesty.

Read this book, as you may read the Diary of Anne Franck, not as a document of sorrow, but as an affirmation of life, as a window into the heart and mind of a sensitive, special person. What a loss. What a life.

Roy Morrison, editor
Warner, NH
January 2006

Nancy and the village children of Bereketa

The South

One

The Call

April 9, 1996

It was 5:25 p.m. The telephone rang.

"Mrs. Coutu?"

"Yes."

"Mrs. Constance Coutu?"

"Yes, this is Connie Coutu."

"Mrs. Coutu, this is Mark Gearon, Director of the Peace Corps in Washington D.C."

"Oh, no!" I sobbed and I sank into my chair. I knew! All day long I knew something was wrong, very wrong!

"Mrs. Coutu, I regret to inform you that your daughter Nancy is dead."

A knife went through my heart and cut a hole as large as the Grand Canyon.

"No, Oh God! No! Doris, Nancy is dead. How-? Why-? How did it happen?" I blurted out with a river of tears.

"It appears that she was the victim of foul play," he said.

"What do you mean, foul play? (I could not think—didn't want to think what foul play meant.) Was it that amoebae that got into her body?"

"Mrs. Coutu, it appears she was the victim of foul play."

"Was it some disease that she got. Oh God! How could this happen?"

"Mrs. Coutu, it appears Nancy was murdered," the cruel words rang out and poisoned my ear.

"No, oh, no! Who could have killed such a beautiful person?" I wailed. "How did it happen?"

"We don't know yet. We can't tell you much yet. The communication from Madagascar is so poor that it takes a long time for a message to get to us. Mrs. Coutu, I can't tell you how sorry we are. Nancy is a great loss to us also, for she was an outstanding volunteer and a great friend to all who knew her."

"What will happen now? This is not the way she is supposed to come home!! Oh. God!! How? Who? How could anyone kill such an incredible person?"

Mark responded, "I know. It is beyond understanding, Mrs. Coutu."

Nancy came home after 7 days, not with hugs and kisses the way she was supposed to, but only with her body in a coffin. There were family gatherings, tears and more tears. The funeral took place.

Her belongings came home, too. While she was alive the family was always asking what she needed, what we could send her. The clothes that came back told the truth. There were blouses and skirts that were almost completely faded. Her pajamas, which had 4 patches on them, were so thin that one could have read a book through them. I guess she had decided to live like the Malagasy villagers.

Nancy's journal was among these "treasures". As I read it, I remembered that Nancy had told me that she intended to write a book when she got home. Immediately, I felt compelled to do it for her. Here is Nancy's gift to you. Enjoy.

Two

Expectations

Excitement filled Nancy as she launched her new humanitarian career. She had gone through years of, "Should I or shouldn't I?" She bounced her desires off the six members of the immediate family, off relatives and close friends. In spite of our unanimous, "No's", she just had to follow her heart and filled out the necessary papers to become a Peace Corps Volunteer.

I remember sitting with her to fill out her will–a Peace Corps requirement.

"Mom, no one wants to do this with me. I don't know what the big deal is. We all have to die sometime."

"I'll do this with you but we better not have to use it."

We also talked about what we wanted for funerals while completing this task.

Within a few weeks she was accepted and was on her way to

orientation. Nancy learns, among many other things, that she'll be on her own in her village, 15 km from other volunteers.
— Connie Coutu

Peace Corps training group in Madagascar.
Nancy is center bottom. Traditionally, in family photos,
Nancy was always put in the center-front because she was
youngest of five children. This habit took.

August 21, 1994

Here I am at the orientation session for Peace Corps in the Barclay Hotel in Philadelphia (quite ritzy!!) There are twenty-two of us, and it's not just environmental volunteers. It's also English teachers. There are two married couples (early sixties), and the rest in our early or late twenties, probably an almost even number of men and women.

August 24, 1994

Well, I fell asleep writing above. Twenty-two of us are in the group. One girl decided it wasn't for her. We're in Heathrow Airport on a thirteen-hour layover. Donna's meeting me soon, so that we can spend the day together. I'm really psyched to get to Madagascar.

It's been exciting to meet everyone, but I find myself getting upset because I'm making such an effort to become friends with everyone. I seem to feel the need to be accepted. There's really no reason for it because we all are getting along fine. I'm not feeling as strong about myself as usual though. It's probably just because I'm going through so many changes at once.

I find myself comparing myself to others in the group and feeling a desire to possess the traits I like about each of them: Chris's introspection, Bruce's "tough if you don't like me attitude," Michelle's healthiness and confidence, Linda's carefree, but quiet style. I guess I don't normally question myself so much. I'm so rarely surrounded by people with such inviting traits. I think I'm starting to realize that everyone in the group likes me, just like I like everyone in the group.

I didn't plan to talk about that. I wanted to write my expectations of Madagascar, to see how much I learn from here on in. Anyhow, I just spent the day with big sister, Donna, in London and I seemed to regain my confidence by being with someone who knows who I am. I realized, with her input, that I have no reason to feel a need to compare myself to others. I'm a sweetheart, too. I had a nice day with her, although I was beat. She'd like to meet in Europe next year, possibly in France for Easter, for a vacation. That'd be fun. So, on to my main message: what my expectations of Madagascar are.

I expect to live in a hut in a heavily forested area, but with a large opening for the village, but not a very big village. I don't expect to have electricity or running water. I'm hoping it will be fairly mountainous (not only to get use out of the warm clothes I brought, but also to get in some good hiking). I don't know if I'll get that though... no biggie if I don't.

I had expected to be with one other P.C. volunteer, and within 20-30 km of others, but at orientation I learned that we will probably be only one P.C.V. (Peace Corps Volunteer) on a site and we'll be about 15 km from other volunteers. I guess that news disappointed me some, but I'm sure I'll grow from whatever experience I'm in. Being alone may be tougher though. Yet being with one other person may not allow me to rely totally on myself, so who knows which would be better.

I don't expect to be very close to a market... I picture myself doing a long bike ride every other day for food. I also hope to have a garden. I'll probably lose weight since I won't be able to have dairy products much with no refrigeration... life, without cheese, yogurt, milk, and ice cream. Everyday will be different, but probably healthier. I will most likely get sick now and then from different foods, bad water, bugs, etc., but I'll be careful enough to keep it to a minimum. I picture the cities with more sturdy houses than my grass or wood hut. I also picture them bigger than my one room hut (with no bathroom of course, only an outhouse in the village). They're made of stone or clay and jam-packed together. I picture biking to a city on rare occasions to go to a big market.

I'm not exactly sure what to expect from my job. I also really don't know how to picture the people, or how they'll react to us. Taking a stab at it, I feel that the job will entail:
- Working to improve management plans for protected forests
- Working with the Malagasy rangers to teach them these plans
- Now and then, walking the protected areas to see that they're not being abused
- Reporting it to the Malagasy rangers if they are
- Communicating with the natives (excuse me...host country nationals), to get an understanding of their thoughts about their life style
- Working with the host nationals to start new less harmful ways to feed their families

That last reason is one I have a problem with. How do we tell people that what they're doing is harmful to them and get them to listen to other ways of doing things when they have been living this way for centuries?

I feel sad that nothing has been done sooner. Part of me feels that it's just too late to make a difference. But yet, it can't be too late because, if it's not stopped, then life will all be extinct, the trees will be gone and humans will also die. So I must feel that we can, at least, make a difference and make a change for the better if we get started now.

I hear the people are very friendly, and love company (respectful company, of course). By what Monsieur Jocelyn, the host national, said, they like people who show respect, who value women and who are open to new people. I'll soon see if that's on the money.

Well, I'm falling asleep as I write this. I'm on the plane to South Africa (Johannesburg). In order not to mess up my new book, I'm going to sleep. Good night.

August 26, 1994

Well, it's my second night in Madagascar. The transition has been very gradual...not abrupt at all, as I thought it would be. We took a bus to our training area. We went through Antananarivo, better known as Tana. This is the capital city of Madagascar. I saw no whites; the earth and huts were mud. There were small market huts on the road. The roads were narrow, and the people drove a bit crazily (on the right side, as in America). Things that were not what I expected there were clay bricks lining the river, which flows through the city. The bricks lining the banks were made from soil, which were eroding away. It was sad to see. So were the conditions of the houses and the ripped clothes of the people.

On the larger scale, flying over Madagascar there was a ring of red around the island edge, which flowed into the ocean. This was erosion of the red, clay soil of the island's edges. Now I know why it's called "The Bleeding Island." I also saw smoke from fires all over the land in the mountains. The mountains were extensive. Come to find out, it was slash and burn, which caused much of the erosion we saw. I, at first, thought it was brush fires from low humidity, but I don't know if that could be true. The river seemed to run throughout the island. It looks like a beautiful country.

Our training accommodations are off away from Tana. There are some small houses around it. It's quite plush though, compared to what I expected...We each have our own room with a bed, a huge connected window, a desk, a closet and a sink. There are showers also, hot ones. There are toilets. Although, the toilet paper is like those brown industrial paper towels, but thicker, the paper can't be flushed down the toilet. We go to eat in another building where our food is prepared for us. Our laundry, other than our underwear and socks, is done for us. There are about eight Malagasy host country nationals working for Peace Corps to teach us French first and Malagasy later. We also have the environment organizer, a teacher organizer, Helen, the director, and Larry, the country director. The French teachers only spoke French to us, which is making us learn it very quickly. Yet we're very protected. I feel like a child being led by the hand.

I've not been to the city yet. I've not had to deal with speaking French with no one to turn to for help. It's been far from scary or hard. I think such protection may make it harder for me when I'm on my site alone.

The country's gorgeous. Red clay mountains with scattered trees (some pines, some cacti with flowers), cows here and there walking freely, the river flowing through, three clay huts, skinny canoe-shaped boats in the river, flooded rice patties, people carrying items on their head, straw chapeaux... It's really beautiful! I'm feeling very much at home, as it was meant to be, for me to be here.

August 26, 1994

Marowano, Denise, Leroy & Caleb (sister, brother-in-law, nephew)

YaHoo - I'm here! I am learning French Dee! It was a long flight (twenty hours with a fourteen-hour layover in London with Donna) but we made it. I'm with twenty-one other volunteers. Twelve are here for the forest/wildlife project and eight to teach English to the Malagasy people.

It's really beautiful here - the mountains are all red clay. There's a river running through the whole country. The houses are made from red bricks and there are cacti all over with huge red flowers.

Our training site is pretty plush...I thought I'd be living with a Malagasy family, but it turns out, that's only for one week during training. Instead we all have our own rooms in a big house/dorm. There is running water and electricity here since it's near the city (but I won't have such luxuries at my site in the "bush"!) The Malagasy chefs here cook incredible meals. The food is really good; also someone does our laundry. So I'm far from roughing it yet. It's kind of like a party actually, hanging out with so many people all the time. It'll probably be weird in three months when I'm shipped off on my own...But I'll be close to one other Peace Corps Volunteer and within biking distance of two more. We'll get mountain bikes...we have to because the red clay roads are really bad. The terrain's pretty mountainous and rugged here, and the erosion from slash and burn by the natives is so obvious. We'll be going to a rain forest in a few weeks or less, for a week, to a site similar to the kind we'll be living in. I'm psyched for that.

Money here is in Malagasy francs, which is basically nothing to us...the average income per year here is $200 (I'll be getting more)...People are so poor here. We went to the city, Antananarivo, a couple days ago. What a reality check that was for me... I've never seen such poverty - that's actually when it hit me that I am in the Peace Corps in a third world country. It was sad and hard for me, but it's about time I learned that America is not the norm and that most countries are this poor, or close to this poor.

So anyhow, I'm really happy the people are so nice and accepting of us and I'm learning French and I'm learning it pretty quickly. I'll learn Malagache starting in two weeks. Life's easy now. I'm enjoying showers, etc, while I still have them! By the way, when we refer to the people or the language, we change the "d" to an "l". That should clear up any confusion you have.

Love ya! Nancy

August 27, 1994

I was talking to Roland (PCV) this evening. We drew pictures of Madagascar. I drew abstract pictures of myself and Madagascar's effect on me and I realized that many things have not been as I had expected. I thought I would be living with a family for training and only with the other volunteers in the daytime for classes. Therefore, I thought I'd be living in the same type of environment, as I will be in the field, with no toilet and no sink, no one cooking or cleaning for me. I figured I'd probably have electric since training is in the city.

But yet, I'm living in the training center with the other

PCV's, going to training with them also, and I have plush accommodations. Life is easier for me than at home. So I must admit that I am incredibly happy here...I'm a bit concerned about this because I was prepared to be alone before, with no water, no electric, by myself in a Malagasy village. But now, I feel it won't be as easy to do so because I'm so content where I am now. I think that's what Bill may have meant when he said one of the training goals is that he hopes we'll be so sick of training by the end.

I've never been faced with reality in such intensity. There were more poor people than I have ever seen...children following us begging, sweaters with the wrists or sleeves ripped off, dirty faces, skinny arms and legs. I had a hard time not crying on the way back on the bus. Everyone else seemed okay... I think they've all experienced this before to some degree, or were prepared for it. I wasn't, and I know I wasn't. How could I have been? I've never seen such poverty before. But I don't want to be naive any more, and I want to understand what's going on in the rest of the world. I realized today, that this is the norm. Life as I know it, is not. America, along with a few other countries, are the exceptions.

I realized today that I am in the Peace Corps...I'm in a third world country... and I'm beginning to really understand what that is. It is nothing that I could have ever imagined.

September 11, 1994

Well, it looks like I haven't written for a while. I've gone through some fun times and some hard times this week. At the beginning of the week I was bumming emotionally. I had to leave French class or I would have started crying. I'm not sure what it was all about. The day before I had taken mefloquin, to prevent malaria, and it was about time for my period, and I was just getting confused as to my feelings and beliefs, how to feel around so many people. I seemed to manage to get my act together from Tuesday on, and for the rest of the week I was on an up.

Wednesday afternoon I studied French when most everyone went to Tana for the day. Friday evening, we went to the ambassador's house for a little cocktail party. We went out dancing after that, to a disco in Tana where they played awful American disco music. It may have been because we were there. There were about twenty-six of us - but maybe they always play that music. Anyhow, I had a great time.

Saturday afternoon I started feeling suffocated and getting a bit selfish. I just didn't feel like sharing with people. I feel like that's a bad problem of mine. And today I'm feeling guilty, like I don't know when to keep my mouth closed. I feel like I talk about people more than just casual conversation. So I guess, instead of feeling like shit and like people don't like me, I should just work on that...on sharing more with people, and on not talking to people about other people...It makes me doubt myself and like myself less. I should be able to be with all these people and like myself as much as when I'm alone. If I don't, there's something I'm not doing right when I'm with people. I'll work on it.

September 12, 1994

Well, I feel a lot better today than yesterday when I wrote. I talked to Linda (instructor) about how I was feeling and she made me feel a lot better. She told me it's human and all of us need to do it so we can survive with each other, as long as it's just with closer friends and it's not something that becomes habit. Michelle (instructor) talked to me this morning about people or a person she doesn't want to work with and it ended up being the same thing I had talked to Linda about, so I felt much better. I understood what Linda meant. I am still going to work on being particular about it though, and if possible, keep bad thoughts to myself. I would hate to hurt someone.

So today I did tres bien (very good) in my French exam. I'm on my own now to learn more. Tomorrow I start Malagache and the next day I go to the family until Sunday. I think that will be a lot of fun, but probably also an eye-opener as to how other people live.

September 14, 1994

Hi Mom!

One of the volunteers is going back to the U.S., so I figured I'd whip off a quick letter. She has to leave because the mefloquin, the medication we're taking for malaria prevention, isn't agreeing with her at all. I was having dizziness and a bit of sleeplessness from it, but I'm okay now.

So, I'm doing great, Mom. I've been really happy and so far my life's been very easy, good food, my clothes are being done for me, and I'm learning a lot.

I took our French test (oral) yesterday. We are only required to know basics in French and I passed with a tres bien from the language director. Today I started learning Malagache, which is a beautiful flowing Asian language. It'll take a lot of practicing, because it's not like anything I've ever heard before. I only learned a little French, for shopping in the big cities, but where I'm living, I'll need the Malagache. That will be my main language. Uh-oh - I just got the word that the volunteer already left without my knowing. I have to sign off. Love ya', Mom. I'll write soon. Tomorrow I go to stay with a Malagasy family for the week.

Hi again. Oh well, I missed her (the volunteer). She's on her way to the airport. So anyhow, where was I? Oh, yes, I'm going to stay with a Malagasy family from Wednesday to Sunday this week. All twenty of the volunteers are doing it. It's to get a better taste of the culture. I think it will be a lot of fun. Some of us are going to Antananarivo, the capital, and others are going to Antsirabe. I lucked out because I get to go to Tana (the first one) where the families talk French and Malagache, so I'll be able to communicate with them more. The families in Antsirabe only speak Malagache.

When I'm back from my family visit I'll get to find out where I'll be working when training is over. It will be in one of three places - either in a forest on the coast (two sites are in forests on the coast) or in Isalo National Park, which I've heard is utterly amazing. So it sounds like no matter where I'll be, I'll be happy. I'll either be living near one or three other volunteers. My work will be mostly social because we need to talk to the villagers to find out why they slash and burn for agriculture (a clearing the land method), and if there are alternatives for them. The approach itself wouldn't be so bad, but they went back to the same areas and burned. The soil is not given a chance to heal because of it. There are huge crevices all over the mountains from the soil erosion, since the trees are no longer here to keep the soil intact. A lot of the good soil flows into the ocean, too. They also dig up the bottom of the rivers and use the soil to make bricks and build houses. This is doing more environmental damage and the habitat for wildlife is being destroyed. I'll be doing environmental education with the tourists and the villagers to try to help them understand the big picture. I'll also be doing wildlife research since information is so lacking here, and I'll be planting trees. It will be hard, but fun.

I'm already learning so much living in a dorm setting, which is new for me, but I'm adjusting. Well, Mom, hope you're well - I'll probably write again soon. I hope you're okay through this rough patch. Let me know.

Love, Nancy

Three

Family Visit

Nancy made her first "faux pas". She also had her first experience in a taxi brousse (taxi bus).

Chicken is not bought in grocery stores there. What an experience! Suzette (the mom) threw Nancy another curve concerning the chicken at breakfast.

The PCV's all went to a host family for 3 days. Culture shock? Oh, yeah! But Nancy writes, "I'm in the right place for this point in my life."

September 14, 1994

I'm at my Malagasy family's house. The family's father is a pastor, Phillipae, and his wife Suzanne, and they have three little girls.

26

They are really sweet people. I like their house. The main part of it is upstairs, with the bedrooms, and the kitchen. The living room, bathroom, and Phillipae's office are downstairs. The house is, of course, very different from any American house. It's made of cement, possibly.

The little girls (four, seven and ten) helped prepare dinner, using a huge knife to cut the veggies. That was something new to see. I walked to the market with two of the daughters before dinner and we saw a dog, right after it had been hit by a car... not at all fun. The kids didn't seem phased.

At dinner, Phillipae and Suzanne asked me about my family and my work before coming here, and my work here, with a little English here or there, mostly French and some petite lessons in Malagache. After dinner I talked with Phillipae about the bad state of the environment and how odd the city of Jhirama is, because it represents everything we're working against.

After dinner, Suzanne heated some water for me so I could wash and then we watched a bit of TV.

Suzanne, Phillipae's wife and their children

It ended up that Phillipae and Suzanne gave me a lesson in Malagache...very helpful. Phillipae said he wants to take me to an environment conference tomorrow, maybe the queen's palace also, and to the Zeema on Saturday. So it sounds like I may be spoiled instead of having to work. I'm glad to be here. I'm going to crash now.

"Rareka aho"

September 15, 1994

Aujourd'hui (today) was an interesting day. Miratsum (Host daughter) and Philber (I shortened Phillipae) and I went to the castle of the queen today. Not in Tana, but in the town of Ambuimangg. It was great to see. After that we came back for lunch and I then went with Philber to an environmental conference avec [with] the youth of about twelve churches. I talked about the definition of the environment, the problems with it and possible solutions. People asked questions of me, and Philber helped translate. I didn't know how people were feeling toward me if I had said anything that had bothered them, but after; two people asked me for my autograph and five asked me for my address. It made me feel really good.

When we came home there was an English class in the church by the house. Helen, Anna, Jeremy, and Kirsten (PCV's) were talking with the groups. I joined in. Then after, the man Anna was staying with told Philber and me that he was going to visit friends in Tana with his wife and Anna. He invited me, and Philber said I should go. I went but I felt wrong about it, though, since Helen told us Malagache people wouldn't tell us how they feel. But Benjamin told me it's different between Malagasy's and if there were a problem Philber, would have told him. I'm not sure how true that is, but I was already on my way with him, so I tried to not worry about it.

Nancy, Phillipae, and his children

At their house, I made my first major faux pas. I asked for the salle de bain (not the toilette) and one of the daughters directed me to it and turned on the light for me. There was a tub, a sink, and what seemed to possibly be a toilet. So hesitantly, I peed in it. There was no flusher so I pulled the plug so the drain opened and then I turned on the little faucets to rinse it. After I washed my hands and went out.

Anna (PCV) needed the bathroom, too, before we left. I must admit, I was quite surprised when she went into the door next to the door I went in. I was more surprised and truly embarrassed when I heard the flushing of a toilet. It was at that time I realized I had peed in the clothes-washing basin. I nonchalantly entered the salle de bain again to thoroughly rinse out the basin. I really should have known; the house was tres chic. Oh well, at least my first major faux pas wasn't majorly public. Anyhow, I had a wonderful evening at friends of Benjamin's and Yardei's (Anna's host couple) after. When I asked for the salle de bain (bathroom) I was shown where that was and the hostess also pointed out the toilette. It was then that I figured out how I got myself in the predicament in the first place.

Yet, it also made me realize how much your environment directs your actions. I had been in a poorer house before this, so a toilette itself seemed luxurious, never mind a wash basin!

September 16, 1994

Something I didn't write about yesterday was my first experience with the taxi brousse (taxi-bus). I got in and sat down, which was my first mistake. People on every side of me practically sat on me. It was really amazing; 'cause people just kept piling in. It was a feeling of sardines in a can. I learned from that, to either stand or get far back in the taxi brousse. No one could sit on me then, because there was no room in front of me to stand. I also know to have correct (or pretty close) change, so I don't have to worry about pickpockets and to have it easily accessible (because it's not easy to get a hand in a pocket when it's jam-packed). I must admit, I wish smoking wasn't allowed on the taxi brousse, too.

Today I was a bit tired because I went out with Anna and the couple she's staying with (without their kids) and I had quite a bit of wine with dinner. This morn we went to Tana. Suzanne, Robert, and Midatsu and I went to the market and the zoo. When we got home, I was beat. After lunch I pulled out my French and Malagache to study a bit, 'cause I just needed to do something on my own. Well, Suzanne and Phillipae were so psyched with my lessons they sat down to study with me. After fifteen or so minutes it was pretty obvious I was beat and not into it, so I was going to go for a walk, but Suzanne asked me if I'd help her prepare the chicken for dinner. I said, "Yes, of course," and we went into the kitchen.

Suzanne put some water on to boil and I looked around for

the packaged chicken. She signaled me to go downstairs with her and Midatsu, so I figured the chicken was down there somewhere. But she went outside instead. I was a bit worried when she started chasing a chicken around the yard. She and Midatsu were laughing as they tried to scoot it into the house... It was obvious they had done this many times before. Suzanne finally got it in and caught it... when she started walking upstairs to the kitchen with it, I pretty much stopped telling myself that she was just catching the chicken to put it somewhere to collect the eggs. Anyhow, that idea wasn't really flying with me, since I knew Suzanne had bought eggs at the market. So as we walked to the kitchen, Philber was once again following me, pointing out articles and telling me the Malagache so I'd repeat it... I was worrying that I'd either throw up on him, or haul off on him.

I was really freaked out when Suzanne got a knife and put a bowl below the head of the chicken. She asked me how often I did this in the U.S., and I said it was actually my first time witnessing it. That's when Philber caught the hint and walked away instead of talking Malagache to me. Suzanne then slit the chicken's throat. Midatsu covered her eyes while smiling with discomfort, and I tried not to shake and not to leave the room. It was the first time I had ever seen an animal killed by a human. After, Suzanne put the chicken in boiling water for a few minutes and cleaned the feathers off. Although I couldn't help, I at least stayed in the room and talked to her about other things while she cleaned the chicken.

Soon after we walked to the school, Suzanne had a pretty shawl on. I thought, it's amazing how much I would never picture this woman killing a chicken. A stupid thought, but it was true. I thought about it, and I thought it's about time I realized that somebody has to kill those chickens that come in a package at Demoula's (a supermarket chain in N.H.).

September 17, 1994

I got up thinking, Okay today will be easier, but I got up at 6 a.m. like normal here (because people walk through the room my bed is in to get to the rest of the house). For breakfast, we had the leftover chicken and spaghetti from last night. No big problem, but the mother threw me off again 'cause I looked over and she was eating the chicken's head with her meal. So it made my stomach a bit queasy again. After that, everyone was laughing as she had the beak sticking out and was causing it to open and shut. Next she shared the excess of the head with the cat that ate on the table with us.

I went to the bathroom and forgot to duck and whaled my head on the stone door casing. I sometimes forget that the Malagasy are short and I am 5'10 1/2" so, the houses, ceilings and doorways are lower. I did the same thing in the kitchen when I went upstairs.

After breakfast, Suzanne, the kids and I went to a market close by. We walked. Helen and the family she's staying with picked us up and shortened our walk. Later we took a taxi brousse back. We cooked some manioc and ate some sugar cane, both new for me. After lunch we went for a two-plus hour walk to the river, and the kids splashed around a bit.

I had raviloto for dinner, which I didn't like much. It's the leaves of manioc cooked.

We then went to a shindig in the church for a going away party for a couple French soldiers who were stationed here. I guess they spent time with the youth group while they worked here. Because of this the kids from the town, with the other volunteers (Jeremy, Anna, Kirsten, and Bill - not Helen or Todd, who were in our town) did some dancing outside. The young here seem much more united and friendly to each other than in America. Even the three sisters I'm staying with have shown nothing but love towards each other in the time I've been here.

September 18, 1994

Church today was really long - almost three hours. It was very Catholic-like even though it was Protestant.

I took the kids for ice cream after lunch. Then it was time to return to our training camp. I had a good time but I'm glad to be heading back. The culture shock was a bit more than I had expected.

September 20, 1994

Dear Mom,

As I read my last letter to myself, I still feel the same way - that I'm in the right place for this point in my life. And the way I wrote that my transition to here wouldn't be abrupt and it would be, probably, totally gradual. That, I'm learning, is only partially true. I'm learning that I'm feeling it little by little, with abrupt spurts slapping me in the face that I'm in a new land. That reality is more real than I ever realized it would be.

My first abrupt spurt was spending a day in Tana. I've never seen so many people who were homeless wearing such ragged clothes, with dirty faces and runny noses, begging to everyone that passed by. That was an awakening.

The next abrupt spurt was during my family stay, when we chased a chicken around the yard and slaughtered it for dinner. The poverty of the families and that basic survival way of life, and the actual witnessing of an animal being slaughtered have broadened reality into things that I've always thought were real, but have never given it much thought. It's never been a first hand part of my own existence.

Life is more real. The people here are more tied to cause and effect. They do what it takes for basic survival. In America we do things to get a result, but it's usually that some ten people before us have done the basics to get us to that result. I'm definitely not taking life as much for granted here. It's just because I'm viewing others working for survival. I think when I'm doing it for myself in a couple of months, I'll start feeling as real as these people appear to me. I look forward to that.

Love, Nance

Four

Back to the Ranch

Sickness from the meat and the mefloquin malaria prevention med-ication did not over shadow Nancy's outlook. She was a vegetarian before the Peace Corps and her body was having a hard time adjusting to eating meat again.

She was surprised with a rather large crowd when she was asked to give a talk to a "few" teenagers. No stopping this girl!!

These people, she finds, are more loving than Americans. There was good coffee, good chocolate, and many cultural lessons.

September 23, 1994

I'm having a really good time "back here at the ranch." I

studied Malagache for four hours, which was a huge boost of my understanding. Charles and Bonnie (PCV's) left yesterday, which got me down some. They said the program's just not for them. Bonnie gave me a couple beautiful yoga books that she didn't want to lug back with her. I'm psyched to have them. I've been feeling a strong desire to do some meditation and read my "Shambala" book.

We had a cross cultural class today on culture shock. Helen gave us this handout, from a book that a man had written to foreigners who visit America. It gave thirteen traits that most Americans have... it revealed many things. One thing I really noticed was in trait seven, how Americans are competitive and how other countries value (cooperation). Number eleven is how Americans are direct, open and honest, and other countries are indirect, ritualistic, and "save face".

I thought about how Americans really hate it when someone lies to them and it probably connects with number seven, how we're so competitive; lying actually comes off as maliciousness to us. Yet in other countries "saving face" (what we think of as lying) isn't lying or malicious at all. It's just saving face, and people here have no problem with it. It's probably because the people here are cooperative. They're a more unified people, so when people tell white lies, no offense is taken by it. People aren't initially defensive due to it. I think that's something I really need to work to remember, so I don't become offended by it. The people here are more loving and more unified, more one. The children don't have a love-hate relationship like we do... they love each other. It affects their whole attitude and relationships to everyone else.

September 29, 1994

Hi ya Mom!

Thanks for the letter! It got here really quickly - nine days. Thanks for the pictures, too. It's obvious my mail going to you is not as fast, because no one's written that they've received my letters. I wrote to people August 26th! But I'm sure you've gotten the other two letters by now-or one letter and one postcard. I'm going to write in cursive so I can write faster, 'cause I should be studying my Malagache!

I just wanted to return a letter to you, to answer your questions and also to send you this, Mom. Don't you think it's an impressive picture from the newspaper of me with Mr. Ambassador? On the other side of him are actually two of my favorite volunteers out of all of them, Kirsten and Joe. Todd is beside Mr. Ambassador, beside him is Joe and Kirsten. What's funny is that Joe and Kirsten are the people who I'll be working with in Isalo National Park. It's kind of odd that we're in the photo together. We didn't know we'd all be working together at the time!

Mr. Ambassador is a top-notch guy, though. He was saying his job's a bit tough, because he can never go out of his house in just a pair of jeans- so I said to him, "Mr. Ambassador, you and Rose (his wife) are welcome at my hut anytime and you can wear your jeans, too!" (Why do I get the feeling that where I'm going to be is a place he can comfortably wear jeans?) He said he might take me up on that.

So, to answer the beginning of your 1001 questions in case I didn't cover them well in the first letter, since they were questions I don't know that I thought of in all my excitement of being here. The flight was long but a good trip, and I didn't get sick. I flew on American Airlines to South Africa, and South Africa Airlines to Air Madagascar. I landed at 2 p.m. (here), five a.m. your time. Our Peace Corps trainer met us. It's a small airport so we got out quickly and the training site is only twenty minutes from the airport, a quick trip. And you know, Mom, to your last of many questions for the first letter, I'm feeling really good!

I'm definitely drinking only bottled water, and I'll have to purify H_2O when I arrive at my site in December. But we're incredibly well cared for here. Our food's cooked or peeled, or chlorinated so no one's gotten sick from the food or water. However, most everyone has gotten sick from culture change or jet lag at first or mefloquin side effects, our malaria medication, but I'm one of the few who hasn't gotten sick. I've got the sniffles a lot here, though. I think I'm allergic to the trees, or maybe the burning of all the trees - ha, ha, ha! Actually, it's not that funny.

I went for a run yesterday. Do Malagasy get a kick out of that...to see a vazaha (white foreigner), running for no reason whatsoever... not carrying anything, no water, no trees, no sticks on their heads even! What was I saying before I so rudely interrupted myself...ah, yes, when I was running, the entire side of the hillside was on fire (except the road, of course). They're constantly burning here...that's the whole problem. They burn to make more grass grow for the livestock, or to kill the plants so they can make rice patties.

I've never eaten so much rice in my life, Mom! Two times a day without fail. We get loads of vegetables and fruit here too so I'm really healthy. The coffee here is nice and strong, too. I like that. It's actually almost too strong! The chocolate here is really good, too, and there is ice cream here - what a relief! I'm definitely not hurting in the food department.

I don't know that I'll be as lucky at my work site in Isalo...I hope so. I've been starting to eat meat more, too. Because where I'm going it's a big part of the diet. My system is a bit confused with the changes, so I'm trying to do it little by little. I'm happy and healthy here, but I'm anxious to be done with training to get into exploring my new National Park and get settled into my home.

Everything that I'm learning here is necessary before I get out in the bush. The language is really pretty, but really tough. I feel like a child learning to talk again. It's nothing like learning French (which I'm getting quite good with, even though classes in it are done).

I'm getting along well with all the other volunteers and I really like the two I'll be working with, which is great. I'm also going to look into doing some marine biology work in Toliar on the west coast, four hours from the park. There's a lot of extra

U. S. funding available to us for secondary projects, and the university in Toliar just opened a marine program. If I get into a small project and can put it on my Peace Corps job- description when I'm done, I'll be set up for a government marine job if I choose that avenue over wildlife conservation What's nice about my job is that a lot of what I do with it will be open ended.

I'm really enjoying being single again. I have always felt like I get in touch with myself, who I am and what my values are, more when I'm alone than when I'm with someone.

Mom, I hope you're well and happy. I'm well and happy. But I need to sign off and study. There's nothing I need yet - there doesn't seem to be much I can't get here actually and Peace Corps gives me plenty of money. Thanks for asking. I'll let you know when I need something. Sorry I haven't called, but it's about $30 for 3 minutes! You can always call Ginny at the Madagascar Country Desk in Washington if you want information on how things are here. I'll probably call around Christmas. If that's not soon enough, write and tell me. Letters work fine for me, but I don't know how everyone else feels about it. Well, Mom, I love you! Keep writing!

Love, Nancy

October 2, 1994

I see I didn't write all last week, yet I wrote about eleven letters so that's okay! Yesterday and today we went to Perinier, a forest reserve. It was the first time that I've felt like I'm really experiencing Madagascar. It was a dryer rain forest, with lots of trees wrapped around trees, vines hanging everywhere, birds singing, and six species or more of lemurs. We went on an afternoon walk yesterday and saw the brown lemur eating first in the trees and jumping through the trees with about four others. We also saw chameleons and geckos (is this the little lizard geckos or a mammal).

Last night we went out from seven to ten o'clock after an incredible chemise dinner at a restaurant across from our hotel (best mushrooms I've ever eaten!). We saw ghettos and oloo lemurs (I have to look that one up), another brown lemur, and a mouse lemur that was hardly any bigger than a mouse! It was pretty amazing. This morning we heard and saw the indrie, the loudest territory calls I've ever heard! So, needless to say, it was a great couple of days.

After we went to an agro forestry place to see their practices. It was pretty amazing because they planted coffee; other crops and trees on almost a straight up and down slope... not easy work! I learned that planting legume plants with other plants is beneficial because they fix nitrogen. Since the soil in Madagascar is pretty bad, this is really beneficial.

I also found out on this trip, a little more than I was already starting to realize that running over animals is the thing to do if they don't get out of the way. Our driver killed two chickens, and just barely missed a third, as well as a dog! He slowed a slight bit more for people, but I do believe that if they left their safety in his hands they'd probably be dead too! What else? They seem to chop eucalyptus off above the stump, and then burn the area around them. I think it's done to clear off the fallen leaves, and also, maybe to assist in getting the stump to get sprouts coming off it. New trees eventually grow from the same stump. I guess they can repeat this way of growing trees a few times before production starts to decrease. (I tried a fruit yesterday that Michelle was eating - it was heavenly. It was a cross between a date and a banana! I'll be psyched to be eating those for the next couple years!)

So I have to buckle down on my language for this week 'cause we're tested on it Saturday and I'm not feeling overly confident in it. It's good to have that pressure though because next week we're going to Ranomafana for the whole week. I'll be having too much fun there to get a lot of studying in.

It just started thundering and now it's raining...the first time since I've been here in this area.

October 3, 1994

Hi ya Dan! (Brother) Aquaria boa Hun?

I wanted to whip off a letter to you, 'cause one of the volunteers is going back to the U.S. tomorrow 'cause his mom's having surgery. That's the fourth volunteer heading back. What's up with that? Actually the other three were older and decided it wasn't for them.

But anyhow, I'm not going anywhere. This place is awesome - No, no - it's incredibly awesome! I've been hanging in the rain forest for the past two days listening to the indries - it's one of the larger lemurs-and they sound like a pack of baboons! I also saw the brown lemur, the Oloo lemur, and the mouse lemur, which is about 3 or 4 inches long with a monkey like body - it's pretty hysterical to see. There's what's called a giraffe beetle, too! With a neck as long as a giraffe in proportion to its body that stretched it out to reach food off other leaves. There are a few poisonous snakes here, but they have no teeth so they can't bite you. They're actually harmless - a bit odd, eh?

This has been the first real taste of Madagascar I've had. Until yesterday, I've been within ten miles of the capital since I've been here. I've learned a lot about the culture being lost to the city, though. I realize how poor this country is. The government here hasn't helped the people at all, which is why the environment is in such bad shape. It's going to take a lot to get things turned around.

I've finished classes in French and have been studying Malagache, the Bada dialect, which is the dialect of the south central area. It's pretty, but tough - "A lasopy my halaoko fa etsaky vary iaho," for example means, "I'm sick of rice!" (Already.) We have rice two times a day.

The food here is limited but good. It's hard to get juice. It's not overly available, which is weird considering all the tropical fruit here. Yet Coca-Cola is everywhere (yuck! - just what I don't want on a tropical island). I tried la bur fruit (I think that's the name) and it is the most heavenly fruit I've ever tasted. It's round with a thick skin like a mango and soft yellow inside that tastes like a cross between a date and a banana. I've also had one of the grossest foods ever, ravitoto (pronounced-ravitootoo), which is the leaves of sweet potatoes finely sliced and mashed to the same consistency as pesto. It's taste and smell is really disgusting.

I stayed with a Malagasy family for a week. Each volunteer did this to get a better taste of the culture. The family I was with was a pastor, his wife and three little girls, and we ate this ravitoto for dinner. My bed was in the room the dinner table was in and the smell made me feel like I was going to lose it the whole night. So that's food I'll be avoiding. I've been trying to eat meat little by little because they eat so much of it here. My body's having a hard time adjusting to it.

I actually haven't been sick much though, except Mondays. I'm always wiped out, 'cause Sundays we take mefloquin (malaria pills), which has some side effects - dizziness, nightmares, exhaustion at times. The effects seem to get less intense each week, and maybe they'll fade out. I wanted to tell you what happened at my home stay with this family. I went to Antananarivo one day with the pastor and his wife to the Zuma, which is the big market every Friday with more people than you could ever possibly imagine (more beggars, more pick-pocketers, too.)

Later, the pastor asked me to go to his church and say a little bit to his youth group about the environment 'cause they're having an environmental week class. So I told him my French wasn't great (the Malagasy's in the city areas speak French and Malagache). He said that's okay, just say a little bit so they'd know why I'm here. So we go to the church and there are about sixty teenagers there. No big deal. But then the pastor puts a desk and chair up on the stage - like part of the church, calls me up and hands me a microphone. I was like, "Oh great." I should have expected it. So Dan, it ended up that these kids really got into my talk and I was up there struggling my points across with bad French...for over an hour! But they got the gist of my information on the environment and I was actually asked for my autograph and address from two other pastors and four students!

Needless to say, by the time we got back to the house, I was burnt and happy to go back to the house.

Next week twelve environmental volunteers, that's me, and our trainer are going to Ranomafana for one week, a national park/rain forest, ten hours south of here, to learn about the environment hands on. I'm sure we'll be doing a lot of hiking and relaxing and beer drinking too! It'll be a fun time - it'll be nice to have a break from classes for the week. I think a few weeks after that I'll be doing a week visit at Isalo National Park where I'll be living. I'm psyched to get done the training soon (we're half way done!).

Well Dan, take it easy, Bro. I hope you're doing as well as I am.

Ciao and peace! Nancy

Madagascar - Notes Culturelles

- Don't stop for animals in the road...if they don't move run them over.

- Speed limit...what's that?

- Don't sit on the southwest side of the hut in a village because this spot is for the most respected, for either the Reimen Dreny (the village leader) or the father of the house. If you do, you've insulted not only this respected one, but also the ancestors. You may need to buy a bull and possibly sacrifice it to make amends for this.

- The Malagasy pull the bones of their dead out of the tomb annually and unwrap them from their silk lamba swaths and rewrap the bones in new silk lambas. If the body has not rotted yet, they may put lotion on the body before rewrapping. They then parade the body or bodies around town, playing drums, valias (I'll send you one of these instruments sometime, Dan) and flutes as they celebrate the spirit of their ancestors. A bull may be sacrificed at the ceremony, also.

- In many areas of Madagascar, a man can have many wives. It is the duty of these wives (be it one or six) to have as many children as the man requests.

- Snapping your fingers of one hand and hitting them against your other hand after which is in the shape of a fist (try this so you'll understand it, it's what Fonzie does some-time) means "#&*! Your Mother," in Madagascar. (Yes, it was embarrassing to learn this.) Ta Osh Be = "Three Horses Beer" is the only beer of Madagascar.

- That's all for this letter - new update of Madagascar, Notes Culturelles on your next issue of "Madagascar Live."
  -by Nancy

October 4, 1994

I'm still hanging in through this week, which I knew would be tough, 'cause I knew I'd be getting a typhoid shot, taking mefloquin, getting my period, and having the same sense of not being my usually healthy feeling self, on top of it. I actually have refused to get sick, which has just barely been working. I've been trying to eat light, 'cause my stomach is always a bit queasy. I've been with a constant headache, and I'm taking Tylenol too - so I'm hanging in. We had the afternoon off and I studied Malagache all afternoon for my test on Saturday, but I'm still feeling really unknowledgeable. I'm going to study some more now.

I got really bummed after dinner, 'cause I got a desperate sounding letter from Mom that I needed to call her 'cause she couldn't stand not knowing what was up. It was dated Sept. 15. I sent a letter to her on September 29 and two more after that. Hopefully, she's gotten them. I can't call her though, it's fifty dollars now for three minutes. I talked to other volunteers and found that most of their families have received their letters, so I stopped worrying about it... she must have all three by now. I guess the letter got me down, 'cause I was homesick and missing Dan, my former, so a frantic letter didn't help. But I'm okay with it now.

I got a letter from (my brother) Danny, which was great. He was sounding resolved to the fact that everyone in his life is somewhere other than U.S. and he's not traveling. Who knows, maybe I'll talk him into visiting me, saving up a little each week to get a plane ticket and I'll take care of him once he's here. Ah well, we'll see.

I'm off to study for a bit, staying on top of it. I will not let things get me down just because my body's a bit out of sorts right now. I need to buy a guitar soon!

October 5, 1994

I just had a great experience. I was out running, which was a tough endeavor because my period just started (I'm so glad I was wondering where it's been!) and I just got a typhoid shot which is supposed to have some side effects of nausea and fever, but I got out there. I'm so glad I did. As soon as I started up the hill, I passed about six people on the side of the road, two being young girls. The girls started running with me up the hill - one was probably seven years old and the other thirteen. They stuck with me the whole way up the hill.

They knew no French, so our communication was limited to me now and again saying "tsada be." They led the way on a path through the village. As we passed through, people came out of their houses as we passed yelling "Bonjour" or "Manwana," (Good day) and kids kept following us! There must have been about fifteen kids with me - I felt like the Pied Piper for a second there! They were laughing and whooping, and I was laughing, yelling "Misortra, Tsada Be!" They all did the loop through the village with the two girls and me. Then we all yelled "velumo" (good-bye) to each other. The two girls and I ran on, back down the road to the path to their house. I said "velumo" and "misotra" to them, and "makay hun," but I don't know if they understood that comment. It didn't matter. It was just a great experience. I'm so glad I went running and I'm so glad I'm here. (All these words meant as much to me a month ago as they do to you.)

Five

Ranomafana

Nancy visits a rain forest on a camping trip with 13 PCV's (Peace Corps Volunteers). Madagascar reveals several of its magical species of lemurs, the cat-like five foot long fossa, and trees that were unknown to her, as well as leeches and epiphytes. Her endurance is tested. Nancy writes, "I'm starting to realize that my mistake is often living in a time other than the present."

Nancy has just learned that she's to be alone in Bereketa, her Village, a 3-hour bike ride to a larger town. It actually turned out to be a 5 to a 5-1/2 hour trip, one way.

Why weren't the volunteers told about being alone before they even made out their application papers? This was not honest on the part of

Peace Corps and it angered several in the family including myself.
Nancy, who always looked at the positive, just shrugged it off.

October 10, 1994

Here I am in Ranomafana, a National Park and rain forest of Madagascar. It was about a twelve-hour drive, and well worth it. It wasn't really that bad. Our campsite's really beautiful with a river running a bit below us. We have five tents for the thirteen of us. It's a great setup. We went for a walk this morning and saw brown lemurs. One who almost jumped on me! We also saw 3 Diademed and Sifaka lemurs together.

The forest is so thick, with bamboo, guava (from China), pines, eucalyptus, epiphytes, vines hanging down, moss on everything... I try to take pictures and the number (light meter) in the lens flashes 1.8, it's so dark! I managed to get a few pictures of the lemurs, though. I'll try again another day.

A Sifaka Lemur

October 12, 1994

Last night we took a walk through the rain forest with a tourist guide. We first went to an area where there were other tourists, and the guides had put banana pieces on the trees, baiting in mouse lemurs. They were also cooking meat to attract the fossa (a slender, cat-like animal, that grows to about five feet). We lost Joe on that one - he was pretty disgusted. Supposedly it is illegal but it's just not being enforced yet. We asked our guide to take us for a walk before the fossa came and we went into the bamboo forest, in an attempt to find the golden bamboo lemur, which is supposedly only in Ranomafana. We didn't see the lemur (it's not easy to see), but it was raining hard so we saw tons of leeches. They were all over all of us. I must have gotten twelve bites on my feet and a couple on my chest. Michelle and

I stripped down when we got home and washed. I felt so gross. It's really amazing how dark a rain forest is at only 7 p.m. I was a bit nervous we'd run into a boa, but I guess it's not common to see them unless it's the rainy season.

I skinny-dipped with Rachel and Michelle yesterday, which was so nice. We might as well get use to it. It's a way of life here. We swam today, too. I'm not in the mood to write anything down, so I'm going to sign off.

October 17, 1994

When I asked Helen when the rainy season starts, she said October 15th. I was surprised to get an exact date, but in Ranomafana, it rained hard some and soft some. But from October 15th on, it down-pours every evening. We're on our way home - not actually home - back to Jerama.

It was a great trip. I feel I learned a lot... I'm not referring to how much I learned about park management, although I did learn a lot in that area. I think I'm referring to learning how much this is where I want to be, and how to get the most of it. For a while I'd been questioning if I should have left. I'm starting to realize that my mistake is often living in a time other than the present - either debating the reasons for my past or trying to plan my future. In the mean time, I'm missing a lot of good stuff. I'm realizing that to try figuring out my emotions for Dan (my friend) and to try comparing him to the image of the complete man I'd like is not really any use. I think I'm just going to enjoy having my friendship with him, and that is the only way we can have it.

I need to enjoy my time alone here for what it is -time to get to know myself and grow in the ways I want to grow. I think that every day I learn more about whom I am and what I want to change, or should I say how I want to grow. I see it so much more easily here than at home probably because my environment is so different.

I'm so excited to go to my village in two weeks. I think for the next couple weeks I'm going to make my focus a lot in learning Bada, (a Malagashe dialect) so I can communicate with the people in my village when I get there. I don't think they'll talk French, if I don't have the language down very well. I don't know that I'll have anything to fall back on. I don't yet know which village I'll be in. I just know I'll be glad when training's done. I'm feeling confident enough to be on my own here. Actually, I think I'm more comfortable alone here. Less beggars and more intimate encounters with people than when I'm with a big group.

"Awareness is everything. People worry a lot more about the eternity after their deaths, than the eternity that happens before they were born." From Animal Dreams by Barbara Kingsolver.)

October 23, 1994

Akoy, Donna & John (oldest sister & brother-in-law), Alex, Ryan and Lauren (nephews & niece), (Denise got the same letter).

How is everyone doing? Donna, please excuse the fact that this is done thru carbon, but it's because I wrote a letter to Denise and Leroy (sister and brother-in-law), Dan (brother), and Bryan, and Joanne (brother & sister-in-law). I'm really busy, but I just wanted to drop you all a letter to let you know where I am. I just got back from Ranomafana National Park, where we (the environmental volunteers) were for a week studying park management techniques and learning about plants and lemurs. We camped right by a river for the week and it was great! A few too many leeches for my liking!!! Luckily, I'll be working in a dryer forest with no leeches!

I'm back at our training center cramming on the language, which is coming very slowly. It's oriental like and I feel a bit retarded speaking as I sound like a child, but I'll get better. I wanted to write because I just found out where I'm going to be living. I'm going to be working in Isalo National Park, which is supposedly as gorgeous as the Badlands and the Grand Canyon (sorry if this is repetitive). I'll be living in a village called Bereketa, which means "Big Cactus". I laughed at that...I never pictured myself living in a place named Big Cactus. It sounds really beautiful...it's near a river, and a bit away from the village, there is a second river. The village is in a prairie below an incredible mountain range at the edge of the National Park. There are about 300 people in the village...it's actually not one of the smallest that the volunteers will be in. I can get fruits and vegetables and berries in my own village. I'll be a three-hour bike ride from a bigger town for other stuff. Peace Corps is giving me a mountain bike so I'm set. No Denise, this doesn't mean you can have mine! It can't come home with me... and I plan to beat it to hell while I'm here. It sounds like I'll be going most everywhere on my bike as they get around with bulls and wagons where I'm going, (I'd expect nothing less of a place called Big Cactus.)

Six
My Village Visit

Many self-discoveries surface for my daughter. Nancy, Kirsten Leonge (PCV) and Joe Schaeffer (PCV) with Parfait (PC driver) visit Isalo National Park where the three were to be working. They left behind civilization as they ventured to Ranohira, Kirsten's village, which is near the park where the three will be working. Joe's location was deeper into the unknown. Nancy's village of Bereketa was the farthest out of any of the volunteers. Each was to spend three days in their respective villages. Nancy writes, "I knew I couldn't have a healthy relationship with anyone before finding contentment within myself."

October 30, 1994

I'm on my way to Isalo after which I'm going to Bereketa, my village! I've been under "mother's wing" a bit too long for my liking. I haven't written in a while - I think it's because I've been going through such a whirlwind of emotions that I had no idea how to start writing.

A book I read, <u>Animal Dreams</u>, brought out some really strong emotions in me. The girl in the story miscarried. She had a hard upbringing, and she had a really hard time getting into relationships with people she really loved. She had been in a relationship with one guy whom she really didn't love; when she moved on and met someone she could fall in love with, she ended up saying she was moving at the end of the year, as she always did (moving on, that is). She managed to keep love and, therefore, vulnerability to being hurt at arms distanced from her.

It just reminded me all too much of myself and it made me come to grips with some things that I didn't know I actually had strong feelings about...that I had kind of let slip through the cracks. So I guess I've just kind of been trying to take a good look at myself and my life, and my being here. I've never been content staying in one place too long, and I definitely feel like a big part of it is because I feel like I'm looking for something I haven't yet found.

In the meantime, like this girl in the book, I'm constantly not feeling satisfied, and I feel as though I'm often "missing the moment." I often miss the main point: to enjoy now, because that's actually all there is. I had to ask myself if I was running from something by coming here - especially if I was running from committing to Dan, my friend. Yet I have to say, I feel in my gut that this is what's right for me. I'm also feeling that I wasn't running from a relationship with Dan, but that I knew I couldn't have a healthy relationship with anyone before finding contentment within myself. I realize that to find that contentment within myself, I need to slow down long enough to notice the now! God, I'm such a maniac!

I think I actually needed to get out of the U.S. to get out of my fast paced life. I needed an environmental change...the U.S. is just so busy. Almost everyone and everything is rushing, and producing. It's different here. Here, it's kind of like, if you have food on your table, you're okay. They work hard here, but yet they have fun with it... work is not a necessity to live here, work is life. When people here aren't working it's not as if they've just started living because their workday is done as it is in the U.S. it's just a continuation of life. People don't rush here. They take things one thing at a time and live in the now. They don't stress much and they smile a lot. Overall, they take care of each other...all things I want to be a part of me.

So anyhow, here I am on my way to Isalo for the week. It's our site visit, but I'll only be in my village, Bereketa ('Big Cactus'!) in three days. I'm so psyched to finally see it, see Isalo and the villagers.

My village has three hundred people. It's in a prairie by a river and below a natural range that's the edge of Isalo. People get around with wagons and bulls... no taxi brousse go through. It's big on agriculture-some animals and crops, so I expect to be waking to a rooster each morn. I think they grow veggies, too. Jackie , an instructor, told me the men only wear swaths for clothes...I wonder how I'll feel in that setting!! I guess women wear dresses. I don't know if I'm staying in a temporary house that the police used during cattle thief search or if I'm staying with a family. The APN's will let me know if I have to hook up with the village builder this week and ask him to build my hut. I'm very psyched because I get to design it myself.

It'll be (hopefully) four by seven meters and I set it up with a stairway on the right side of the living room that goes up to a loft bedroom. I want a lot of windows, and two doors, one going to the garden and latrine. I put a front porch on my model, too. I made a model, 'cause Helen said that if the carpenter's illiterate, he won't be able to see my drawing in three dimensions, and therefore, won't understand the loft. So my little model will give me more of a chance to get what I hope for so I'll look through the window to my future tomorrow. For now I'm just enjoying the scenery and ride (it's comfy with only six in the car).

November 1, 1994

I'm at my site visit for the second night. I wanted to write last night, but I was too tired and having too many emotions to be able to write. I was happy to find that the men wear trowsers and shirt as I'm used to seeing. So much for loin cloth concerns. We're basically out in the middle of wide openness-the wild west! The whole park is "incredibly isolated". We left civilization a few hours before we arrived in Ranohira, and we're about four or five hours from Toliar, in the opposite direction.

Kirsten's town is the "big" town, which has one thousand

people, but is hidden in the middle of nowhere and it appears very small. There are a couple good-sized hotels by Malagasy standards, but they still didn't have much for food. Not many fresh veggies, and not much variety of anything else... and that's where we're all supposed to shop... or in Ihosy but it didn't look as though they had a much greater variety.

Joe and I are going to be bumming. After Parfait dropped Kirsten off, he took Joe and I to our villages...Joe first. We drove off the "main" road, which was a mostly dirt rough road onto, a road that was four wheeling material, We drove a long way, past beautiful rock outcroppings, and otherwise absolute non-civilization in wide-open Ravana.

We got to Joe's village after driving this back road for about fifteen minutes. It was really small only twelve houses, and fifty people. We went into one house with pretty much everyone and sat with (I think) the Reimen Dreny to discuss Joe's house construction. I could tell Joe was really scared, understandably. It seemed more like a tribe than like a village.

Before we left him (we stayed a while to make sure he felt okay) I pilered rice (pounded rice to remove the seed coats) with some ladies of the village. They all laughed really hard. Joe gave it a whirl after, too.

Villagers pillering.

When we left, we took a few of the villagers with us because one person was sick and they needed the hospital in Ranohira. Their clothes were so ripped and dirty, and the APN's who went with us brought them lots of rice. I don't think they eat much else.

Then we went to my village. The rock formations on the way were incredible. We were told by the APN's which road to take off the "main" road and it was barely noticeable. We drove 19 km down it seeing no sign of civilization and traveling down turns that made me honestly wonder if Parfait, our Peace Corps driver, would ever come back!

Before we arrived at the village, I was feeling elated that I would do this. I had played the Grateful Dead with Joe's villagers in the car, and they laughed and seemed to enjoy it. I felt I could get into the cultural exchange, and I felt definitely strong enough to deal with the hardships.

When we got to my village, we were approached by tons of children and everyone also looked on. A few adults approached and I felt what Joe felt - fear. The village was about three times bigger than Joe's and the scenery was as nice. The villagers and APN's got out five chairs for the APN's, the village chief, myself, and Parfait. Parfait was such a comfort. One APN explained Peace Corps and me, then I talked a little, and then this drunken guy stood up and rambled. A couple others talked, and then we put my stuff in the APN's house. The president of the village and his wife insisted I stay in their room ("more secure" he said). They stay in a different house.

The room was small with a bed and dining table in it. It was also their living room, so I'm only alone at night. I'm feeling that fish bowl effect...the people come in or stand at the door and watch me. It's difficult. The people are very dirty, without nice clothes, and without any food except for omby akoho, and mangos. They seem happy though.

We went to the church the first night and they sang and set up electric lights (that was weird). The service was so long that the president's wife walked me home to sleep.

I'm not sure how I feel here yet. It's so isolated...with not many fruits or veggies and it's probably four+ hours to bike to Joe's Angratsy (village). I have trouble with the dirtiness of everyone, and I also think some of the guys here could be a drag; it seems like they drink some, too. The villagers gave me rice and akoho as a Bada Fomba (culture) to welcome me. We killed the chicken for dinner. Oh, yes. I've seen that before. There's a river on either side of us, one being fast, probably no schista (a parasite).

Where will I put a house? Can I deal with so many kids and a few guys often drunk? Will the poverty bother me so much that I can't be happy? Ah, I'm just not sure. I'm feeling today I want to stay here more than not.

November 2, 1994

Well, it's my third night in Bereketa. I feel as though I could easily be happy here. Although I know that some times it will be really hard being so isolated and being such a magnet for the people here. The people are very loving, very patient and accepting. I don't know that Americans could live this close and in such a small group without really disliking each other.
 The kids here are really loveable. Even though I have a lot of trouble with the dirtiness, they show much more love to each other than American children do. They and everyone are really psyched on teaching me the language, and a lot of the adults really want to learn English.

There's one man, maybe the pastor here, who had a Malagache and also an English Bible. We read them both together with many other people and kids of course. I feel like the Pied Piper! It was a lot of fun actually - Donna would flip to find that out! It's nice talking with the villagers because they are patient and they listen...I'm used to everyone being in such a rush and having too much on his or her mind to listen well.

Parfait and Kirsten came today. He talked to the president about making my house but found out there's a house already here for me. It's not in the town center, so that's good. It has two pretty but small rooms, not many windows, and two doors. The Reimen Dreny said a latrine on the north side of the village would be no problem. Today I feel like I should stay and I'm still a bit shaky on being definite about it, but I think I want to stay. I hope I feel the same tomorrow. I just think it would be a good experience for me, considering the things I want to learn and change in myself. Yet, I didn't realize I'd be with so few people. I'm probably going to get really attached and it's going to be tough to leave. But that is one thing I feel I need to change in me. It is to stop avoiding situations where I get attached to people. My life would really be a lot richer if I stopped being timid about attachment.

November 3, 1994

It's my fourth and last night in Bereketa. I felt really good being here today. It was a bit up and down to start, but things smoothed out. It seems that if I'm having doubts and I mesh with the villagers my feelings get better. They're really good people. I'm going to come back. I'm feeling like I'll miss them all some this month and I feel I'm going to have some good friendships in the future. And, of course, some good hardships, too.

Bereketa villagers in front of mud hut.

Villagers were afraid of geckos. They thought their ancestors' spirits lived in them.

Seven

Return for More Training

Nancy, Kirsten and Joe were picked up for a day's tour of their surroundings before returning to the training center at the capitol. Nancy finds a retreat that she could bike to in the future. They have dinner at a hotel that was so beautiful that it looked like it was accidentally dropped in the wrong place. The owner was in Madagascar during World War II and determined that he would return to build his "castle".

Nancy spends time trying to accept life in this very foreign, beautiful land. She writes, "I'm sure sometimes two years will pass so slowly, but in actuality I know it's a very short time. It's definitely the most important thing I've ever done."

November 5, 1994

Parfait picked us all up today. The one request of my village was a "football," a soccer ball. I heard they're expensive. But since that was basically their only request, I want to get it.

After a meeting with DEF and the head honcho in Ranohira, Kirsten, Joe, Parfait and I went to the "Fenetre d'Isalo," ("Window of Isalo") a big hole in a rock, that we could look through and see the saints. It was a pretty spiritual place.

I sat with Kirsten and Joe in the window. It was kind of a landmark for me, because I know I'll be going back there in the next two years. Before I leave Madagascar I'll be looking through that window with different eyes.

We drove a little further after and hiked some incredible rocks with wild shapes from the ocean and sand rocks in the shape of flat coral reefs. It was pretty incredible how much the history showed in the formations and shapes of the rocks. There were mini-baobabs with fat trunks; fat leafed brown cacti, lizards sunning on the rock faces, and lemurs climbing some of the rocks. After, we went back to the Window and watched the sun set through it. We stayed about an hour until the sky was pink and there was a skinny crescent moon above. It was really gorgeous. We all decided we could definitely enjoy years of this. I need to remember that when the going gets tough.

Parfait drove us to the hotel in the rocks after that, where we had dinner with Landell Mills, who works for an English consulting agency that ANGAP hired to research a management plan for Isalo. (I'm sure we will be working with them.) The hotel was utterly beautiful. It is in what I consider to be the prettiest part of Isalo I've seen so far...with tons of huge rocks jutting up, and the lines of all the different rocks going in the same direction, where the wind or water shaped them. The rest was rustic, medieval, and really classy. We were really styled-out with an incredible dinner. It was great to hang out with Englishmen with that fun, dry humor. I met the owner of the hotel, too, who said, "You poor girl" when he heard I was living in Bereketa, because it is "difficile." He said, "This is your home," when I told him I'd be stopping in now and then on my bike for a drink on my ride to Ranohira. Not bad for a second home!

I've decided that since I realize I'm going to have a hard time being in a small village, now and then I'm going to make camping trips and take vacation times often, before I get to a point of depression, if possible. I think Joe, Kirsten and I may be going to Toliar for Christmas. I'm sure I'll need a break at that time. If we don't do that, I'll throw a pack on, grab my compass, and explore Isalo.

November 8, 1994

"Akoy" kin! (To Mom)

How are ya', girl? I'm just dropping you a quick note because one of the volunteers is going back to the U.S. tomorrow. He decided it's not for him...too bad, I really got along well with him. I just had a site visit to see where I'll live and work. I'll be moving there on November twenty seventh, after having Thanksgiving with an American family in Antananarivo. It will be a ritzy celebration, I'm sure. I'll enjoy it before going to rough it in a taxi brousse.

I wrote to you about Isalo Park. It's incredibly beautiful. It's a huge area of big rocky mountains with natural rivers within and places to camp and hike. There are three kinds of lemurs plus tons of birds.

The village I'll be in is right on the edge of the park, and there's a river on either side of the village. One river is fast moving, with no problems for me to bathe in. The other is slow flowing. I won't go in it until I know there are no parasites in it. I'll ask the villagers this. I cross the nice river and walk up a mountain and I'm in Isalo. It's quite an easy access get away when I need a break. The people are very poor, but very sweet. It will be a very different learning experience.

Mom, I was so well accepted, you wouldn't believe it! To think a "vazaha" (white foreigner) can just be dropped into a village to be taken in with open arms and no suspicions. It's quite amazing. I definitely feel in good hands. I think I'll have a fun time, taking lots of vacations with the money the Peace Corps pays-that I can't spend any other way! I'll be beaching and snorkeling in Toliar a lot! So, Mom, I'm well and happy and things are great.

Can you send me a few things in a bubble envelope? They travel faster than boxes. I need a set of calligraphy pen refills, and a 4 pack of AA batteries. Thanks, Mom!

I love and miss you, Nancy

November 11, 1994

Well, I'm just hanging in my room. I was a social butterfly tonight. Maybe it's 'cause I know I'm going to be away from these guys and missing them all soon. One of the volunteers is going back to the U.S.... he decided it's not for him. I gave him some letters to mail for me. I was sorry to see him go.

I've been trying to play my guitar more, but I don't feel like I'm very good, so sometimes I get bored with myself. If I can get many chords down well, I can probably do a lot of learning with it after. I'd like some music paper to write out the chords and understand what notes are in each chord. It would probably help me better understand theory when I start learning them.

I haven't been meditating. That's another thing I really want to start doing more of especially in my village. I should try to start doing it before I go, so that it won't seem so foreign to me there.

I hope I'm happy there. I feel like I can be... it's just going to take a certain mindset. I felt so drained for a few days after I returned here from there. I know that's how it's going to be a lot, seeing the poverty and dirtiness and feeling so distant from the way of life I knew in the U.S. I can't let it get me worried about living there, because I know that will change. I felt tired and drained after the first time I went to Antananarivo, because it made me so sad. Now, I go to Tana and I'm okay. I sometimes, like yesterday, enjoy my time there. It gets easier the longer I'm here. It will probably be like that in my village. I just have to ride the waves and remember how much I'll learn and grow through this and how many other people than just myself I'm helping. I'm sure sometimes two years will pass so slowly, but in actuality I know it's a very short time. It's definitely the most important thing I've ever done.

Nancy and a little friend washing their clothes in the river.

Nancy on her homemade mat in front of her hut .

Eight

Starting Life in the Village

Nancy's final acceptance as a volunteer had arrived.

On her trip to Joe's village, she demonstrates her ability to fit in and to make everyone comfortable around her. She seems to think her acceptance was because of "her" villagers. In reality it arose from her.

When asked about being a volunteer, Nancy wrote, "I'M READY FOR IT." And also, "I have to admit I'm incredibly happy here." Plans, plans, plans are what fills Nancy's life as she recorded with lavish detail all that is around her.

Nancy notes that she was 16 hours by car from the PC Headquarters in the capital of "Tana". She was the furthest out of all the PCV's. She was also 47 km from Kirsten, the nearest PCV to her.

November 15, 1994

Hi, Sweetie, (Mom)

I just received two letters from Helen, along with my invitation to be sworn in tomorrow. Helen, Mupemba and Mike [instructors] talked to me about how I did in stage 1. Everything they had to say was beautiful and very complimentary. They said my energy and smile makes people comfortable and happy to have me around. The way I try at things and work hard makes Helen feel I'll be really good at my work here. I know I'll have a good experience here. They also said I do pretty well at French and Malagashe.

When she said, "Am I wrong in inferring that you'd like to be a volunteer?" I responded "That's a given." I'm quite excited. It'll be a fun and a hard path. I'M READY FOR IT.

As for my letter from you that I just read, I already feel my growth from my first letter to you. I feel I was right in both respects that change is very gradual, yet there are times of "growth spurts" where I'm slapped in the face with new realities. Entering my village was like that. It was more intense than I had imagined it would be. That day of arriving was another big eye opener. We drove for four hours in flat plains with very few people anywhere and finally approached Ranohira, the "big tourist town." I laughed long and hard. I thought, "If this is the big tourist town what the heck am I living in, an ant hill?"

The town was probably a twentieth the size of Hudson, New Hampshire. It was quite civilized though, with a couple hotels, a school, small and big houses. But then, we drove 20 km down a dirt road on the edge of the beautiful mountains of Isalo. We passed no one and no villages at all. We arrived at a small village with about 13 huts, small ones. Many people came out; adults and children... about 50 people. The headman wore a striped shirt ripped down the front, ripped on the sleeve. The other people's clothes were the same: ripped dresses, pants. The children had dirty faces and messy, braided hair. I looked around and as I stood by Joe who was very scared I said, "No crap, Joe, we're in the Peace Corps!"

He said slowly, "a-yah," and I laughed! I pilered rice with the village women. They love it, and so did I. I had to try. Joe tried it too.

After leaving Joe, we had a few villagers in the car with us going back to Ranohira. I decided on the way there that this is where I wanted to be. I put on some Grateful Dead (rock music) and the villagers smiled at it and laughed. Yes, these were people I wanted to know. I was content. I prepared myself for my own village.

When I arrived. I had the initial fear I felt that Joe had had. I got to know many villagers through the week. They're wonderful people and I feel I'll be happy to spend some of my life here with others. I have to admit, I'm incredibly happy here. When I joined the Peace Corps this is pretty much exactly what I pictured. The villagers are very poor but much richer than most Americans. They are real and very happy. They smile a real genuine, love filled smile. If they're not smiling, they're still accepting of me, even when I do act different.

When we got there, I asked the children to take me to the river where I splashed water all over me and then on them. We washed our faces off. Mom, I went down to the river with 7 groups of kids. This may have to be a daily ritual for their dirty bodies and runny noses that bother me. We can have fun learning that this is something that you do everyday. Well, Mom, all is well so far. I am filled with joy. I'm really in the Peace Corps.

Love, Nancy

Children are bathing in the river where cattle cross, people wash dishes and clothes. This is also the drinking and cooking water for everyone.

November 17, 1994

I have to admit I'm incredibly happy here. When I joined the Peace Corps, this is pretty much exactly what I pictured. Joe's not as happy in his village. He said people aren't overly friendly - and he said where I am, is exactly what he, too, pictured P.C. to be. Kirsten agreed. I wish they had the same situation as me... I feel kind of bad. Kirsten's happy enough, but she still hasn't met many people and she doesn't yet know what Ranohira is all about.

I know I'll go through times of homesickness, but I don't feel like I'll feel out of place a lot here. I think I know what I am doing here. Questions won't come up for me as often as for others, because I've been so well accepted.

While I'm working on my house, Jardinier's family has lunch for me every day. I bought them oil today - they asked me how much and I said I wanted to buy it 'cause they've fed me so much... then I was brought a plate of food again! But I think they appreciated it, and I appreciated that they asked, "How much?"

I bought Gredy a loaf of bread, too. So anyhow, things are good for me. I think these people are as sweet as they appear. The fact that Jillian rode me the 47 km to Bereketa and 47km back to Ranohira and wanted nothing pleased me.

Xavier helped me mud and paint my house, with many other people pitching in, people feeding me, giving me fruit and veggies. I can see in their smiles, many of them, an instantaneous love, with a lack of judgement. It's such a welcoming feeling. Farana's smile, and the smiles of a little boy and his mother are so full of love, there's no way I could ever not trust them. Many people here are like that. If they're not smiling like that, they're still very accepting of me-even when I do act different.

November 20, 1994

Hi, everyone! Akoy aby! (Donna and John Powell, Alex, Ryan, and Lauren in the U.K.)

Last week I went to where I'll be living and working. Isalo National Park is absolutely breathtaking, and I'll be living right on the edge of it. We had to drive about 16 hours to get from Tana to our villages. The last three hours were through flat prairie lands, with not much civilization. All of a sudden up crops this huge mountain range, where the mountains are clay or rock, with diagonal parallel lines, where the ocean and wind carved them. It's really an incredible sight. It's sort of a circle of rock mountains that covers about 80,000 hectares. In the midst of the circle of mountains is forest patches, many rivers, and more mountains with three species of lemurs, tons of birds, and tons of reptiles and small mammals. I'm going to have two years of incredible hiking!

The village I'll be living in has a population of approximately 300 very poor but very nice people. There are a lot of children, who make great language teachers. I was very well accepted into the village, and was invited to stay in the huts of the president and his wife for my visit. I'll have a two-room hut when I live there. It's with a lot of other huts, but not in the village center. I'm very pleased about that. People were in the hut so I didn't see it. A cyclone whopped the hut of the present tenants. They'll have a new place by the time I move in. I have to have a latrine built, too. If it turns out the hut's not great, Peace Corps will pay to have a new one built for me.

There is a river on each side of the village, one with fast flowing clean water, so I can bathe in it without worry of schista, a parasite that lives in slow moving waters.

My village is out there though - it's a 47 km bike ride from the nearest big town, 27 km off-road and 20 km on a main tar road. One of the two volunteers I work with, Kirsten, will live in "the tourist town," Ranohira. The other volunteer, Joe, lives on the other side of the park/mountains from me. So I can bike to him (one or two day bike ride or bike around the park to him. We plan to all meet in Ranohira once every other week to see how our work's going, and so Joe and I can get supplies and mail. I'd like to go in every week, but it's a rough, long (4-5 hours) mountain bike ride. Therefore, I don't know if it will be possible. I may have to make it possible just for sanity reasons, to not feel so isolated.

There are a few other villages within 4 km of my own, but on a daily basis I'll be in just my little village. Yet, when I need some space, the park boundary is right on the edge of the village, so I just need to throw on my backpack and hike over a mountain and I'm in the park.

As for food, the villagers grow rice, carrots, and onions. They also have chickens and omby (cows), which I doubt I'll be eating because I refuse to slaughter one! There are also wild mango and banana plants near the village. I'll start my own little garden, too. I'm going to bring coffee, sugar and flour with me, ingredients like that to make breads. I'll buy a gas stove 'cause I won't have time always to deal with charcoal or wood. (Our training director taught us a way to cook breads on a gas stove.) Anything else I want, I'll have to bike in the 47km from Ranohira. Yeah, I'm likely to get very skinny!

That's my future life. It's a bit more intense than I had realized as far as isolation and the poverty in the village. But Isalo is so gorgeous that I think I can handle it. I'll take a break whenever I need space.

I'm getting sworn in tomorrow evening along with 17 others, and I'm ready to do this! I love you guys! Please write to my new address.

Love PCV, Nancy

November 24, 1994

Hi ya', Mom! Ahory!

Happy holiday! I'm a volunteer now, Mom! As of a few days ago I was sworn in at the U. S. Ambassador's house. Now I'm trying to buy things to fix up my little hut. We have the next two days to do that and then we spend Thanksgiving with different American families who live in the capital. I'm going with Joe, one of the two volunteers I'll work with at Isalo, to a couple who works with U.S. Aid and had been Peace Corps Volunteers. There are a lot of returned Peace Corps Volunteers that work here now. They work with Peace Corps or U.S. Aid or World Wild Life.

After that I head to my village. Peace Corps has given us so much money. I have more money than I had at home with a paying job! I won't really be able to spend it in my village, so I'm now buying some nice things to bring with me and I'll save the rest for country vacations.

At Christmas I'm going to Toliar, the town on the west coast near Isalo. I'm meeting about six other volunteers and we'll rent a house on the beach for a few days. We think we'll all need a break from our villages by then. It's going to be such a different lifestyle. I'm also going camping in Isalo for a couple days after a week or two in my village. I'm sure I'll need some time away from all the children, and away from the new language...it's draining speaking a new language, so I'll need to build in "mental breathers." Isalo is definitely good for that - it's so incredible. Well, Mom, you have Happy Holidays and I'll have happy holidays, too. My next letter will be sent from my new address, so it will take a long time for the next letter. The mail may be slower there.

Nine

The Beginning is in View

Christmas celebration for a small group of volunteers in a "real" city reveals, the hotel standards in Madagascar were much different from the U.S. So was bus transportation. Taxi brousse (a van-bus which was always overcrowded) had no time schedule. People just sat and waited and prayed that one would go by with room for them.

Name derivation in that country is interesting. When a child was born, a first name was given. The last name became the first name of the father. Therefore, every generation had different last names.

Nancy writes, "I feel safe here and I have my own three-room hut which I'm fixing up. Three rooms is incredibly nice here..." But she also finds, "I'm having trouble finding any boundaries. I think this is because I don't know their intentions and I'm scared to trust them."

November 27, 1994

Dear Mom,
Mom, I have the biggest cockroach I've ever seen in my life! He's in my hut now! It's the size of a small mouse and it just flew at me 'cause the candle is next to me! He has a tusk coming out

of his head! No lie!

Excuse me while I find a way to move him out of my house! ... He turned out to be quite docile. I wonder what the tusks are for. The female of that species must be scared out of their wits, or maybe the female are those hissing, spitting cockroaches (which Madagascar is known for, and which also live in my hut!). They hiss and spit to keep those overbearing males away! Oh well, as long as he doesn't use his tusk to dig his way back in here tonight!

Let me try to draw him now!

Love, Nance

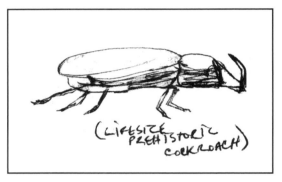

Cockroach drawing

December 10, 1994

Hi, Bryan (brother) and gang,

Odd card, eh! It's even odder to be making Christmas cards in 100-degree weather with not a drop of rain yet in sight and no aggravating commercials and jingles daily to try to brainwash us as to what Christmas is not all about! I can't say I miss that part...

But as for this Christmas, I'll picture all of you sitting by the wood stove at Dad's, drinking eggnog and rum and eating pecan pie and going skidooing at your place, while I'm basking in the sun drinking T.H.B. (Three Horses Beer) and wallowing in relaxation under a waterfall. What an odd concept, huh? Sometimes I do realize it's true that we are half a world apart, but most of the time I don't feel that far from you. I'll be with you in spirit for Christmas.

Love, Nancy

December 16, 1994

Hi, Dan,

How are you? I'm doing fine. I've been in my village for a week and half now and I'm very happy. It's nothing like home, but yet it's not that foreign either. I'm getting really comfortable here, although at first I was really nervous. The people here are so accepting of me. I don't feel judged at all here. It's quite a contrast from being with the other volunteers. It's nice to be away from them for a while.

So far I've learned how to mandesa (piler rice), and mehola rice (get the husks and rocks out), I learned how to plant peanuts, I know how to make "mofo gasy" (rice bread) and godro godro mofo gasy (made with bananas and as good as banana bread). It's amazing, Dan; you don't need flour to make bread. The dry rice is put in water to soak for about five minutes, then the water is drained out. After pilering it, sifting it, and pilering again the stuff that didn't sift, it's like flour.

Nancy pilering rice.

I have to say though the Gasy (Maligasche natives) laughed their heads off watching me piler the rice. I did, too. I've been laughing at myself a lot here, with good reason. I started a vegetable garden here and they got a major kick out of my technique with that, too. A Reimen Dreny (elder) of the village was farming next to me and he decided to teach me the Malagasy technique instead of laughing himself into a hernia.

I'm learning a lot, including the language, although it is going a bit slower than I expected. French wasn't that hard. However, I have to go back to it and improve it once I have Bara down. Learning a new language that is nothing like our own is a real challenge. It can be frustrating, if people aren't patient. But I'm lucky to be in a village where everyone's pretty lighthearted and patient with me. Of the three villages around Isalo,

I think I got the best placement. The hut I was supposed to get had people still living in it when I got here. I was just about ready to cry when I found out, because I had all my stuff with me and it was an hour's drive (47 km.) back to Ranohira. I had psyched myself up to "this is it." Yet the doctor (I didn't know there was one here) told me he'd let me rent his hut. It worked out better, because this hut is in part of a closed in area, where one huge extended family lives and they're enjoying having me here. I feel safe here and I have my own three-room hut (three rooms is incredibly nice here), which I'm fixing up with the doctor's help.

Today, after I went with a bunch of the people, who were all about my age, to plant peanuts, we started re-mudding inside my hut. (Once I got beyond the mud mixture, I was o k - cow dung, soil and water. It makes a great cement.) I thought we'd just patch up the house, but we totally re-mudded one room inside. It's really nice and it was incredible fun. We got so dirty...about four other guys helped us. I guess Bara women don't do work like this normally and they laughed hard when they saw me mixing the mud and start throwing it on the walls.

I don't think the doctor, Jardinier, realized what I meant by help. This guy's been great, he helps me a lot with the language. Yesterday he taught me how to make a basket. Of course, I loved that, and I'm already starting to make other stuff for my house.

So, Dan, things are going really well. I was feeling a bit melancholy, missing all of you during the Christmas season but I learned how to deal with it...I taught these guys "Lean on Me" and some Christmas tunes like "The 12 Days of Christmas," "Jingle Bells," and with my guitar, too, Dan! It makes me feel more at home when people are walking around whistling and humming familiar tunes. I'll have to tape them and send it to you guys. It's funny to hear them singing in English. They sound as funny as I'm sure I do to them in their language.

I did a major faux pas today and said, "Teaks ravitsy," instead of, "Tiako ravotsy," which means, "I like the wind. It's hot here". Everyone died laughing and one guy put his finger to his mouth and said "Ssh" while cringing. I don't know what I said I liked, yet. But I'm sure when I find out, I'll laugh like crazy or turn red as hell. Well, Dan, I'm well and happy and eating well, although the variety's not great. I've eaten more mangos in the last week and a half than I have in my life! And okay, okay, I'll say it...I love rice! There, I said it...it's happened. Are you happy? I'm part Gasy now!

Well, Dan, I love you!

Love, Nancy

P.S. Malagasy people love your music. Sometime if you can, will you make me a tape of your piano playing...for when I miss you? If you do wrap it well and tape it well, so no one rips it off and write "school supplies" on the envelope. Or if you write "church supplies" that's not likely to get ripped off, either. Why do I write like this every letter?

December 17, 1994

Hi, Donna,

How's everything going for you? I am doing really well here. It is a gorgeous night here, and the stars are truly spectacular, as always. There's no noise at all though, which is really surprising 'cause it's only 9:50 p.m. There is usually at least a flute or kabosy (Malagasy guitar) to be heard. But it's just quiet and peaceful and comfortably cool. It is only hot here during the day now, and cool in the morning and sometimes down right chilly at night. (It's the beginning of winter here now...if only they knew.)

I am enjoying life here, although sometimes I crave familiarity...it's so different here. Yet there is a "city" on the coast. If I bike the 5 hours to Ranohira I can taxi brousse there in about 5 hours so it makes for a good change of pace now and then. Ranohira's just a little town, so it's sometimes not different enough from my village when I am needing a change. All in all though I like living in a village, lugging my water up from the river, planting all my food (my garden's pretty impressive. Joy!) and writing letters by candlelight every night. It is a nice life style. Sometimes, though, I have trouble adjusting to the slower pace and I often wonder "What did I do today?...nothing, again." It is hard to change my whole view of things, to see life as how content I am, not how much I have produced. I think this life style is just what I needed for figuring that out. I spend a lot of time alone just thinking, and at home I was often going too fast to do that. So it is a nice change in pace.

I am still single, but I want to be. It'd be nice having a relationship with someone while I am living way out here - even if the person was right in Ranohira, it'd still be a long distance relationship! And I sure as hell don't want a relationship with someone in my village. With only 350 people there is no such thing as privacy!

There's such a cultural gap, too. People living the village life have often not seen much more than that. They could not even fathom the world I am from!

Well anyhow, Donna, I hope all's well with you and you are still enjoying your work, and having fun with the kids. Take care, girl!

Love, Nancy

Here I'm gardening with two villagers.

December 18, 1994

Hi, Denise!

I had this urge to write to you. I'm leaving in two days for Toliar, an exotic town (actually north of Toliar) to spend Christmas with friends and four other volunteers. Tonight, I'm sitting in my hut eating rice and traka (legumes) and drinking wine that some people (merchants, friends of the family I live near) brought on a charrette, which is a wagon pulled by two bulls. The wine's very good.

I closed my door tonight while cooking and eating, which I rarely do, but I felt I needed some space tonight. I also didn't feel like sharing my wine!

The hut I live in is in a little complex of the village, fenced in; it's only an extended family in this one area - three generations.

I didn't realize it was a family alone when I accepted to rent this hut, but it's worked out fine...they're good people and they respect the fact that if my doors are closed to leave me alone. Yet I'm having trouble finding any boundaries. I think this is because I don't know their intentions and I'm scared to trust them. I mean, if you were a bunch of natives living off the land, making your houses of mud, living off rice and a few vegetables, travelling the 47 km to town to sell vegetables and wearing nothing but one outfit, (or maybe two), that you got with a little of that money, then all of a sudden this "vazaha" (white foreigner) drops in out from nowhere to protect that National Park next to your home - what would you think? These people really enjoy giving - they're loving, sweet people. I can see it in their eyes. Kids don't fight here, Denise. There's no maliciousness...people just take care of each other. The people, the family I live with, are constantly giving me food and helping me work on my hut, (mudding two rooms and painting). Tomorrow I mud the third room. They're truly happy to have me here. But since they share everything with me, I think they expect the same of me...yet they're thirteen and I'm one. Now that I've written to you I know how to handle it - I'll just follow my gut, like I always do. For example, I bought them oil in town and when I got back they said, "How much?" I said I wanted to buy it because they'd been feeding me all week while I worked on my hut. Tonight I bought wine, they wanted to feed me tonight, I felt because they wanted me to share my wine. I said no, I wanted to cook, because I shared my last bottle with them and I wanted to drink this alone tonight and eat alone. So now, I'm content and I don't know what they think. I can only control my own feelings. They can make of me what they want. Anyhow, I think no matter what I do they're happy to have me. Well D, thanks for helping me work through that - I love you! Yes, I know you said nothing, but you listened. Yes, I'm buzzed!

Love, Nancy

P.S. Hey Dee, give Caleb and Leroy a major hug for me!

Nancy mudding her hut.

Nancy and friends building her hut.

Ten

Christmas Like No Other

A celebration in the village imposes customs that Nancy discovers with an uncomfortable situation. We follow her through the village partying, getting a 40minute nap and resuming the party for over 24 hours. This was a usual celebration in Bereketa. She was happy when it all ended.

Nancy writes, "I'm starting to think that there's no reason to not trust these people. Yet, my guard's not down yet, I guess because I'm not accustomed to people like this."

December 25, 1994

It's Christmas day today. I'm at the Bamboo Hut with volunteers; Linda, Todd, Joe and Kirsten. We've been here two nights now, after two nights in Toliar, one without Linda and Todd. The first night in Toliar, after a three and a half hour bus ride where some young Malagasy with the help of his family tried to pick me up, we stayed at what turned out to be a dive. The shower smelled like urine, the beds were squeaky and uncomfy, and the club next door was loud 'til 3 am...We got out of there early the next morning.

Kirsten and I found a nice hotel with little bungalows, the next night. It was so comfy I didn't want to leave. Todd and Linda met us there that day; we went out for pizza and caught up on our experiences.

The next day we took a taxi brousse on a 3-hour ride to go 50 km. to the Bamboo Hut. Todd paid for us. I said "dimy vazaha"...anyone in earshot laughed hard (we were the only vazaha on the taxi brousse). We looked very touristy, too, all with big packs, and each carrying a basket or two of tropical fruit, breads, wine, pasta, and small gifts for each other. I felt very European and rich. The locals on the brousse definitely thought we were tourists and laughed when they heard us speak their language from time to time. So it's been great being at this place.

Our little hut is great. We've just been lounging, swimming, eating and thoroughly enjoying each other's company. Joe's been more relaxed and happy now. He was really stressed out for a while...I think 'cause he's not as happy at his village as he had hoped. So we're all together - and actually yesterday, Bo (PCV) and his friend Barbara from the States showed up. So now there are seven of us.

The last two nights we ate at the restaurant here, but it's quite expensive. So today we went to lunch down on the beach, and tonight we'll cook spaghetti Christmas dinner with flambéed bananas and 3 bottles of wine. This morning they all woke up to Christmas stockings, of course, and we all had other gifts for each other. It was really special. Linda gave me a necklace, Todd gave me earrings, Kirsten gave me natural toothpaste (the practical type!), and Joe gave me a carved box that I'll use for pencils.

After, we had coffee, biscuits, cheese and fruit. Then we rented a boat and snorkeling equipment and went to the reefs. It was amazing. And now I'm hanging in a hammock, the wind blowing, the sun shining off to my side. I'm picturing my family getting up having coffee and waffles, getting ready to open presents and feast. I'm very content. I also wonder what my friends are doing. I think I want to buy myself a hammock for a Christmas present.

December 26, 1994

Here we sit, waiting at the Bamboo Hut entrance for a taxi brousse. One just went by fully overloaded. The reality just hit us that we may be here a good long while. Linda just said she'd give a lot to have a Domino's Pizza car go by. Wouldn't that be nice? I really don't even like Domino's! It would be heavenly right now, though. Ah, the luxuries of home.

I'm going to have to do two aerobics classes a day when I get back to keep from getting fat! So anyhow, we sit and wait. We racked up a 610,000 francs bill at the Bamboo Hut, $190...Not bad. I spent more than I had expected to on this vacation, but yet I always do. I've already spent my whole moving-in allowance.

I'm feeling a slight underlying depression today-maybe from mefloquin, I don't know. I don't know if it's 'cause I'm leaving here and don't want to, or if it's 'cause I've been away from my village too long and want to get back or if it's cause I've spent too much time here, or because I'm slightly holiday homesick. Maybe that's it. It's kind of weird to be depressed and have no idea as to why. It's the same feeling I had visiting Kirsten in Ranohira. Mind you it is slight. I thought it's 'cause I was anticipating having to go back to my village and didn't want to... Yet when I got to my village, I realized that the depression was due to having been away from my village. Well, it's not strong enough to worry about... just a bit unnatural feeling. Enough of analizing my feelings.

December 30, 1994

I'm back in my village now and I am very happy to be here. I came back to find some village men had worked on my shower, mudding the whole thing. I was so psyched... but I again didn't understand it and had an underlying thought of "What do they want?" The more I get to know these people, the more I think they're just helping me 'cause they like to, and they're appreciative of my being here.

My house is not the only one that's been worked on-where Jardinier (the doctor and my landlord) now lives is all new now with cement, new mud inside and out, and painted 2-tone white and blue (fotsy and manga). Bota's house is painted, and Jardinier's mom's house is all new, too. They needed to buy nothing but cement - they used white earth to paint - I didn't ask yet how they made blue, only 'cause I'm not quite sure how to ask.

Jardinièr and I painted my third room and shower yesterday. Saban 'Bota put in my two screen windows for a bottle of wine. When I went out for a little while I came back to find Jardinièr doing the bottom half of the big room blue, like his and his mom's house. I like it, but I must admit my hut looks more like an apartment than a hut! I left my bedroom earth tone so I would remember where I am!

Everyone here was really happy to have me back - Jenny and Xavier (young village friends) said they missed me. It was nice to feel like I missed being here. The underlying depression I felt in Ranohira is gone again so I guess it was due to being away from here. I was supposed to go to Ranohira January first to have dinner with Cindy and Buff McKenzie at the Hotel de la Reine, with Joe and Kirsten, but I told the people here I'd be here "Bon Annei." I thought that was New Years Eve only. Here the first, as well, is considered Bon Annei. So I don't think I'll bike in to Ranohira. I set a date of the fifteenth with Joe and Kirsten in case I didn't get in, so I'll just wait. I bought some wood today off a charette and Bota's making me a coffee table, a table for my stove, and a bookcase. He wouldn't give me a price, he said, "...Whatever you like..." He really didn't want to name one. I think it made me realize that he helps because he wants to and he likes to work, too.

I'm starting to think that there's no reason to not trust these people. Yet my guard's not down yet, I guess because I'm not accustomed to people like this. (Is it real, or is it Memorex?)

Bota's wife, Bota and Nancy posing by his new charette.

Eleven

Bon Annei

Nancy's love for me brought joy to my heart and tears to my eyes. It was the greatest gift she could give me.

Nancy is becoming part of the village with a focus on friendship, laughter, discovery, and jealousy. New insights were constantly immerging for this volunteer. She was learning to accept the emotional roller-coaster ride. Nancy is also learning to abandon the American characteristic of judging others. The insights in this chapter are profound. Ponder these ideas.

She had Christmas from home on January 16th. There was no mail going into Bereketa. For mail she would bike the 47 km. to Ranohira. This trip took 11 hours that day.

Her first physical problem occurred at this time. Popping corn had village problems, too. Oh what we take for granted in the U.S.

January 1, 1995

"Dimy amby sivy polo sivan jato sy ariva" (Today's the first day of the New Year.)

It's almost eight in the morning here, which means I've been celebrating for eight hours+ and it will soon be New Year's Eve in the U.S. (midnight). I had a fun but confusing night. I only slept forty minutes because in Madagascar, at least with the Bada culture, which are the people of my village, they don't sleep until the evening of January first. We danced all night. I wanted to go to a few houses other than in the area where Jardinier's family lives.

Hoasa, Mama's father, who lives next to Jardinier's family but outside the fence, showed up at a house I was dancing at, he got drunk on tokoa gasy (moon shine), and said he didn't think it was right my leaving Jardinier's area. The dancing stopped, the music stopped and he lectured. Xavier with many other people defended me. Then Xavier told me what was up, so I said I wanted to leave. I didn't want to spoil the party. People told me to stay but I left with Xavier, Abodo, Roger and Boda, too. I was really upset-pissed off is more like it. One of them woke the president to discuss it, which bummed me out more. He said I should go back to Jardinier's until morning until it was light. I did, and worked things through with him. Unfortunately Boda and Abodo went with me, but not Xavier. They were both a bit drunk and loud. Things turned out okay. It was 11:15 p.m. and we danced 'til midnight. I was sad, but Jardinier's mom danced with me and cheered me up.

At midnight a lot of people came in and kissed each other on the cheeks (three times), and danced. Farana and his brother came in really drunk and asked Jardinière if they could take me to another house. He said, "No problem, just walk Nancy back." People clapped and hollered when I entered. I think some of them had been at Xavier's uncle's house and were glad to see me happy and dancing again. So we danced a lot.

Farana could barely stand. The president stopped in, about as drunk as Farana, and took me to Xavier's house to dance. A few people from Farina's house soon showed up, too, including Farana. So I danced a bit more and at 4 a.m. Dori and Farana walked me back (or I should say I walked Farana!) We visited Jardinière and then I went to sleep for forty minutes, and got up and went visiting people and dancing again.

I visited the church. I like listening to the singing - the kids singing and dancing was so fun I had tears on my face. After, I took about forty pictures for people to buy. It was a bit frustrating after a while though. At first I danced between photos at each family's hut after I was tired and I wanted to stop. It got so I wasn't having fun anymore. Before I had had lunch and wine with Jardinièr and his family, I was ready to party, but half way through I needed to rest. When I finished taking two rolls I went and found Xavier to pig out on mangos, unfortunately, he was at the president's house, who was still really drunk and hung on me to dance again. I was glad Xavier was into leaving fast. We had a good talk about last night on the way. He also told me people aren't happy with us hanging together so much...I knew that was coming. I'll have to think about how I want to deal with this new situation - I probably just won't change, and let them think what they want.

Now there's a storm, and I'm happy for it...the dancing and singing stopped, so I'm not feeling obligated to party. Now I'm sitting here writing and making tea, about exactly what I want to be doing. So although I've felt like I've been on an emotional roller coaster for this holiday, it's been fun. I must say, I learned quite a bit about the culture this holiday. And man, can they drink!

Villagers dressed for church in their Sunday best.

Village teens, Nancy, and Xavier after church.

Omby (cows) outside my living room door.

Twelve

Problem Solving

Speaking three languages has problems when you lack proficiency in two of them. Also, being a "rich" American gives a false picture to the family Nancy rents her house from. She was really struggling with the family's cultural differences. It was very un-American and foreign to her. The plus side of this was that she started to develop friendships outside the fenced in family group.

Nancy wrote her impressions of what Peace Corps really is. The reader can, at times, feel Nancy's tranquility settling in while she is accepting the Malagashe culture, and showing the villagers a little of American culture. You can also feel the emotional struggles as she lives this different life. Malagashe children show much love to one another. There was no competition there.

Nancy writes, "I dream now in Malagasy Mom...I'm also starting to throw in Malagasy words when I speak with my American friends."

Christmas was celebrated Jan 16th with packages from home. Nancy had to bike to Ranohira to get her mail and packages which she did about every two weeks.

This chapter, also has many profound insights.

January 7, 1995

Hi, Mom!

Have I ever told you what a sweetheart you are? Thank you so much for taking care of me! I feel like you're helping me through everything...I have to say I miss you the most of everybody. But your last letter said you were sorry to have neglected me so. Mom, you have far from neglected me! Most every time I bike in to Ranohira there is a letter or a box from you, or a letter from your class - you and my friend Andrea are always there for me! It's a great feeling - I don't actually feel very far from home!

So you got my negatives. Were the pictures answers to any questions? I need to take a roll of events in my village for you and your class so you get a true taste of the village life - it's hard though, 'cause whenever people see my camera, they want me to take pictures of them. I just shot two rolls of only villagers and their families to give to them, but I haven't yet taken a roll of film I'd like to take for everyone at home. I'll do it soon. I'm presently making a cassette for you and your class with the villagers singing and talking... maybe I'll take a roll of pictures and send that, too. It won't go out 'til fara fara Fevrier (end of February).

I dream now in Malagasy Mom, did I tell you that already? It's good in some ways, but I never feel as well rested as I did at home - I don't sleep really deeply because of it - it's like I'm working in my sleep. I'm also starting to throw in Malagasy words when I speak with my American friends because they now come more naturally. That's weird, huh? After only two months in the village I do believe I'll sound like quite an idiot in the States after being here two years. My first instinct in many ways will be to talk Malagashe! And Mom, when I go to Ranohira I visit Kirsten, we often speak and work with French researchers and I need to speak French...well, have you ever seen the Looney Tunes Cartoon? Dr. Jekyll and Mr. Hyde take off where there's a sweet little man walking down the road and all of a sudden he starts having body convulsions and starts turning into a monster? Well, that's what I feel like now when I try to speak French.

I was getting pretty good with my French before, but I had to stop and start learning Malagache, and now that I'm in nothing but Malagache speaking environment, I've lost a lot of it. I try to even say, "Hello, how are you," in French, and it comes out something like "Akoy! Ca va henas!" with a bit of English to follow...Then I usually follow this with a bit of laughter by me. So I get quite a kick out of it for now, but after I'm more fluent with Malagache I need to go back and learn French. It doesn't look very professional this stage I'm at now. I was getting pretty fluent with French before so I'm sure it'll come quickly once I go back to studying it.

So, Mom, everything is going great for me. I'm starting to get to know enough people in the village to start getting some good friendships going. Unfortunately, none of them really being the family that lives right around me. They got in the habit of asking for anything and everything - coffee, sugar, oil, money, a little here, a little there. With ten kids, a mother, a father, an uncle, a grandmother, and a great grandmother, this can get a bit tiring. I put an end to it last week. I lent the mother and grandmother money they said they'd pay me back the next day. When they didn't, and didn't again the day after, and then one of their kids asked me for oil, one for vinegar, and the next for coffee, I got visibly angry and refused all of them.

The last one who visited me I said, "I will not give you coffee... go buy it at the market next door" (there's a little stand). I will not give you anything else, because I gave your mother and grandmother money they haven't paid me back and I don't know that you'll replace the food I give to you either!"

The great grandmother's hut is attached to mine and must have heard it all. She told the whole family, 'cause no one's asked me for anything since! Yet there are no hard feelings. I'm buying vegetables and mojo gasy (Malagasy bread) from them without giving them money 'til they pay off their small debt. So I'm very glad it all happened 'cause they visited me way too much before and I was feeling suffocated in my own home, especially since my hut is in the middle of all theirs, and the whole area is all fenced in.

Since that happened, I've been visiting more people. There are some people I'm spending a lot of time with and becoming good friends with. They don't ask me for stuff like most of the other villagers do. They just hang out with me because they like being around me. I don't give stuff to people when they ask, because so many people ask (especially for medicine. I've had to lie and say that I have none...). Before I was giving to the family around me because I was so intermeshed with them and they fed me a lot, but now I don't and I think that's best.

I'll tell you, Mom, I get invited to a lot of great meals. In the Malagasy culture, they just love to feed people...it works out great 'cause I just love to eat. There's this one woman next door with a husband and son (who I'm a good friend with) that is an incredible cook and who often yells over the fence for me to come over for lunch. It's great, 'cause I don't like to cook much 'til evening. In return, I give her vegetables now and then. For awhile there, everyday was a major emotional roller coaster, where sometimes I wanted to be around people and sometimes I just wanted to shut the doors and keep people from visiting (in this culture if the doors are open it's an open invitation and people just walk in).

I've started picking my friends instead of them picking me, I'm feeling happier and more stable. I know I just needed to get my personal boundaries set up, so I wouldn't get "walked on." After the incident with the family and, also, after calling the guys back who built my bookcase to rework it 'cause they did an unacceptable job, I think people realize a bit about who I am.

I'm very happy to find that many people here do not want to have friendships with me for the sole sake of having a friendship. I knew it was so obvious I have so much. I knew many people would be "testing me out" initially. But I've "passed the tests" and I'm starting to feel at home now.

Well, Mom, I'll let you go for now. I love you more than I can write. Stay well and happy and if your life is stressful take up yoga! I've been doing it every day and it's a great relaxer and food for a sore back.

January 8, 1995

Hi, Dave W, (friend in Brother Dan's band)

Thanks so much for your letter. It was a great one. It was nice to hear that you feel a lot like I do about people in third world countries. Maybe they don't have much, in America's view of having much, yet I've never seen people as happy as these people. They're poorer than anyone I've ever known is, that is, the way I've learned "poor." I'm learning that that doesn't matter. They're rich in the ways that matter. People don't fight here, Dave.

Children don't hit and yell at each other, they play with each other; and carry their younger siblings around. It's as if, because they're living closer off the land and they're closer to survival than we are, they cooperate more. They don't compete.

I've never felt as taken in and unjudged by people as I have here. They're like that with each other, too. It's not just a first impression thing. I've yet to be laughed at, although I'm constantly laughed with! So, I have to say, I don't think the people here need to be "westernized," as we'd say. In fact, as I sit here writing this, there is a full moon, I'm sitting outside, and about ten of the villagers are outside singing together. They do this every night. I've gotten in the habit of coming out and listening and humming along and giving them my guitar to use. I've taught them a few American songs too. I'm teaching them the "Twelve Days of Christmas," and tomorrow "Jingle Bells"...or maybe tonight.

The bulls are lying down to rest after pulling the charrettes all day. The chickens are in their house now. I just "pigged out" on mangos and I'm stuffed. A lot of people are walking around singing. It's very tranquil.

Today some villagers and I planted peanuts. There were about twenty of us, Later about five of us re-mudded my hut inside. Tomorrow I'm painting. They're very accepting of me, even though, in a lot of ways, I'm different. It's nice, because I like them, too. I'm not questioning myself, either. I'm starting to just accept myself.

When people laugh with me, I can feel their fondness toward me. A little voice says to me, "Of course they like you, Nance. How could they not?" It's new for me to hear this voice and it's happened a few times in the last couple of days. Maybe it's my own self-confidence starting to blossom. It's weird, Dave, because I'm not even sure that it's my voice! It makes me realize how rarely I've been in an environment where I don't feel judged.

So how did I get off on that tangent? I was starting to respond to your question about Peace Corps. I think the bottom line is, yes, I think the Peace Corps is very tied into the government and is concerned with getting our foot in the door in these countries. The government is helping them to progress and get "a piece of the pie." That's the way the American government is, I think. Yet, it's nothing to worry about, I don't think, because everyone I've met in the Peace Corps were once Peace Corps volunteers. Although the government has its ideas of what Peace Corps motives are and they fund the Peace Corps, the people who work directly in Peace Corps especially, the volunteers, really are here because they care about the people. They want to learn about the people. It seems many people in the Peace Corps come to the realization that these people are not in need in the ways we initially thought. We end up helping them in ways that truly will improve their lives, like better health. We learn how much they actually know about what really matters, which ends up improving our lives. It's a great cultural exchange.

Although the government has plans for our work, we're just a few people working in a few small villages. Rarely does a project get big enough to "westernize" any third world country. The people working in the Peace Corps are cool enough that the government's underlying plans are rarely felt by the countries we work in. The volunteers working first hand do not represent the governmental attitude. Some of them do. They don't work directly with the people, though. They are more in the capital of the countries, working and living in big houses and having hoity-toity parties. I think people remember Peace Corps by its volunteers. We're pretty cool people usually, Dave, just like you.

Dave, I am so glad your house is beautiful. Mine is, too! I have a three-room hut. I am totally in seventh heaven. I have a river on each side of me and am getting in shape biking the 94km. round trip weekly to Ranohira. It's not an easy life, but I am really enjoying it so far.

Keep in touch, Velumo
(Good-bye), Nancy

January 8, 1995

Well, I took off on my bike today after sleeping 'til eight, going outside and visiting for a little and sleeping again 'til noon. I'm feeling a bit melancholy and suffocated. My house is done and it's beautiful, but I'm having trouble feeling at home here. Whenever I open a door, the family I'm renting from walks in. So does Xavier. I like Xavier visiting though, but he comes over a real lot now, a bit too much. I think he'd be cool if I told him not to visit so much. I don't know how to go about saying it to him and the family that I live with. Basically, I'm realizing that so much of the growth I want I need to be alone for. It's hard to be alone in my home, unless I have the doors closed. Then it can be really dark and stifling.

I'm now at my favorite spot on the river, trying to figure out how to be happy in my environment without making other people unhappy or uncomfortable. It's hard, 'cause even when the doors are closed, people still talk in to me if they know I'm home. I've come to this spot on the river a few times now. I jump under the waterfall to bathe, and then I meditate. My brain has yet to shut down enough so that I can focus on my breath.

I just did 60 sit-ups, which was the second time I've done that since I'm here. I'm just having trouble doing any of my usual stuff here, like sit-ups, playing the guitar, drawing, reading a lot, or studying a lot. I tend to always have people in my house.

That's exactly what I said I knew I'd have a problem with. I said I'd have a porch so that wouldn't happen. I either need to make an abrupt change and tell people I'm starting my work now so I can't visit, or do it gradually. I am happy here, but I know that if I don't get some boundaries set up, decide what I need for space and let other people know, then I won't be happy here for long. It's a matter of learning their culture and working within it.

January 16, 1995

Hi, Mom!

I can't believe how much you did for me for Christmas! And I can't imagine how much it cost! But you said not to worry, so I won't. Your present was an incredibly good surprise after a long hard day. I biked in to Ranohira, after getting a bit lost. I was very tired, so to find your present, as well as the box that Dan G. sent me the day I left, was spirit lifting. Everything I sent myself was still intact, as I'm pretty sure it was with your box, too! The next day I went to the post office to find a box from my closest friend, Andrea, with many small gifts, too. I also got a necklace from Denise and about ten Christmas cards! So I just had Christmas on January sixteenth! But I have to admit; I was so excited about your gift that I was pretty burnt out when I got to my other stuff! I waited a day before I opened the rest!

But God, Mom, you make me really happy...my life is complete...a mud hut with a Mickey Mouse pillow! There's something very ironic about that. I don't know that you could have done any better Mom! And the tee shirt was great. I needed it, the quality of clothes is bad here. It felt great! And the toilet paper...Ah, sitting is a pleasure now! (Ha! Ha). And I, Kirsten and Joe thank you for all the junk food! I'm glad I could help you by giving you an excuse to buy a bag of Snicker's...I love them and I know you do, too! Ha! Ha! The harmonica hit the spot too, Mom. The visor is quite tacky, a very good gift to send to give the villagers a true sense of Americans. Thank you, Thank you, Thank you!

In my own box that I sent to myself is the book you gave me on how to draw and do calligraphy. So I'll probably get into those projects soon. Although, right now I'm learning to weave a floor mat, tihi, (te he) for my bedroom.

I head back to my own village the day after tomorrow. I'm still at Kirsten's in Ranohira and helping her move into her huge hut (house), 'cause it's been remodeled and cemented. She's been living, 'til now, in the building that'll be our office at the National Park Service. Tomorrow we're going into the park with one of the researchers studying the tree species. ANGAP, the national park service of Madagascar, hired them, and we're going along to pick their brains. We're kind of starting from scratch on the knowledge of plant and animal species here, since 95% of them are nowhere else in the world.

In 2 weeks I'll be going with a researcher studying for 5days the reptiles here. I'll take good notes on the snakes for you, Mom! I'll probably get the luxury of taking a car ride to my village the day after tomorrow. I think a nun here is going to visit my village. I don't mind the bike ride, but with all my stuff I just got here, I need a lift! (I feel like a spoiled brat).

left to right- Nancy, Niener, Angelin, Jean-
Baptiste, Achille, and Angeluc.

Ma, I'm exhausted and want to sleep, so I'll sign off. Just wanted to tell you thanks and I love you. I have to get out of Kirsten's comfy sleeping bag though and go to the vase first. They have a saying here, Mom; "Oko inbo tsy akche" which translates to "people aren't chickens"...people say this when they have to go pee, and chickens don't pee they only crap (this was news to me!). So if a bunch of people are riding in a taxi brousse and one needs to pee, he or she just yells out to the chauffeur "Oole mbo stsy akoha" (i.e. I am not a chicken!!) Then the chauffeur will pull over. It's pretty funny.

Well, Mums, love you and miss you. I'm not as far from you as I actually am!

Love ya, Nancy

January 20, 1995

Hi, Powells, (Donna's family)

How is everyone? Hope you had great holidays and hope your trip was great, John! Thanks for the Christmas card and Ryan, thanks for the post card! I'll write you soon and send Malagasy money!

My three-room hut is all finished. I'm renting it from the doctor. I've mudded it with his and other people's help. The Peace Corps paid for cement, so all the floors are done now. There's also a small room off the back for taking bucket showers. I just pour water into my shower bucket, which is high up. It actually has two faucet handles, a shower-head and a drain in the floor. No heated water though. The back room is off the kitchen, and I have a porch. There's also an out-house off the back door.

I bought paint and painted one room and I left one earth tone brown. I painted one with white earth on the top half and blue tinted earth on the bottom, so my kitchen is two tone! I also bought big woven floor mats and made curtains and door curtains out of a pretty sheet I bought. So I probably now have about the nicest looking hut in Madagascar! I'm feeling pretty at home. I live in a fenced in area, actually in an extended family unit, a woman and husband with their ten kids (ages three months to my age) and her brother, the doctor (from whom I rent), and their mother and grandmother. They've taken me in as their own, which is both good and bad. As is their custom,they visit way too much. But I'll figure out what I need for boundaries and work them in - no biggie!

All in all, I'm very happy here. I eat rice bread and have coffee for breakfast, mangos and bananas for lunch, and rice and veggies for dinner. I think that about covers the food. Now and then we have milk from the cows. There are guavas, and mangos which are almost done until November. I'm sad about that! I was up to eating about eight mangos a day!

Once every other week I bike in to Ranohira, the "tourist town" where Kirsten lives. Joe, who lives on the other side of Isalo, the national park does the same. It's 47 km for me and it takes me five hours. So I'm getting in pretty good shape.

How were your holidays? Mine were great! I spent Christmas on the beach, four hours west of me, at a great beach resort with 5 other volunteers. They were little bamboo bungalows and the place was right off the reefs in the Mozambique Channel. We snorkeled Christmas day. New Year's was spent in my village and we danced all night - didn't go to bed at all! I visited about eight huts and every new family I went to was so psyched the vazaha (that's me!) was visiting. They'd put in a new tape and start dancing. I didn't rest 'til the evening of the first. I felt like I was doing a dance-a-thon!

I'm just glad I'm in a village with spirit! My language is coming slowly, though...it's hard for me, but I'm getting a lot of help. I'm starting work a bit, now that my hut's done. I went with a researcher for four days last week to study plants in the park. I got many plant presses. I am going with someone to study animals next week.

Well, all, I love you! I'm well and happy. Hope you are, too!
Nancy

January 21, 1995

I spent the week in Ranohira, after going for three days with Landell Mills, a researcher. We went to study trees in Ala Lava. I was here for a couple days in between. I didn't mean to stay in Ranohira so long, but there were people there with Landell Mills and ANGAP that I talked with. Montere went to Andreamanero I wanted to go along to see Joe. I also was a bit intimidated by the bike ride, 'cause I got lost for six hours on my way to Ranohira.

Here I am now, back in my village. I've undergone so many emotions since I last wrote. This experience is such an emotional roller coaster. My emotions can absolutely flip-flop in a matter of minutes. I can go from thinking these people are so special, two years will go by way too fast; to, man I need some space, these people won't stop asking me for things, how am I going to make it two years? I guess it's all in perception.

Sometimes I feel at one with the villagers, and feel like they accept me and take me at face value. Yet, sometimes I feel like I'm being laughed at, like they just want me here to get what they can from me. Every time I open the door (the door to me, not the door to my house) I feel content with everyone. I feel the good vibes. Sometimes it's easier to just sit in my bed, read and not deal with anyone. I could see myself getting into a real rut if I did that often. I'm sure I'll do it now and then, and just say I'm sick, but I worry about getting on a low and staying there, by doing this many days in a row. Oh well, it's just something to be careful of. Now I'm content enough and I'll be really busy the next couple months, so I should be fine. I do realize that most of this experience will be what I make of it, more so even than what it does, or what reality actually is.

Maybe people are laughing at me, yet I break out laughing, too, and I perceive them as laughing with me. Does it matter if they truly were laughing at me? I don't think so-not from what I experienced of life so far. I think perception counts a lot more than I ever realized.

January 26, 1995

I wrote to my family today. I'm starting to get the hang of how to live here happily. I think that I have to accept the fact that it will be an on-going roller coaster ride... simply because the way of thinking is different here. The culture is entirely different. When I forget that (which is often), and look at people here from U.S. eye, it doesn't work. I end up misperceiving people's intentions a lot and feeling angry or offended, or homesick! I often feel like I'm being laughed at or teased when I look at the people here from U.S. eyes because in the U.S. we're constantly aware of what we're doing. Whenever people are around we feel we're being judged. It's because in the U.S. we are. Here, it's not the same. People don't judge you; they just accept you. I don't know if it's because the people here have to work together to survive. This makes them more unified. In comparison, Americans are more competitive. Their togetherness could be because they live on such a basic survival level that they think of people the way they think of other aspects of nature, not something to be judged, just something to be accepted.

I thought about that when I was studying trees in the forest near my village. I thought, if I was looking at a tree with big thorns on the branches, I'd just write down as a characteristic of the tree, "This species has thorns." I wouldn't like it any less or more than trees without thorns. I think the people here, at least the people living on the village level, think of other people that way, maybe themselves too...(using thorns just to get the point across) they seem sincerely happier. So I learned that when I'm feeling frustrated and I'm feeling laughed at, to just laugh. The only difference between being laughed at and laughed with is that when I'm being laughed at, I'm the only one not laughing!

There are times when I just want to go into my little cozy three-room hut and lock the door, but I'm starting to find that those are the times I most need to go out and socialize. Every time I do this, I'm okay after. I always feel better after I let the villagers in. If I don't, I end up looking at them from my own culture's eyes, because that's all I have; I end up isolating myself (it's not them, it's me). That is when I get to feeling depressed and feeling like I don't belong. I can easily see how people "know who they are" after this experience, because every day is a roller coaster ride. If I can stick through it without giving up, I'll have a good idea of who I am! The question is, will I understand who everyone is in the U.S. when I get back? They say the culture shock's a lot more intense going home than coming to the new country.

I believe I have it in me to hang in there through the downs. I've been starting to do yoga and a short meditation every morning. That seems to ground me a bit. I need it here, since once I open my doors, more people than I would personally invite in visit me! It's the culture here: with no TV's, no cars, no books or pen, only 350 people and no one else for 5 km., you tend to visit people a lot!

It'll take some getting used to, especially since I have books, paper and pens/pencils, a bike, a guitar, oh yeah...and work (although I'm not sure what it is yet). But the world here is really beautiful and I'm pretty content. There are the rivers on either side of the village where I go to every morning and evening for water, and across the river are the mountains of Isalo. There are wild fruit trees all over... mangos, quavy, tamarin, tapa, samoty, oranges...I'm also so much more laid back now- something I was hoping to get out of this experience. I don't rush anymore, I don't stress, and I don't really worry about things now.

February 25, 1995

Hi Dan!

How are you? I'm doing great, although I have my ups and downs and ups and downs and in between a couple ups and downs. But all in all, I'm feeling quite stable (ha, ha!) Dan, I got your letter - thank you so much! You sound great. Decisions, decisions, huh? I can't say I'm going through the same, though. For once in my life, I feel like it's okay to be just where I am, and I'm finally managing to enjoy the present instead of always looking toward the future. It's as if I've been given permission, by me and by everyone else for that matter, to do this for two years and to not question why I'm doing it. The fact that I'm doing it is enough.

Why is it not like that in the United States? Why is it that no matter what I did, I always questioned, "Is this what I want to do for the majority of my life? Am I doing enough? What should I do next?" Yet here it's like, "Who cares what I'm going to do next? This is where I want to be now."

Yes, it's tough sometimes. I find the times when it is tough are usually when I'm really homesick and lonely and my perspective is negative. So many things here that are happening to me and are making me realize just how much you get out of life is determined by how you view it, not by what it actually is (what things actually are). Did I say that right? I don't know. Okay, I've thought about it. I want to re-say it.

I'm realizing that how meaningful our lives are is determined more by our perspectives of things, more than on what things actually are. Simply because we don't see things as they actually are; we see things from our perspective. What is meaningful to us is totally dependent on who we are and what we've been through. (Does that all sound profound or stupid?) Oh well.

Anyhow, since I've started to realize this, I've started changing my approach to things. I'm starting to change my perspective on things that I don't like instead of changing the thing (or person) itself. It's much more enjoyable and relaxing, because I don't feel like I'm always trying to control things anymore, just my own emotions. It feels much more natural. What right do I have feeling like it's my right to change everything? It's just my perspective of the thing that needs to be changed. That doesn't mean it actually needs to be! Well, that's enough on that - I'm heading to the point of babblation.

Dan, I just got back from a 9-day hike through Isalo National Park ("my back yard") with some researchers who are studying the reptiles and amphibians. The place is utterly gorgeous, Dan! I can not explain to you the beauty I saw. We walked through areas where I could stand on the trail and look straight down beside me into a canyon 200 meters deep. In this canyon was a forest and river. When I looked to the other side, I could see huge limestone mountains jutting up in a line, going from a small mountain to a tall one which was made up of tan and red granules. I could sometimes hear Sifaica Lemurs in the canyons below. I had some really breathtaking moments.

Once, on the walk, I was behind part of the group and way ahead of the rest of the group. So, I sat at the top of this massive rock, looking into this incredible valley with rock formations jutting out everywhere, with a clear breeze going by and thunder starting and I just sat and admired and thinking, "So this is my back yard." I thought of you as I sat there. You'd love it, Dan. As I meditated, I labeled this "thinking" and you passed. Ha, ha! Only mentally did you pass. I think, spiritually, you were still sitting with me! It was a nice few moments.

I hiked a good portion of Isalo on that trip, hiking about 80 km (1.6 km. = 1 mile). It was a hard, fantastic trip. My foot's now elevated, though, because I had a bug bite on my foot that got infected from the dirt and water and is now swollen and numb. I'm at Kirsten's in Ranohira, and need (or want, I should say) to return to my village. But I'm just going to hang here for a couple days to make sure it'll heal okay. There's a doctor here if I need him. Once I'm in "the bush," it'd be tough to get back here if it gets worse. Not bad, though, being here six months and this is my only problem I've really had in the way of illnesses.

Love, Nancy (Rakoto)

March 5, 1995

Hi, Dad!

I just got your letter that you sent to Donna and me. No, I don't mind seconds at all... an incredible letter, Dad, I must say. I didn't know it was to both of us at first, because I saw the name "Donna" and got such a kick out of you sending the wrong letter that I read that one first. I have to also admit that there was a child-like thrill of getting to read something that was actually not meant for me to see (I thought!). But having read it, I'm so glad I didn't make you an "old" joke card to send. This year sounded like an age realization year for you, one of the ones where you feel like saying "Get lost" to someone when they give you an old age card! Ha Ha! But I did make you look a bit haggard on your birthday card, didn't I? Then again, I made myself look pretty haggard, too!

I'd like to respond to your letter, but I'm going to have to read it again first. First of all...a bit surprised Mom's coming, huh? You're not the only one, dude! Amazing!! Amazing! Just amazing! (To quote you) And yes, she will be living in an African village- mine! Amazing!

I think my biggest joy in having her come is the joy I will get watching her reaction to things. I do think I'll be getting a lot of belly laughs during her stay here! How will she react watching women step out of a taxi brousse and lifting their skirt to pee right next to the road curb along with the men? The other older people pouring an extra shot of moonshine for their two-year old? Two old men with spears walking into my hut at six a.m. to join me for a cup of coffee? Ah, yes, it will be an adventurous and learning experience for both of us!

I'm going to set us up one or two country flights here to see some of the best parts of Madagascar, so I'll only be in my village with her for about five days or so. I think that'll be more than long enough...I don't know as she'll like it. We'll see.

Okay, let me keep reading your letter. I'm going to pop popcorn first. I'm at Kirsten's in Ranohira, which, as I've told you, is nothing like my little village...it's a town, and her house is a bit on it's own, so it's very private. The fact that I can make popcorn here is a total treat, because in my village I only pop it when there's a loud rainstorm. Otherwise, tons of people hear it and come running. They only sell it in Antananarivo, so my villagers have none, and I get it rarely. Especially since the rainy season's over and there are hardly any loud storms now. So, this is quite a luxury to fearlessly pop and eat popcorn...ah yes, the things we take for granted.

It's funny, Dad, 'cause you say you don't at all feel the way people think you'll feel...like when you reach sixty. Isn't it weird the way that goes? We all have these ideas about what is old and what is young and what this is or that is, simply because we've

99

never been there. We guess it's out of ignorance. Then we find out we were wrong.

I laugh at my ideas of Madagascar before I got here - I was so naive! It's the same with age, I think. We don't know how it feels 'til we get there, and then we usually find it's not what we expected.

Ya know, to tell ya the truth, it's like that with anything, isn't it? And then once you do get to that point in life, or do get to that place you've never been or imagined, it's all much simpler than you realized it could be- just another day in your life. "60" is no big deal, Dad, it's just another day (but then again, how would I know? I've never been there!).

I must tell you something I've learned here, Dad, that may help you diminish that feeling of lack of in your life. This is my perception only. I don't know if it's fact. Happiness in life has very little to do with what you're doing, it weighs almost entirely on how you perceive what you're doing. There ya go, life's meaning, by Nancy Coutu.

It's funny, 'cause so many people have written to me how incredible it is that I'm doing this, and that I'm strong for undertaking such an adventure that they never could. Yet, now that I'm doing it, it's just my life. No fireworks or anything. It's just what I'm doing right now. My perception of it is pretty remarkable, and that's why I'm growing so much.

I see other volunteers in almost the same situation as me - with negative perceptions. They are not really giving a lot of worth or value to their situations. I don't quite know what I'm trying to say. I guess just that the trick is giving worth to where you are now, because that's all you have.

If you take a look to the past and it wasn't enough and there was something lacking, it may be simply because we've been taught so much in our society that one of the keys to a "successful" life is how much you've done. What have you accomplished? Well, I have to say that, now that I've lived in a society with an entirely different set of values, where "life" as they know it is growing veggies and pounding coffee and scraping enough money together to buy a blanket for cold nights, success of life is not dependent on how much you have done. It has to do more with what you are getting out of now, no matter what it is that you're doing.

It's society's view as a whole that's taught us the more you accomplish, the better quality your life is. Yet we live as individuals so society's views, as a whole, don't pertain to us on an individual level- they don't even relate. We all know in our hearts as individuals, that what makes a successful life is being happy and what makes us happy is giving worth and value to whatever we're involved in from minute to minute.

That's why doing what I'm doing is so damn incredible-not because I'm doing it, but because I'm finally giving worth to something I'm doing. I finally feel content with living in the moment, not judging my past or planning my future.

As I look back at my life, most everything I've done is amazing and worthy of my living in it for the moment, enjoying it fully. While I was doing it, I was constantly thinking, "What'll I do next?" I've wasted so much time judging my past or looking toward the future, that I'm constantly missing the now. It's all basically been negative energy in a way, because it showed I devalued my present life to some degree; it was worthy enough to be focusing on just that. Now that I feel I am starting to live for the moment, planning my future doesn't seem necessary. It'll just happen as a continuation of my "now", and my past seems beautiful whereas it didn't before. I hope this doesn't sound like babbling, 'cause I'm not. It's just a hard topic to correctly convey my thoughts.

Let me tell you, Dad, you've done many worthy things in your life. Don't feel dissatisfied with what you've done if you can help it 'cause it's a waste of energy, energy that could actually be positive energy if you focus it on your present moment. If you do sometimes feel that way about your past, slam it down with this undeniable truth: you have us Dad, you've made us. We are your progress, and we show your progress through your life.

I'm not a parent, so I don't know if looking at it that way is enough, but we're all pretty incredible people and there's reason for that. Most everything you've done in your life has been valuable, Dad. You just have to see it as that and accept that. Once you do that, you'll have enough time freed up to focus on what you're up to today. And you don't really have to worry about your future because it'll happen for you.

You're far from old Dad, you still have about a lifetime of mine to live, which is quite a long time. You have plenty of time to have your life with Paula and the boys, and then later do your dreams with Paula. You are as young as you feel and it's only a number. When people tell you otherwise, just laugh and shrug it off. They're either talking out of ignorance, because they're not there yet, or they have been there and it's just their own perception, which doesn't matter anyhow because it's not your perception! Too deep?

I love ya Dad! Rakoto

P.S. Sorry if it wasn't light enough for ya! Tell Paula I'll write soon. I'm building a tolerance to the kickapoo juice here and I'm not deaf or blind yet. Ha Ha!

I thought you would like a picture of the
villagers with the omby (cows)

Thirteen
Trying to Find the Chords

Brother Dan was in several bands playing the synthesizer. The tape he sent Nancy brought her closer to home and gave her much joy. She liked his plan for a homecoming party. The two loved and missed philosophizing with one another.

Nancy so wanted to learn music theory but found it very difficult with no teacher on hand. She pen-paled with my class of third, fourth, and fifth graders. It was great for her, great for my students, and great for me. The students never complained when they had to correct and rewrite a letter for a second time. Science and social studies took on real meaning for them. We received some slides to help here.

(Teachers, call 1-(800)424-8580 the Peace Corps in Washington D.C. Ask for World Wise School. You can have a pen pal, possibly in the country of your choice, for your class of classes.)

Nancy was given Ra-koto instead of Coutu. It stuck with her and the villagers. She was feeling crippled by her inability to help in situations where she thought she had a cure. Nancy writes,"Here it's the custom to simply walk into someone's house and plant yourself if the door's open...My boundaries are constantly feeling broken down."

My youngest child did a super job weaving a mat (tihi) for me out of palm tree prons. I shall cherish it always.

March 5, 1995

It's been way too long since I wrote, but I'm writing now. Here I sit, on a mound of hard dirt that faces the mountain range, a mound I've claimed as my own. It's not a long walk from the village, but far enough away that it's very private here. I'm listening to Dan's demo tape that he sent me. It's evening and the clouds are dark with a pink tint. The wind is incredible after such a hot day. It's so strong, I'm having to anchor myself on my little sand mound so I don't topple off the back. What a perfect feeling it is to be so far from home, but yet Dan's heart is pouring out into my ears...I'm really not so far after all.

I already cooked an eggplant, green bean, squash, tomato,

dish so I'll just have to cook pasta when I get back.

This past month I spent a lot of time hiking throughout Isalo with researchers. Some of the spots along the trail were absolutely breathtaking, as is the song that Dan's playing right now. Some of the sandstone ridges were like none I've ever seen. And the canyons dropped straight down into forests and rivers. The walk was a long and challenging one, too, only adding to the beauty. It's truly a gorgeous place.

The researchers were a great bunch of guys, too. Dr. Chris Raxworthy from the U. of Michigan, was the head reptile and amphibian researcher, a person I'm so glad I've met.
The other five were Malagasy, a bunch of wonderful hams. I, at first, felt really in the way 'cause Joe and Kirsten went, too - there wasn't enough for three to do. But after I got to know all of them and they me, I felt very happy to be with them.
I spent some time in Ranohira after, 'cause my ankle was in bad shape. Then I went to my village and went out with another research team studying birds and lemurs.

After, I was in Ranohira for a few more days, 'cause the PC director, Theresa and Dr. Boda were also visiting. Now I'm back in my village and very happy to be here. I am feeling more solid on what I want to accomplish here and more solid in who it is that I am. I do still get pangs of suffocation in my house 'cause; when my doors are open, my nerves are tight. I'm always waiting for someone to come in when I just want to be alone with some light in my house (it's more suffocating to shut the doors). Other than that, I'm so glad to be here. I've missed a lot of people here. But I must go home now and cook some pasta, because I am now writing in the dark!

March 8, 1995

Akoy, Dan!
Thank you so much for your letter. I just got the one that you wrote on your advertisement page, which is really professional. I have to admit, if I wasn't 14,000 km away, I dare say I'd be calling you for a lesson! Dan, what a wonderful letter! I so much miss having meaningful conversations with people, as I told you in my last letter. There's really no one here I have deep

conversations with, which does make one more in tune to oneself. I do crave it.

I get an incredible amount of mail from many people, but everyone's so busy that they often tell me the basics in their lives and never get to the heart of things. I have to say that your letter was a tearjerker and I loved it. The idea of having a party when I get home - where we'll dance and sing and feel the joy of celebration through your music - sounds perfect (in the true sense of the word). To tell you the truth, Dan, it doesn't sound all that far away. I'm sure it will by the time it is actually here. Time is flying right now. My schedule looks like this:

I'm working with researchers now. I'll have a language training in March. I'll have in service training in Antananarivo in April. This one is a maybe -I'll be cutting (crops) in Isalo in May which is near the end of summer here. After, I'll be spending much more time with long periods in my village, where time takes on an entirely different meaning. I'm happy there and when I'm away for long periods of times I truly miss it, but it is such a different world. It is so far removed from the rest of existence. I need to find a person or two in my village who knows Isalo and will hike with me and show me the trails. So, when the village life is foreign to the point of unhappiness for me, my escape is in my back yard. I've always hiked and experienced nature for my sense of wholeness. Being stationed where I am is a gift for this opening and growing part of my life, and is very significant to me. But Isalo is such an enormous and untouched place that I could get totally lost without someone initially showing me the route. It's definitely a magical place. I'd like to get comfortable enough with the terrain to take off on my own there. The trail systems aren't really defined in many areas, but I can fix that. My writing just got a bit better, huh? I'm not in a car anymore.

So, Dan, I was really impressed with your description of music. It is magic. I was not surprised. I know it's your closest way of connecting to what's real and what's perfect in the world for you. I would love to find that, too, but it doesn't click for me. I try and try and I can never play from my heart. It's all just chords. I need to see the music on paper and I don't understand how it all flows together or why. I want so much to feel what I know you feel and what you make me feel when I hear you play.

It's a sense of continuity, a flowing one, and one with a deep sense of meaning and feeling - magic as you call it. Yet when I play, it's choppy, and it's hard work. It doesn't flow. I don't understand how to make it flow or to play from my heart. It's a door that's closed to me and I don't yet understand how to open it. I can do it with a drum, (somewhat). I have the rhythm, but yet with a guitar I don't understand how the notes go together. Yet, I don't plan to give up.

Yoga was downright painful and not enjoyable when I started but now I crave it, if I'm not doing it. The same with meditation, although I definitely am not at the point of craving it. I'm still in the stage where I have to discipline myself. The same is true with running (I crave it if I don't do it). I know I've had to work hard for the things that are now important parts of myself, yet it's hard to get started. Because there are so many incredible things I'm learning now, that disciplining myself to practice my guitar is very tough. I just wish I could understand the theory of it. Dan, how's it all go together and why? I've always had a hard time understanding how the parts of things fit together.

I can see a whole of something right in front of my eyes, but yet not realize that it's a whole because I only see it as parts. It's an odd trait and it makes for slow learning. For example, in Malagasy language every action verb starts with an M: manome = to give, mangalatsy = to steal, meanatsy = to learn. All that needs to be done to make the action into the person doing the actions is to change the M into a P: pangalatsy = thief, pianatsy = student. No one told me this rule (probably because it was so obvious) and it took me quite a long time to notice the pattern. It's like that with a lot of things with me.

It's like that with the notes of music. Why do chords fit together? What's the pattern? I remember Dad once showing me some theory of 1-3-5 of chords or 1-3#-5? Something like that. It was all so simple when he taught me - if it's explained to me, I learn quickly. But now I've forgotten his explanation and I'm again lost on how it fits together, and I can't learn very well from books alone, so my music book without a teacher is a bit tough going. I'll stick with it Dan, because I really want to feel the music.

I don't feel the magic in myself as I do in other situations, like in hiking, feeling myself connecting to the earth, being in tune to the sounds. I hear who's singing or chirping - feeling the breeze in my hair, and feeling the strong comfortable weight on my back and see the beauty that was created by Someone far more powerful and majestic than us. That's when I feel the magic, the magic that I can connect with. Some day I hope I can feel your magic of music coming from myself.

Well Dan, I'm pretty beat and ready for bed - it's 3 p.m. there and 11 p.m. here, siesta time for you and bedtime for me!

I love you bro! Nancy

P.S. Hey Dan, I'm going to be 28 soon - a magical number wouldn't you say?

March 19, 1995

Hi guys, (Mom's class)

How is everyone? Sorry I haven't written for a bit. I haven't heard from all of you, and I have to return to my village tomorrow. I only get and can send mail when I bike here to Ranohira. There is no post office in my village. I won't be back here near the post office in Ranohira again for two weeks. But I'll write back to you again when I return if there's a letter from you. I'm presently making you a cassette of my village and sometime this month I'll be doing a roll of slides for you, too. I want you to see what life is like here. I guess I should work fast, as you must have a summer break soon, right?

Things are going well for me here. I've just had a weeklong language training with our Peace Corps language trainers, in the town of Ranohira. It's a very tough language and I can communicate simple thoughts with people, but I don't understand a lot in long conversations. I'm getting there, though. So much of communicating isn't through words, anyway. I can most always get my point across.

This last week I made my garden bigger. Now I have more than corn, zucchini, and green beans. I have onions, tomatoes, peppers, asparagus and cucumbers. I don't know what will grow. We'll see. It'll be nice to have a big variety.

The people here are pretty content without a great variety in vegetables probably because they've never had a great variety in foods. Coming from America, the land of "whatever you want, we have it," I want a variety in vegetables. I'm bored with rice!

This last week I've been helping a lot of the villagers pick peanuts because they're done now. They were planted in November, huge fields of them. The whole plants are pulled out of the ground in March. Then the peanuts are picked off the plant (the peanuts grow underground and the leaves are above the ground). They are then dried in the sun for about 5 days. I've eaten so many peanuts in the last week that I can't eat any more of them! I'm going to piler (pound, grind) some to make peanut butter.

I need to go to sleep now, because I will bike back to my village tomorrow morning early before it gets too hot. So I'll sign off now, but I'll drop a letter to you and maybe a cassette with some of the village singing and the Malagasy people speaking, so you can get an idea of how different their life is from yours. I'll try to get going on taking some photos, too.

Veloma! (Good-bye) Take care guys and stay cool! Nancy

P.S. Dear Mom, I am sorry I didn't get a personal letter in here to you, too, but I've got to catch some shuteye. I love you and miss you, though. I'm doing really well, Mom. This is still right where I want to be!

Love ya sweetie!

March 20, 1995

Hi, Mom!

I just got my third birthday card from you. Man I'm doing all right! I loved this one - I've always wondered what was going on out west when I was born!

So I just got your letter with the date of your arrival here, July 2nd. I still don't know the dates I go to Uganda...if you can change your tickets to a week later (July 8th). If not, don't worry about it. These dates may work out okay.

Well, Mom, I don't know when your vacation starts, but enjoy it when it does! I won't write to your students anymore unless I hear from them again, 'cause I doubt it'll get to them before school's out.

Love ya', Mom! Stay Cool!

Love "Rakoto" (Rakootoo)

P.S. Don't bring me your T.V.!!! It defeats the fun of this and I don't think anything would come in! Maybe I could use a dark colored blue or red T-shirt plain color with no writing would be nice. A used one would be fine...it's just the tee-shirt quality here is really bad!

March 22, 1995

I'm confused lately as to what my work is here. When I go to Ranohira, things seem clearer to me. When I come back to my village, I get in this rut where I don't really have any direction and each day passes by without my actually doing much. Not even just concerning my work with the people but also my own personal activities. Every morning I want to do yoga, meditate, practice the guitar, study, and read part of whatever book I'm on. Every day I end up doing very little of any of these. I end up socializing all day, maybe managing to farm my garden a bit, or to wash my clothes. I often help the villagers here with picking peanuts or whatever they're working on. I tell myself that it's okay to do that, because I need to gain the trust of the people here before I can expect to make progress with them in other respects. I still feel as though I'm accomplishing close to nothing.

I know I've shut down a big part of my sensitivity too, because it'd be really hard to live here, otherwise. Like when people are asking me for medicine, I'm actually lying and saying I don't have any, even to the people I'm becoming close to, which I hate doing. If I were to give medicine out, I'd have 350 people approaching me for it. Yet some of these people are justifiably sick.

One man died of what was probably malaria last month and I probably could have changed that had I given him my mefloquin. Now another guy's sick with malaria and he's a friend of Abodo, and I'm tempted to give him a couple mefloquin to see if he can knock it out. He has the chills, a fever, and looks drawn out and horrible. I feel so callous not helping when I have so much. The children here have swollen bellies...they're malnourished and would benefit greatly by just putting veggie oil in their food, yet I don't think it's my place to give it.

I think I'm feeling a bit crippled here. I don't know where to start. I'm sure I've put on a pretty thick shell of insensitivity so that I can survive, and happily namanako. Yet it's not overly natural for me. I don't know. I have to find some ways to get money in here so they can buy meds, because there are so many sick people here. I need to teach them about nutrition, too. I've got to catch some shut-eye. Mokotsy be iaho.

March 26, 1995

Hi Mom! Akoy neny,

How are things going for you? Well, I hope things are going really well for me, although I've been a bit homesick today. At least it's not a common occurrence. Fa many iaho amin'ny neniko! (I miss you!) I made you a gift and am writing this letter, so I'm sure it will help me feel not as far from you.

The gift is called "tihi" (tee hee) and the people here make huge ones for floor mats. I myself made just a little one for you, because if I made you a huge one it would take my full two years here and I'd get nothing else done! This one is for cutting vegetables or for serving cheese and bread and crackers to your guests or as a placemat. I've made one for myself and use it as a chopping board. Don't be afraid to use yours like that - that's what it's for and it can take the chopping, it doesn't get cut through. Just wet it in water, Mom, and it'll flatten out. If it gets ruined (for example, if your pet mouse likes the taste of it as much as my pet mouse does), I'll make you a new one at no extra charge.

What a ham I am being, huh? That's one thing that's hard, Mom, - I can't joke near as much with these people because I don't yet have the language down enough to express all my thoughts. I'm getting there, though, although it's coming very slowly. I've never really learned a second language before, so it's hard to know the best technique to learn. French seems easy in comparison...it'll be a breeze to go back to learning that after I get Malagache down enough.

Yet, I've learned a lot about the culture here through learning the language. It's an oriental type language, and the concepts show their acknowledgement of natural beauty (for example sun= "masoandroe" which translates to "eye of the day"). There's so much to learn about people through their language-I hadn't realized it. So, although, I don't feel like I'm making a lot of headway with it I am enjoying it. It seems I have to study daily, writing words I hear that I don't understand and looking them up, to feel like I'm making progress.

Mom, I'm writing this to you by the river, way upstream from my village, simply because I needed a break. I just washed my clothes and I was just sitting in a tree above the waterfall (my favorite "get away spot").

Xavier, my friend who wrote to you, passed by cattle guarding, and came down to talk. I'm sitting by a calm part of the river. It is losing shade by the waterfall and it's got to be about 95 or 100 degrees today. The rainy season's over now and it's getting hotter (but not muggy, I'm happy to say).

I just planted a second beautiful garden this week. My first one was little and more experimental than anything. I did get some cukes and a couple squash and some green beans out of it. The corn's not yet big enough to eat. I planted too many seeds and everything basically suffocated. I've got it down this time. I had to lug a lot of cow manure and thin out the seedling. Hopefully that will do the job! I planted onions, cauliflower, asparagus, tomatoes, cabbage, cukes, green beans, carrots, sakoy, peppers, eggplants and spices like basil, parsley, celery and mustard. Whoopee!

I have to go to Antananarivo, the capital, where we had our training (blah, I hate that place!). We will have two weeks for our first in-service training, so I'm going to pay a kid 2000 Malagasy francs (or 75 cents) to water twice a day for me while I am gone.

I'm lazy in the morning and I never feel like doing anything when I am here. I never get up before 7 a.m. Mom, everyone here is up by 5:00 or 5:30! I can't seem to change my bodily schedule of staying up late and getting up fairly late. I've been trying to change it, too, because I could get a lot more done in the cool of the morning if I got up early and went to bed early.

It's hard to get much done by candlelight and it's dark by 7:30 or 8:00.

I seem to need so much sleep here, no less than 8.5 or 9 hours. That's understandable I suppose, huh? At least I'm not exhausted anymore. There were days in December and January that I could barely get out of bed and had no motivation to do anything.

I'm not alone in that, though. I just had a week of training in language in Ranohira (the town I biked into last week to be with four other volunteers and four teachers). One of the volunteers, Jeremy, went through the same things. It was so refreshing to spend the week with him. He's one of the few volunteers I really hit it off with and it was a nice break. Jeremy is really upbeat and happy and it was nice to see someone else enjoying himself here.

I'm a 5.5 hour bike ride away and I only go into Ranohira every other week. It hasn't affected me much. I'm happy I got the site I did. I like experiencing a lot of this on my own, and there are so many really sweet people in my village. I haven't seen many other volunteer sites, but I think I was probably given the one closest to the experience I was hoping to get.

It's tough for me to figure out just how to get started in my work here, though, or to understand what it is. I think that's the goal of this inservice training next week. Up until now, I worked on my house, learned the culture, learned the language, and did some research in Isalo. But when I get back from Tana, I need to start some projects. Some will be with the park, working with Joe and Kirsten to organize the guides, get signs up, mark trails, and get a tourist information center started. Yet, I'm further away, so Joe and Kirsten will do the bulk of that.

My work will be more village based. We'll be planting trees so they stop cutting the forests. We'll be planting vegetable gardens to get the health improved here. I hope to get some campgrounds in to get some income going in the village, so they can buy medicines. In my particular village, I hope to get the school and hospital fixed; both were wrecked in a cyclone last year. I have a lot to do, but it's hard getting started with my resources all so far away and my language not good enough yet to communicate these ideas to the villagers very well. I can totally understand why we've been given handouts on the Peace Corps

Volunteer "emotional calendar," and from month 3-6 many feel useless! It's like okay, what do I do? I've yet to feel like "okay, why am I here?" so that's good!

But anyhow Mums, I'm very happy, very well, and not yet skinny. Soon to be 28, which sounds great to me (the 28 part, not the "not yet skinny part!").

This is a roll of pictures of activities in my village for your class. I wanted to send a cassette, too, but it'll come later, because I fell off my bike my last trip here from Ranohira, and my jug of cooking oil busted and got all over my tape deck and everything else! So once I've fixed my tape deck, the tape will come. It's half done now, with some people talking to your class, and a lot of singing (the villagers' choice).

I may write to you again before I send this, as it's only March 26th today (oops, 3 days left!) and I won't be going into Ranohira to the post office 'til about the 5th.

I love ya', Mom!
Nancy (i.e. "Rakoto")

Rakoto's a common Malagasy name here and once they heard I'm Nancy "Koto" it got translated to Rakoto pretty quickly. Although since I told them what "cookoo" means, they often call me Nancy Kookoo to tease me. (There are no c's in this language. That tells me something about our language...why do we have "c's" Mom, if they always sound like a "s" or a "k"? - Yes, Americans like "sauce!"

March 30, 1995

So I'm 28 years old now - The first day of 28. It was actually a bit of a tough one. This week I've been trying to fight off homesickness and I've really just wanted to be alone. I got really frustrated with so many people coming in to watch me make godro godro on my birthday. The adults went home. It was finally just the kids, and I told them I wanted to be alone.. But, I do fight with myself...I think "get the heck out," and then a voice says back to me "Nance don't be so harsh,...what's the big deal if they watch you cook?" But the thing is I'm going to be here 2 years, and if I feel I need space, I should give it to myself,

113

and tell people to give it to me. They don't know my culture. No, I must remind myself that they don't know how much I like to be alone. I should start telling them, 'cause the anger that wells up in me is a really aggravating, unnatural feeling, a feeling I'm unaccustomed to having so regularly. How can they know if I don't tell them?

Last night was a lot of fun. I had cake and wine with friends. We made a tape of singing for my family (it feels weird to write "my family" as though I'm writing to someone other than me). Everyone was having so much fun, they didn't want to leave for dinner, but I told them to come back and dance, and they all did. We danced to Malagasy tapes first, then a few kabosies played. So it was a good birthday, although I have to say I felt like I was sort of out of my body, not feeling like myself, looking from the inside out. I feel like that a lot 'cause I never feel like a truly intelligent and comfortable person when I can't use my own language.

It's exhausting, too. I'm still having the feeling of suffocation living in the house I'm in. My boundaries are constantly feeling broken down. Even outside of my home, my porch is constantly used. Rasoa has taken to napping on my porch a couple times...I have to ask her not to, because when she does, people come visit and they're not my guests - they're hers. If I'm in my house, I really hate to come out my door to four or so people sitting on my porch. It's too bad, 'cause I really like my village, and I like the people and the environment, but my own space situation is very stressful. I need to open my space up somehow. How do I do it without hurting anyone?

April 1, 1995

Hi, Decey! Hi Leroy! Hi Caleb!

How's it going all? What an obnoxious envelope, huh? You can ignore it, as I'm sure you've written me by now. I write letters while in my village and only get to the post every two weeks, so I never know what's waiting for me when I write...it makes for fairly slow responses. I sent my friend a letter and a tape and I sent one to Dad the same day I mailed this out for all of you guys...along with a roll of film. My friend's got to her in two weeks and she got a letter back to me in two weeks...a month for a full circuit - not bad, eh? The mail system coming my way's proven to be great. It seems slower and variable going your way and I don't know if you guys get everything I send. People have been pretty good about writing, which has been a big help 'cause I'm starting to get homesick...but anyhow, I'm babbling.

So it's a couple nights after my birthday, which was a great dancing bash. Tonight, the stars are bright. It's not unbearably hot, so I should be able to sleep tonight. However, I just took my mefloquin (malaria preventative) this morning and that always gives me nightmares or makes me sleep badly the night I take it. I'm going to get the Peace Corps doctor to switch me to chloroquin, a milder and not so new drug. I don't like to be the guinea pig of such a strong drug - they worry there may be chloroquin resistant mosquitoes here, but yet there have been no causes of such thing here, only in Africa. I'll be glad to switch. There are a lot of mosquitoes in my hut tonight. I'm going to put up my mosquito net - hang in there a minute - okay?

I'm back. Mosquito nets are really cool - they make you feel like you're on an African safari or something. Not only that, they're effective, too!

I'm doing really well overall, although somedays I'm pretty emotionally up and down. It's hard to feel really stable in an environment that's so different from anything I've ever known. Sometimes it's refreshing, but some days, it's downright frustrating. I enjoy starting from scratch on everything - planting all our food, pounding rice, mudding my hut, going down to the river everyday to lug water and do laundry. Yet sometimes I feel I have no other time to do anything else! Days just seem to slip by and I don't feel like I've done anything. Here they're content with getting the basic survival needs taken care of and once that's done (the farming, the cooking, wood chopping, and rice pounding), they just kick back and socialize a lot. It's hard for me to get in this mode, cause I'm so used to doing so much in a day. Here they have no money to buy books or any other hobby stuff, so they spend spare time visiting each other and playing their homemade flutes and guitars.

It's so hot here in mid-afternoon that it's hard to do anything outside, even if you want to. It's hard having people visiting me so much. Here it's the custom to simply walk into some-one's house and plant yourself if the door's open - very un-American. Standing and staring in the windows is acceptable, too! I'm trying to teach the kids that it doesn't fly with me. It's tough, 'cause I'm a hut in the middle of a family unit of 16 and they tend to stop in alot. They don't bug me if the doors are closed, but then my hut is too hot and too dark. So I'm still working on getting my space defined. Oh, how to do it? How to do it?

I tend to take a lot of long walks and draw or write just to stay content. I bike the five hours to Ranohira every two weeks and stay a couple of days with Kirsten, the other volunteer work-ing here (Joe's the third in a smaller village on the other side of the mountains). Kirsten's is a town of 1000 and a much differ-ent environment, so it makes for a good change.

There's also this incredible medieval style hotel built in the rocks on my way to Ranohira. I've become friends with the French owner and the people that work there, so I stop in on my ride and they give me a beer or juice and let me shower. It's an incredibly ritzy, beautiful place, totally opposite from my vil-lage where everyone's dirty and poor with basically nothing but their homes. They speak of this hotel like it's an untouchable castle, which to them, it basically is. The owner's really impressed with my being here and can't believe I'm doing it ("Poor girl", he says) so I get quite spoiled - just what I need every two weeks after living in the bush!

I go to Ranohira in two days because all volunteers are going up to Antananarivo (the capital) again for our first in-service training. We do an overall work plan. I'm psyched, 'cause there's a pool outside the hotel and there's lots of nice restaurants and bars and ice cream, too! It'll be a fun change. I've asked to stay a few extra days and work with my old language teacher on Malagache. They accepted. I'm doing okay with the language but I'm still not fluent...it's oriental like and hard. I also need some help in French, 'cause a lot of the people we work with in Ranohira speak French and are French. Most of the people here are Malagasy, but the ones organizing the park management plan are often French- from Antananarivo, or Malagasy from Antananarivo. They prefer to speak French with us, since we're not yet fluent in Malagache. Joe and Kirsten were fluent in

French before coming here, but I tend to be a bit lost at meetings at the moment. I only had three weeks of French before switching to Malagache during training. So when I do find time to study French instead of Malagache, it comes easier now 'cause Malagache is such a challenge.

So my work here with Joe and Kirsten will be setting up a tourist information center in Ranohira, working with the guides and training them in some basics, helping researchers study plants and animals here and marking trails and then some. I've already hiked a lot of Isalo with researchers and know the percent of lemurs, birds, and reptiles that are here.

Isalo, The National Park, is incredible, too. The mountains are sandstone and the rock mountains are similar to pictures I've seen of Arches National Park. There are rivers running through many areas. Quite an incredible back yard!

My work in my village will be getting vegetable gardens and tree planting going in Bereketa, my village, and the surrounding villages, the closest being 10 km away. There are ten other villages on this side of Isalo and about the same on Joe's side. I shall be trying to get some hygiene education going; trying to get funding to make the road here more accessible to cars. Right now it is rough, all sand and big boulders. The goal is for the villagers to set up camp-sites and get some money out of these rich tourists.

I'm also going to try to get them motivated to repair the school and hospital here that got whacked by a cyclone last year. Sixty kids went to school, coming in each day from nearby villages because there's a teacher in Bereketa. Now only twelve go...it's pretty sad. Sixty was bad enough, considering there's at least as many kids in this village alone. So it'll be tough to get motivated to do this stuff, being so far removed from everything else. I'm basically out here on my own - but I'm sure I'll figure out how to get it all going. This meeting in Tana should help, especially since all the Peace Corps directors up there are former Peace Corps Volunteers, so they can relate.

So guys, other than a constant emotional roller coaster ride, I'm happy and healthy. I've yet to be sick here-actually, one of the very few volunteers here to have such luck. I've been pretty content here, though, and haven't yet doubted that this is where I want to be, so I'm sure that helps.

Hey, Denise, you asked me to write a lot and let you know what's up in my life here, but it seems hard for me to write my emotions and all unless I get letters back from you, too! I don't know why it's hard - it just is. I'll be happy to write to you often, but you've got to keep up with me so I know what's up with you too. There's probably already a long letter from you waiting for me at the post office right now - if there is, you'll be getting another letter pretty soon! I love you guys and miss you way too much at the moment! (Yes, homesickness is setting in, in volume!)

Nancy

Denise, here's a picture of some of my village children. Aren't they beautiful?

Fourteen

Work Planned in Tana

Nancy never received the mace and the speakers that her sister Denise had sent her. Someone along the postal way must have wanted them. Mail is not government controlled in Madagascar.

In Tana Nancy had an "Oh my God experience". I don't know

how she shrugged this horrendous deed off, but she did.

Nancy writes, "One day a guy passed me while I was walking along ...and he put a needle in my leg. I was quite shaken up and yelled at him as he strolled casually past. After we called the doctor to see if I should see him. I had no reaction and the doctor said AIDS isn't a big problem here...I'm not worried"

April 4, 1995

Hi, Powells! Akoy Aby! How are you?

I had a great birthday in my village. I went to Antananarivo for our training with all the volunteers' back together again. It was basically to learn how to apply for project money. It was a drastic change from my village and a nice one.

I hated Tana during our first training, but this time it was a nice reality check. It was beautiful driving there and I felt joy as we approached different large towns that were lit up with lights from the luxury of electricity. It was a sight I hadn't seen in four months and I hadn't realized I missed. I was in heaven eating ice cream again, too. It was nice being back with the other volunteers as well, although our cliques had changed... Everyone I hung out with was different now. It seems the dynamics had changed through who was writing to whom and who was working with whom. It was fun.

I'm back in Ranohira now and I was going to bike to my village today, but I have a flat tire and my pump's busted. I borrowed two pumps from people in town, but neither fit the valve. I'll wait to go in a car tomorrow with a nun here that's visiting the village near mine. My director's coming to visit me next week, so I'll get a lift back with her to fix my bike then.

The idea of going back to my village has taken some getting use to, although I feel ready now. It's such a different world and although I only went to Tana for two weeks, it felt like four months. I'm glad Mom's coming to visit. It'll be nice to have someone who can understand where I've been, when I get back home. I just wanted to let you know I love you.

Peace and Love, Nancy

April 22, 1995

Hi Dee!

Thanks so much for my birthday package. I got it mid-April...not bad! The dress is great for here and the sash I wear as a belt or headpiece the way the women do here. Thanks for the junk food. (My Malagasy friends said thanks, too; they had never had chocolate with caramel in it) Please thank Caleb and Leroy for me. I haven't received the speakers and mace yet but I'm sure they'll make it soon...the order things get here is really variable. I haven't gotten Mom's package yet either, but you've gotten me curious!

Can you believe she's coming? Man is she in for a surprise! It's a different world here. I had to laugh when you said maybe she'll find a honey here, 'cause I joked with myself about the same thing.

As for me, Denise, I'm sorry but I have no juicy stories to give you. I've had an UN-exciting life of celibacy since I've been here! I must admit, that's exactly what I wanted. The last thing I want is to be hooked up with someone and not being able to see them 'cause I live 47km. out in the bush. I definitely don't want to date anyone in my village. I'd get sick really fast of people asking me when we'd marry.

The culture in my village is so drastically different than our own, and many people there have never left the village, so there is always a huge misunderstanding gap. I have to admit, I've not found myself attracted to hardly anyone here. I think it's partly 'cause I have a bit of a wall up. I don't want to get hooked up with anyone here...I want to come home after my two years is through.

There is one guy in Tana (the capital) I had a crush on, but come to find out he's been with one of the other volunteers (who was here the year before us) for some time now. I can't say I was really disappointed. I think I'm getting a lot more out of this experience... being able to concentrate on me. I have been starting to get lonely though. It's more for you guys than for a man to be with. I've just been getting pangs of missing all of you greatly.

Love 'ya, Nance

April 23, 1995

Sorry I've neglected you so, diary. I've been in Tana the past 2 weeks, which was actually a good time. It was nice to see the other volunteers, although it was initially awkward. At first I didn't want to hang with them. After a bit, I started enjoying their company. It was great driving there and seeing a different environment. We got to Fiamaratso in the evening. Seeing the city all lit up thrilled me - it was so beautiful. I almost cried, because I realized just how long it had been since I had been out of my small world of Isalo. It was a nice change to be in the city life for a week. I actually liked Tana this time, and I learned my way around fairly well.

It wasn't as crazy as before, because the gendarmes had done some shooting to get some law and order here. It seemed to work, but I heard it was an undesirable process. There weren't nearly so many people in the market this time. One day a guy passed me while I was walking along with Roland, Chris, Kirsten, Amy, Linda, and Joe, (PCV's) and he put a needle in my leg. I was quite shaken up and yelled at him as he strolled casually past. After we called the doctor to see if I should see him. I had no reaction and the doctor said AIDS isn't a big problem here. Yet he had me take an AIDS test to show that I don't yet have it, and I'll have to take another in three months to see if I do have it. Can you believe that? I'm not worried about it.

Otherwise, no problems. I didn't spend much time with Jeremy, as he seemed to want to be a loner. I hung out a bit with everyone, but more so with Anna, Gretchen, and Michelle who was my roomy during basic training. I didn't see Linda much, either.

I stayed in Tana a couple days extra, and when I got to Ranohira I got into a slump of not wanting to return to Bereketa. I ended up hanging with Kirsten and working with her two days...

Fifteen

Back to the Village

Nancy wrote to my class and answered all their questions. They asked things that I never would have thought of. We learned much and got some laughs, so did Nancy.

Nancy writes, "I saw a sifak (a species of Lemur) bouncing along, when some kids from my village were chasing it. It ...jumped like a kangaroo, very fast (two times faster than a person can run) and swung like a monkey through the trees after... And to tell you the truth, the kids stoned this one to death and took it back to their family to eat."

Nancy's garden was grown to sell produce to Hotel de Reine to raise money for medicine for the village.

April 23, 1995

...I'm back in my village now. It felt good to eat with Abodo and his family today (not lemur). It felt good to bathe in the river and to see my garden. It felt great to see my house, and it was fun to see my friends and hear how much I was missed. It's weird, 'cause I often have a hard time with the idea of coming back here. Yet once I'm here, I'm happy. Maybe soon I'll start always being psyched to come here. I guess it's just still a foreign world for me and I've yet to feel comfortable with it, enough to consider it my own. It probably will, soon enough. Then I'll be whisked back into my own world and that'll seem foreign!

April 25, 1995

Hi, guys! Akoy Ary! (Mom's class)

I'm back in my village now, after being in the capital for two weeks. It's a different world altogether. The life in Antananarivo (the capital) is more like the U.S., with stores and cars and running water and electricity. Most of the people in my village have never seen it, so they don't even know such places exist. There's no electricity in the village, so they can't watch a television, either. But I did bring back pictures for them, which they loved.

So anyhow, I'm sitting by River Fitalana now and reading all your letters for a second time. Thank you so much, all of you. I really love getting them. I don't know if we'll be writing much anymore, since your summer break is coming up and I don't know if you'll be in my Mom's class next year. But if you want to keep writing, just get my address from my Mom. If you're in the same school next year but not the same class, drop by my Mother's class now and then to see if I've written or sent pictures to the new class. So keep writing to me if you like. And Amanda, Jardinier was so happy to get your letter. He'll be psyched if you keep writing. There's a letter enclosed to you from him, too. Alright - here goes answering some of your questions:

Anthony, not many kids here go to school. Most work in the rice fields. The kids feed the dogs, cats, ducks and chickens here - their food is, of course, rice (no Alpo here) but they don't feed the cows, 'cause they eat the grass. They feed the pigs the left-over food; again mostly rice.

Nancy's drawing of her village

Every Sunday the kids play soccer (which they call football). There isn't any football, the game we know, here...that is, I haven't seen it yet! They don't play much more than that. In the cities, they play basketball. I haven't seen baseball yet. I introduced frisbee in my village and they like it, but they like soccer more.

Bart, how old can a lemur get? Ya' know, I don't know. I'll have to see if I can find the answer to that in one of my books. How fast can they move? Well, I saw a sifak (a species of Lemur) bouncing along, when some kids from my village were chasing it. It was by the river by my village and it jumped like a kangaroo, very fast (two times faster than a person can run) and swung like a monkey through the trees after. They don't come up to the village. And to tell you the truth, the kids stoned this one to death and took it back to their family to eat. That's part of my work here-is to teach them why they shouldn't do this often, if at all. It's hard to explain that, since there's not a lot of food here. But anyhow, as far as what the lemurs themselves eat, fruit and leaves. Some species eat bugs, birds, lizards, frogs and worms. Steve said they look just like a cross between a monkey and a squirrel, which I laughed at, 'cause I thought the exact same thing!

As for Steve's question: There is a president here who lives in the capital. His name is Albert Zafy. Having a president here is new, as of a few years ago. The politics here are, therefore, not very organized yet. There are some kings here, too; a Bara king lives in a village near me. Before the country had a president, there was a French King and Queen. I've seen their castle in the capital, but it's not too big. There was actually a series of Kings and Queens before they changed the politics to having a president.

Three little boys just passed me, and they were acting. The two front boys were holding forked sticks to their foreheads like horns and the boy in back was yelling and hitting them with a stick yelling "Ndow, alfefa," which means "Go! Go!" as you'd yell to a bull pulling the cart. It was really funny.

Steve, yes, I really do have to stay two years, but it's going so fast that any less time wouldn't be enough. As for sicknesses here, there's malaria (from mosquitoes) where people get a fever and can die without medicine. There are a lot of sicknesses from drinking water without boiling it, 'cause they get amoebas or parasites or worms in their bodies. A lot of sicknesses here are the same as the ones in the U.S., but they have more here since it never gets cold. (Germs don't die as easily in tropical places).

Kacy, there are many snakes here, but don't tell my Mom or she may not come to visit me! Yet, there are no poisonous snakes here. Actually, that's not true...there are some poisonous ones, but their teeth are in a way that they can't inject the poison into you. I don't quite understand that...what's the use of being poisonous if they can't use it on their predators? Oh well, that's nature. But as for your rattlesnake, I'm glad it didn't bother you. They're more likely to slither away from you than go toward you.

David, there are tons of reptiles here, a lot of little lizards especially...there are ghekkos, salamanders, iguanas, crocodiles, some fresh N20 turtles and lots of sea turtles. There are no tigers here, though. The biggest mammal being the Fossa, a small cat, which is the predator of the Lemurs.

Okay, here's a letter with no name and you asked me if we have a library here or if we need books and if there's a D.A.R.E.

Program here. There's no library here and whoever you are, thanks for asking if we'd like books. Maybe some crayons and paper would be nice to start, as there's not even that here, and also because the books in the U.S. are in English and the kids here wouldn't understand them. I'll keep you posted on what the students could use...thanks. As for D.A.R.E., there is no program in the village because there really is no money to buy drugs. Yet, there may be a D.A.R.E. program in the capital.

Hi Sean, yes, I have a door on my house! I actually have three, one off each room. My hut's quite big, plenty of room for my mother to visit! What do I do for fun? Bike, swim in the river, dance to the Malagasy guitars and play Malagasy rumey (similar to our rummy but not quite the same).

What time is it? Well, take your time and add seven hours. As you sit in school I'm probably cooking my rice and vegetables for dinner. And as far as temperature, it's about 75 degrees now. It's cooler (60) in May - August and gets hotter from Sept - April. It rains November to January, but not as much here as in the rain forest. I'm not used to the heat yet. I'm from New Hampshire and I already miss the snow.

As far as my work here, I'm helping to protect the animals and trees. (i.e. all nature) in the National Park Isalo which is next to these villages. I'm also trying to help the villagers improve their living standards (plant vegetables, learn about good health, make crafts to sell to tourists of the park so they can buy medicine, fix their school and hospital). I'm staying safe Sean, and I am having a blast! Thanks!

Hi, Nicole, I'm getting pretty good at the Malagache language, although it's Polynesian and nothing like our language. It's very beautiful to listen to. As for Lemurs, I don't see many by my village, but there's a forest near here with tons of them and I can see them if I walk through at night.

Wendy, the forest I just mentioned above is a nice thick forest but not a rain forest. The rain forests are on the east-coast, but I'm on the west coast. The animals in the rain forest are a bit more plentiful than those in a dry forest. There are more species of Lemurs and snakes and all...and tons of leeches. Tons! Yuck!

Dear David, Yes, the men here have spears and the boys (14+) have spears while they guard the bulls. The men hunt pretty much whatever they find - Tenrecs (similar to little groundhogs) wild pigs, lemurs,- but not iquanas cause they're scared of them. There are really no animals dangerous to humans...maybe the crocodiles are, though.

Hi Ronald, They do celebrate Christmas here and do so by singing in the church all-day and eating a roasted pig after. They don't really give gifts to each other like us - just on birthdays. They don't sing happy birthday, although they did with me, 'cause I taught them. There are about 350 people in my village. I'm far from alone here!

Sean, I'm so glad you thought my letter was beautiful. So was yours! Yes, there are many parasites here, but I boil my water and wash or peel my food so I don't get them.

Bradley, I'm glad it sounds like I'm having fun. Learning and experiencing all these new things and knowing all these new people is fun. It's amazing here.

Joel, There are termite mounds that are two or three feet high. I see them when I am riding to another village.

Hi Nicole, Did you look up Madagascar on the map, yet? We are in the Southern Hemisphere so our seasons are the opposite from Florida's. When it is winter here you have summer.

Bart; The people in my village have no cars just charrettes; I do go swimming but I don't jog every day 'cause it's too hot and I don't know where there are parasites here. I think it's easy for them to live in hot places.

Hi, Christian. Things are great on the island...it doesn't feel like an island, though - this place is quite big (although it does-n't look it on a world map!) By the way, the women here don't shave their arms and legs but for some reason they don't real-ly have any hair on them, either! I don't understand it. The women that do have hair don't have much. They are quite sur-prised to find that I shave. So yes, that was a novel question! The little girls here loved your drawing. Yet, there are no little girls who speak English here, even the adults don't!

Stay well and happy and if I don't get a letter to you again before school's out, have a great summer vacation! Take care of my Mom!

Veloma! Nancy

Joe, Kirsten, and Nancy, who worked together,
are surrounding Parfait, their PC driver.

Sixteen

I'm going to Uganda! Mom's coming!

Peace Corps was sending Kirsten, Joe and Nancy to Uganda to learn how to train guides to run the National Park. This was to be training for the trainers. These trainers had already been teaching English and how to deal with tourist problems to the guides.

The dates had a possibility of conflicting with my upcoming trip to Madagascar. Time will tell.

My daughter gave me welcomed instructions of what I needed to do for the trip and what I needed to bring.

Brother Dan gets a lesson on the local brew.

Nancy writes, "Narie said he loves me and I tried to explain the difference between like a lot and love, but he said he knows the difference and he's liked me for 4 months watching me bike in, and he's sure he loves me."

May 10, 1995

Todd's (PCV) here at my hut tonight. He biked in with me today. I've been in Ranohira for a week. The one and a half weeks before that I was in my village, happy to be there. It was just that initial day that is always an adjustment. Then, it was probably the most stable week I've had. Only toward the end of the week did I start needing space.

Todd, Chris and Linda came to Ranohira this week. Todd, Chris and I (Kirsten the first day) hiked to the Piscine and the Canyon. Chris, Todd and I dined at Kirsten's last night.

Now Todd and I are in my hut. Todd is sleeping on my living room floor. We had the most incredible time tonight. I feel like we looked into each other's souls. We laughed until we had tears in our eyes. Then I took him through one of my analyzing highs, of how, the perception of a man saying, "Can you get me a towel to wipe this oil up?" is different for a man than for a woman. So much of our perceptions are formed by the cultural teachings.

We talked about how he started fixing things when his parents got divorced. He would try to fix himself since he must have been the problem (in his eyes). When we view situations as needing fixing, it may cause us to view others in the same way we view objects that need fixing. Emotional thoughts cause people to follow the same emotional procedure of something needing fixing. It's not only viewing things in the same process that we need to fix them, but we view the person as one who's needy and needs to be fixed...when they're cuddly, "dependent", instead of believing that maybe they're just like that 'cause they love us. We can't admit to ourselves that we're worthy of such love... we label them "needy" instead.

Yes, it was great to have someone to philosophize with and to laugh with.

This is a Lemur in Madagascar.

May 14, 1995

Hi Garrett & Jessica! (Nephew & Niece)
There are 32 species of Lemurs, and they exist nowhere else in the world but here on this huge island I live on. They have the shape of a cat, but the face of a fox. I'll bring pictures of them when I come back to the United States next year (before Christmas).

I love you both and miss you! Aunt Nancy

May 15, 1995

Hi, Denise,
Thanks so much for the lengthy letter you sent me. It was great to know what's up. I'm sure you've gotten my letter by now saying I've received your birthday package - by the way, some of the other Peace Corps Volunteers thank you for the chocolate and butterscotch, as well as me! I still haven't gotten my speakers and mace package, but mail with packages is variable here...I'm sure it'll make it. You asked me in this last letter if I need anything else but I don't think I do. By the way, send stuff to me here now: N. Coutu / BP5 / Ranohira /Ihosy 313 / Madagascar. It gets to me faster than if you send it to the Peace Corps office in Antananarivo, which was what I used during training.

Thanks for the newspaper clipping - I'm starving for U.S. news...I have a short wave radio, but often I can't get the news

in well, and it's not the most thorough (it's "Voice of America").
I had heard about the terrorist bombing, but not in detail.
Sorry I haven't really sent anything home yet as far as nice gifts,
but I live in the bush and the "big town" near me sells nothing
nice. I only see nice stuff in Antananarivo and when I'm there
it's for work and I don't have much time to shop. I just want you
to know, when Mom comes I'll rectify that and send her home
with tons of goodies, hopefully.

I'm glad Leroy liked his knives. I got a good deal on them. I
shall look for the same or something similar for Bryan when
Mom's here. They really are good for fishing and hunting.

Can you believe it Denise? I've been here nine months now!
I must say, it's going fast. I haven't been in my village for any real
long spurts 'cause I had a language training and then a work
training in the capital. Then I hiked Isalo for a bit with a Peace
Corps friend of mine, and now I'm teaching English in
Ranohira to the new park rangers. Next month I'm going away
and the next month Mom and I travel Madagascar! So it's flying by!

I think I should tell you just where I'm going away in June.
Denise, I'm going to Uganda! It's in east Africa! Peace Corps is
sending two other volunteers here at Isalo and me to a huge
Peace Corps conference on how to train tourist guides. That's
part of our work here. Can you believe it? A ten-day trip to
Africa, all expenses paid! We'll go to see some of the National
Parks in Uganda - i.e. I'll see lions, leopards, wildebeests, and
gorillas in the wild! I am more than excited.

This truly doesn't feel like a job or a sacrifice Denise, it feels
like a gift! Yes, we are an adventurous bunch (which you mentioned after saying our brother Dan's moving to Colorado). Is
he really doing it? I hope so...he needs a change! I'm sure I'll get
a letter on it soon. That would be great - I'll buy a car and travel out and visit him when I'm home. Denise, thanks for the pictures - send me one of you, okay? I'll send some home with
Mom of me. I really, really miss you. It's hard to spend so much
time in my village in long spurts, because I get real homesick -
it's so far removed from everything else. I'm glad I'm so busy and
time's flying. Well, Denise, good luck with your school applica-
tions and I hope the day care scene gets better.

I love you all! Velumo! Nancy

P.S. I'm going to Africa, Denise! Yes, To Africa!! (I'm not rubbing it in; I just can't get over it!)
May 15, 1995

Hi, Mom!

How's life going for you? Well, I hope. School's coming to a close, huh? Mom, I'm so sorry I didn't send you a Mother's Day Card. I didn't have an American calendar and I forgot the date. I just wanted to write and tell you thanks for being such a good Mom to me while I've been here. I've been pleasantly surprised at the amount of support you've given me, considering I know at first that you weren't thrilled about my coming here. My gifts and letters from you have pulled me through some times that could have otherwise felt very lonely. And the fact that you're coming to visit me gives me a support system I didn't expect to have. So, there's your Mother's Day belated message Mom, all summed up to, "I love you and appreciate you very much!"

Mom, something very exciting has come up for me here and I'm hoping it doesn't mess up our plans together. There's a training conference for Peace Corps Volunteers in Uganda. It will be on how to train National Park Guides and my Peace Corps director wants to send the other two volunteers from Isalo and me. I'll be going to Africa for 10 days in June! All expenses paid! The problem is, we don't know the dates of it yet, we won't until May 30th. There's a possibility that the training may run into the beginning of July. I truly don't want to miss the chance to go, but if you're coming within the first few days of July, I don't want you to arrive in Antananarivo before me. I will write to you when I know the dates, but it may not leave you enough time to change your flight if that's necessary.

Can you call the travel agent now and shift your landing date in Antananarivo to some time after about the 8th of July or so (leave US July 6th)? Is it too late to change it?...You can visit me at anytime from July 8th to September's end. If a change is not possible, let me know. Let me know either way. Don't worry, 'cause it's very possible your dates won't clash with any of my dates. I just figured I should take a precaution, just in case.

Concerning malaria, I talked to my Peace Corps doctor and he's instructed you to take 1100 mg. tablet of doxycycline daily for the week before you arrive here. So you only need to take one tablet daily of the pills I sent you. If you never received them, buy some in the United States for the first week and I'll give you more here.

As far as bringing money, I still don't know how much you should bring ($500-$700 probably) but don't bring hundreds Mom, bring 20's or $200 in travelers checks. $100 bills and credit cards aren't useful here.

I love you Mom, Nancy

May 25, 1995

I had a wonderful time with Todd here. Two nights after we got really drunk on tokoa gasy - way too drunk. We danced a lot and the next day both threw up. Something I haven't done in ages, and don't care to do for ages more. Poor Todd. He's infatuated with Linda, who's doing well with Joe now... hard predicament. Todd and I both feel just a friendship for each other, although I sometimes find myself somewhat attracted to him. I'm glad nothing came of it, though. It'd be really hard having feelings for someone so far away.

This last week I stayed in Ranohira with Joe (he got a room by the office). Todd, Joe and I taught the new guides for a week. It was a great time. We taught English, some French (not me, of course). The basic gist of the week was how to deal with tourists if they screw up in the park. I really enjoyed the week. Kirsten, Joe and I worked well together. I feel like we got closer. What a bunch of cuties the ACP's are.

There was a dance in Ranohira on Friday. A lot of them were there. We all danced and had a great time. A lot of them were really drunk. It was great to hang out with the new PVC's out of class. Narie (a villager) said he loves me and I tried to explain the difference between like a lot and love, but he said he knows the difference and he's liked me for 4 months watching me bike in, and he's sure he loves me. I was truly flattered. I am very attracted to him, as well as to his brother, Rivo, who will be living in Bereketa. I'd love to date Narie, but he seems so serious in his feelings that I think it would be more serious than what I'm craving. It's too bad, 'cause he's really affectionate, and not pushy, which is the type of relationship I'd like just...someone I care a lot about to cuddle with. It wouldn't be fair to him 'cause that's not at all what he wants or needs now. I really don't want to feel bad about getting involved with someone that I could break his heart. I must admit, though, the pull of wanting to go to Ranohira-instead of waiting 'til Sunday to go like I planned-has been hard. My whole heart has not been in Bereketa, as usual.

I'm starting to get things going here. Yesterday I planted potatoes with the villagers for the hotel and I will plant more tomorrow. I've been talking to women about weaving baskets and purses for the information center. I'm having a hard time jumping gun- ho into it all, without knowing if I'm going to Africa with Mom. But hopefully, this week coming up I'll know the dates and I'll be able to plan things out a bit. I hope the dates for Uganda and for Mom's coming don't clash...I'll be a bit sad to have to miss a trip to Africa. Well, signin' off now. I've been pretty stable emotionally, only 'cause I haven't stayed put much recently! My village is starting to think I'm not "tamana" (content) here.

May 29, 1995

Hi, Dan!

How's life, Bro? Good I hope. Is it true you're moving to Colorado? If it is, I was wondering if you wanted my opinion on the subject? Yeeha! Go! Go! Go! Yes, you have my support. Change is a good thing. So I've just been listening to your tape "As Birds Fly" with Janice - really beautiful - I plan to meditate to it later tonight. So anyhow, I felt like writing.

I've been writing to you a lot, huh? I was gonna write in my diary, but I decided I didn't feel like it. I did read some of it, though-stuff I had written before I arrived here. I was quite accurate as to what to expect here. Yet, I knew nothing. The picture I had was accurate but not vivid at all to the reality of it. There's no way it could have been. It's all a new world to me. I also realized there's no way I can ever actually describe it to anyone either. You can't see it until you actually see it.

I realized from reading my diary that I'm quite cute. I got a real kick out of it. I think any man would be a fool to pass me by. Where'd that come from? Sorry, Dan, I'm in a real silly mood. Mola mola iaho (I'm a bit looney!) It's funny, 'cause the other Peace Corps Volunteers that work with me say "there's the Malagasy language, there's the English translation, and then there's Nancy's translation."

More notes Culturalle:

Malagasy	English translation	Nancy's Translation
Akoy Aby!	How are you?	How's it shakin' Babe?
Sanabav!	No Way!	B.S.
Vita Miasa Tsika.	We've done our work.	It's Miller Time!

Although here I say, "It's T.H.B. time", 'cause that's the only beer there is here. Its full name is "Three Horses Beer". Why there's one beer here with an American name, I have no idea. There are only about 600 Americans in this whole damn country. The country was populated by French and Polynesian and their one and only beer is called "Three Horses Beer", with no French or Malagache translation written on the bottles, either. It's made here. Unfortunately, it's about as good as Budweiser, which isn't saying much. Even more unfortunate, is that I'm growing a taste for it. We'll know I've been here too long when I truly like it.

Ya know what's irritating, though, Dan, is that many stores have a Guinness sign up and many hotels have it on the menu. I was thrilled when I got here and saw that, 'cause I thought, "alright at last I'll have a good beer with my three meals of rice each day."

Well, Sanabav Zay! (That's crap!) I think it was just a ploy to keep American tourists and Peace Corps Volunteers in the country, 'cause I have yet to run across a Guinness sign in a place that actually has it. It's a total farce. So I'm forced to drink the tokoa gasy (moonshine) here. I think it's about 100 proof, 'cause last week I got quite sick on it. Dad warned me to be careful of it.

I just had a nice rice dinner with barangeli (eggplant), carrots and the likes of Chinese lettuce, with a glass of red wine that a merchant here in Bereketa charretted in from Toliar. It was truly a delicious meal, but I got lazy and didn't wash my rice first and I must have eaten about six rocks. I won't be lazy like that again!

Well anyhow, Dan, I just wanted to say, "Hi."

I love ya, Bro, Rakoto!

June 1, 1995

Hi ya', Mom!

I just spoke to you on the phone (June 1st). I'm so sorry it was so rushed. It's 100,000 fmg. (about $30) for 3 minutes, but I wished I had just paid for 6 minutes, 'cause I felt a knot in my gut after. I don't know if I left you in a bad position, like if you have to pay more or if this messes up plans for you with England with Donna. And I was also bummed, I didn't say, "Happy Birthday!"

Bring a warm coat and warm pj's, Mom, sleeping bag if possible...it's cold at night here! I'm psyched for you to come. I'm not sure where we're going yet, but we'll probably get a hotel in Tana for a day or two and just relax and eat and talk and talk and talk, so you can regroup. We might then go to the Periniet, a park a few hours south of Rana, to do some nature walks and see some lemurs. We can either then go to the east coast, or take a flight north to Nosy Be or south to Fort Dauphin...I'm asking around now to find out what's nicest. So we'll either take one or two in-country flights depending on how much it costs. Don't worry though, 'cause either way you won't be spending much, 'cause I'll have a good lump, too. I took out a year's vacation pay, which will buy us at least each one in-country flight. So Mom, we'll have a great time.

We'll probably go to Isalo and to my village last and will, hopefully, have no problem getting to my village. We may have to take a charrette (bulls and carriage) for 4 hours. I'll maybe book you a flight back to Tana and a night at a hotel by the airport before your flight home, unless I decided to go up with you to see you off. So, Mom, I hope I didn't mess things up for you. Did you decide to go to England first? Please know that I'm not upset at all if you come on July 2nd...I realize it was very short notice. Whenever you get here, I'll be psyched to see you.

Mom, I love you! Nance

P.S. If you go to England after here, you may want to set up a counseling session now for when you arrive back in the states on "How to Deal with Shock from Price Differences between Countries." It's a fear I have of my own on going back to the United States alone, never mind expensive England. We will live like queens while you're here, for very little money.

June, 1995

Hi, Powells!

How is everyone? Two of the volunteers have gone back to the states. They found it wasn't for them. Actually one was a health nut (or so he said) and therefore refused to take his mefloquin. He caught malaria and came close to death. Peace Corps gave him the option to "resign" or be fired. Refusing meds and riding a motorcycle without a helmet are grounds for being returned to the States. I think that if he hadn't gotten booted for one thing, it would have been for another.

What am I babbling about that for?

I'll be biking in on Sunday in two days. I'm excited to get mail this week, for some reason. I have spurts where I could take it or leave it and spurts where I downright need to hear from home... I suppose when I'm homesick, which is now. Just a bit though, nothing heart-wrenching. I'm just missing familiarity... and Chinese food, too!

I'm getting things going here, though, as far as work is concerned. I was in Ranohira last week for the whole week, working with the other two volunteers to train the new park rangers here. The new National Park Service just hired fourteen rangers, a good group of guys. I'm psyched because three will live in my village, so now I'll have some counterparts. They'll move here within a month, and one already lives here, Xavier. He's, I'd say, my very closest friend in Bereketa.

Xavier just got his mountain bike from Peace Corps.

I just got a new Mickey Mouse sweatshirt from Mom. You know you're in a foreign land when you have to explain Mickey Mouse.

I've been planting vegetables with the villagers this week, because I talked to the owner of a big ritzy French hotel here at Isalo, and he said if we can produce enough vegetables and rice, he'll buy all his food here. That would give us enough money to start a pharmacy communitaire here. I have to talk to the Ministry of Health in the capital (in Antananarivo) to set it all up.

We also want to rebuild the hospital that got whopped by a cyclone last year. This was the villagers' second desire, to fix the hospital and get medications in. The first was to get the school fixed, and I'm getting that one set for now, because the Department of Eaux et Foret (under the Malagasy government) is working on getting some money to do that. I'll only help if it falls through with them. I'm also going to start women's group, making crafts to sell to the tourists in the new information center in Ranohira. I'm going to start a weekly environmental education class with the kids here. Later I'll plant trees in this village and others to start incorporating the idea of replacing what they're cutting in the forests. The forest by my village has the most lemurs in all of Isalo Park, so I want to try and get the idea of protection into the villagers' lifestyle. It would be a shame to lose the seven species of lemurs and other animals that live there. I finally feel like I have a direction in my work here, although I'm still not used to the slow rate things get done. It's been good for me, though-learning to take time to just enjoy nature instead of always doing something. It's a nice way of life.

Well, Donna, John, Alex, Ryan, and Lauren, I love you all and miss you! Keep writing!

Love, Nancy

June 12, 1995

Hi, Bryan,

I mainly wanted to write to you to tell you your daughter is absolutely gorgeous. I can't tell you the emotions that picture of her and Garrett brought to me. I guess it was the first slap in the face I've had of just how much I'm missing at home. When I left, Jessica was still just a tiny little baby who was just starting to respond to people. Yet in that picture she is already a beautiful, little girl. I guess I didn't realize that children grow so fast. I felt a serious sadness with the realization that I'll miss seeing the beginning of your children's growth. I plan to start writing to all the kids more, just so they'll know I exist other than by just all of you guys telling them I exist. I believe Jessica and Lauren, (maybe Garret and Caleb, to some degree also), won't know who I am when I get home. At least, if I write often, it will give them something to tie it to. Keep sending me pictures now and then Bry, and I will try to do the same.

ANGAP is the national park service of Madagascar, and they are just starting out. They're going to be working here in Isalo. This is their first big project. It's making my job pretty easy, 'cause they have the money to get projects started. Then I can give the people a kick in the butt to get things going. We (Peace Corps) started here at a good time, since the park service is just starting up. They have us at the village level to help plan in what's best for the people that live around the protected area, too, instead of just thinking of the conservation of the protected area. I'm getting a huge vegetable garden going here with the villagers to sell produce to the Hotel de la Reine, the big ritzy hotel here.

The owner agreed to buy all his vegetables and rice here if

we can grow enough. And then I'm starting a women's group making baskets and purses and stuff to sell in the new tourist information center in Ranohira. Then, with the money from those, I'll talk to the Ministry of Health in Antananarivo to start a pharmacy communitaire here. I think I can get the villagers pumped up enough to rebuild the hospital that got hit by a cyclone last year. I'm also going to start a children's class once a week in environmental education, and hygiene, and making rope swings/games, and stuff like that. I'm going to start tree nurseries in Bereketa and surrounding villages, too, so the villagers can start to put back some of what they're taking out of the forest. So I have some good ideas to get going. I'm actually just having trouble finding time to get started....Isn't that weird! Tomorrow I start planting with the village, so I'll get that project going before I go to Uganda and before Mom comes. Three park rangers will live here with me, so I'll have counterparts now- that's nice. It's easy to feel all alone out here. Yet I've already worked with the rangers and they all know French well, and a little bit of English, which is rare to find here!

It's only Malagache in the village, which I've gotten pretty good with, but I'm still not fluent, Matetitetiky mokotsy be iaho amin'ny mitsara Malagache avao! I sometimes get tired of speaking nothing but Malagache! It's hard to feel overly intelligent with a language where I'm not quite sure where to put the predicate and where to put the subject when I talk. It's quite draining. I was starting to get French down pretty well, but then I needed to start learning Malagache so I never got French down really well. I'd have to say Malagache is my second language and French is my third, and I sound incredibly stupid when I attempt speaking French now. It comes out some French, some Malagache, and a slight bit of English frustration in there.

I've found that many French don't like hearing their language slandered, so I don't speak French unless I have to. I have been studying it now and then, though...I'm sure I'll be fluent before my time here is done. It is tough, because I think in English or Malagache now, and I dream in Malagache, so my brain doesn't switch to French too easily. Maybe Mom'll be good enough to help me when she visits.

Well Bryan, I'm going to sign off 'cause I want to read up some on Uganda and study a bit of French or Malagache. I haven't decided which yet. It's already late (9 p.m., past my bed-time here!). Please give my love to Joanne and the kids, and I'll be sending stuff with Mom for you...

I love you Bry! Velumo! Nancy
P.S. Bryan, hmm. Let me think... is there anything I would like more than some of that maple syrup you said you're attempting to send to me? Can't think of a thing.

June 25, 1995

I haven't been writing much here. It's not because I haven't had anything to write about. It may be because my thoughts are so many and my emotions so complex that it seems like a task to write things out. Also, when I need to "get away," I usually need to walk and get out of my village, where-as at home I'd sit and write. My writing's messy 'cause I can't use my thumb, both my thumbnails are on the verge of falling off, and they're a bit swollen too...I'm not sure what the problem is. The inside of my finger beside my thumb is all burnt, too, I think it may be sun poisoning. The Peace Corps doctor, by coincidence, will be here in a few days. Maybe he'll know. But anyhow, back to the sub-ject.

It's not only writing I'm not doing lately. I'm not really doing any of the things I usually do daily...I haven't been exercising, or doing yoga or meditation, I haven't really been playing the gui-tar. My environment is in some respect paralyzing, and I can't see just why. I always feel like I should be out doing stuff with people, yet when I visit people I only socialize. I truly don't know how to get my work going, other than farming with Anre. It may be because I'm going to Africa in a week or two and then Mom's coming, so I'll be gone for about five weeks. I hate to start anything right now.

When I'm in my house, I don't do anything I'd normally do in my house. It may be because I'm always expecting someone to show up, because someone always does. Yet if I close my door I still feel trapped, like I'm appearing odd or something 'cause my doors are closed...which I probably am, but why should I care? Why don't I go for a run every morning here? Why am I going to bed at nine and getting up at seven, instead of getting up early to do yoga? Why do I feel guilty to take an hour each day to play my guitar? Why must I close my doors? Why do I feel like I have any privacy and why do I still feel like someone will intrude? Why do I always feel like I'm doing nothing? Why do I feel like every one else thinks I'm doing nothing? Do they think that? Am I doing nothing? Why do I feel like I'm at the beginning of losing myself?

I need to start focusing. I need to get back into the habit of doing my things that make me feel like me. I think tonight I'll play my guitar, do yoga, and tomorrow I'll exercise some. But now I'm signing off 'cause my hand hurts.

Nancy sat on the floor at her homemade table to eat, read, or to write. Candles were her source of light; remember, there's no electricity here. Tomorrow she'll start anew.

Seventeen

Africa

I changed my flight plans so that Nancy could go to Africa. Nancy wrote to me in England for I had gone to visit Donna's family before going to Kenya and Madagascar. I was very relieved to get that letter for I had no idea how we would meet without it. She gave me full details on where I would find her, complete with the hotel telephone number.

Nancy proved how strong she was physically from her daily doctor's visits in Kenya. Her park visit in Kenya was the first time that she showed poor judgement. She lucked out on that one.

During her visit to Uganda and seeing gorillas in the wild was the greatest of all her experiences.

Meanwhile, I was on my way from England. My night's travel was filled with fear. I couldn't believe I was going to Africa alone. I leaned on God to get me there safely and without incident. Being able to see my Nancy was worth it all.

Nancy writes, "When they left, I biked back through the park, biking beside herds of animals including a buffalo. I passed a herd of zebras, giraffe, and antelope that ran up the mountainsides as I approached. Their power was amazing to see. After biking 20 km, I returned to the campgrounds."

June 27, 1995

Hi ya', Mom,

How ya doin', sweetie? I'm in Kenya and I'm writing you to let you know I just got in touch with Air Mad and learned that you're going July 20th to Madagascar from Kenya on the same flight as me and that you're staying 'til August 20th. Is that right?....In Uganda I'll probably see incredible sights. Then I'll go back to Madagascar with you to travel some more! We'll have fun, Mom.

My village is going to be so psyched when we arrive, 'cause I'll have been away two months and they're waiting to meet you. They're throwing you a party. It's tradition.

So, Mom, I hope your travels before coming my way go

smoothly. I hope the date change wasn't a problem financially or emotionally. I have lots of vacation pay, so it should be pretty cheap for you to travel in Madagascar...you picked a good travel partner! ...I'll see you at the Parkside Hotel - yeah!

Well, Mom, I love you and I am psyched to see you. See ya' in Kenya!

Love, Nancy

July 1995

I'm in Uganda now. I was in the Nairobe area in Kenya for a week before this. Kampala, Uganda is much different from Nairobe, Kenya. Nairobe is much more westernized and I have to say I liked it more, simply because it was closer to the things we have at home. I realize now that I greatly miss home.

This whole trip started in Bereketa. The doctor made a site visit. When he saw my hands, he said I needed to go to Tana (I have a bacterial infection under my nails). I figured I'd have trouble dealing with culture shock when I go home to America. I expect an overload on the senses. Maybe that won't happen, because I stayed at the guesthouse in Tana near the Peace Corps office. At this guest- house there was a vcr/tv, electricity, hot running water, a refrigerator, a stove, and an oven. I had no problem adjusting. I was more than content, even with the great selection of food. So I don't think going home will be too hard. I believe I'll slip right back into it.

Going to Nairobe was like returning to the United States and I loved it. Everything is written in English. People were speaking in English. There were tall buildings, grocery stores, clothes stores, shops, American movies, ice cream, Italian, Chinese, India, Greek, American food...it was incredible. It's funny because before, I thought that Africa was not westernized at all and I was pleasantly surprised.

I figured Africa would be similar to Madagascar, but with large game, wildlife, and maybe slightly different houses and village set-ups. Unfortunately, I didn't get to visit very far out of Nairobe because I had to visit the doctor almost every day. He made a habit of pulling nails off with each visit! Ouch!

I did get up to Lake Naivasha where I saw in the wild,

wildlife that I've only seen in zoos until now. It was an unbelievable experience. I saw giraffe, zebras, and antelopes all relaxing by the lake. I also saw the back of a hippo in the water. It was quite incredible. At the campground there was cold beer, munchies, and meals were served. I met Tom, a Norwegian, and sat by the fire in the evening with him and three friends of his.

The next day I biked to Hell's Gate National Park. A Kenyan woman named Nancy with her fifteen friends approached me and invited me to go through the park in their van with them. They were worried about me biking through the park, for it housed very big animals, none of which were too happy with Homo sapiens. I accepted and went for a walk with them to the hot springs and had a picnic where they fed me tons of food. Next we drove by giraffes, antelopes, zebras and warthogs. When they left, I biked back through the park, biking beside herds of animals including a buffalo. I passed a herd of zebras, giraffe, and antelope that ran up the mountainsides as I approached. Their power was amazing to see. After biking 20 km, I returned to the campgrounds.

I had dinner with Tom and Valdor. In the morning we met again to take a bus to Nairobe.

It was time for the next doctor's visit. This time he removed a toenail. - ugh! I ignored the pain by going to see "The Lion King." I then browsed the African clothes and craft shops. Then I met up with more volunteers and palled around with them. There were volunteers in Nairobe the whole time I was there, because they're doing their COS medical. So I never spent an evening wondering what to do. I was whisked everywhere and felt very well cared for. I found Nairobe to be refreshing, yet an air of danger was present...maybe the same as Tana. Just watch yourself. Over all, Kenya was fun, but I don't think I got the true taste of the country by only visiting Nairobe and Lake Naivasha.

July 1995

Dear Dad,

I'm in Uganda now, which is not open grasslands as Kenya was. It has continuously, gorgeously forested land. The forests are plush with many devils in them - they look like tropical rainforests with all the vines, fig trees, palm trees, and the African tall flat topped trees (I don't know the species). Since there are so many forests with two rainy seasons, the wild life is different from Kenya. We've seen the ring-tailed monkey; the red colobus and black and white colobus monkeys, baboons swinging through the trees and chimps, one whom we watched groom and eat. It's been quite great.

I do believe Madagascar was probably similar looking to this country before all the forests were cut. There's seemingly no erosion problem here as there is in Madagascar. Uganda's personality seems similar to Madagascar's, except everyone speaks English. It's more developed here. It is similar in the way people are so friendly. The people have the custom of setting food on sidewalk tables to sell. The two are similar in the way there are "haunted Popsicle stands," as Kirsten and Roland have called them, where sodas and crackers and gum and things are sold. They are also similarities in that everyone yells "Hello mazunga," or "Bonjour vazaha" (Good day white foreigners.) It's necessary to wait for the bus about three hours before going anywhere. There is no such thing as a time schedule here (and very few clocks, for that matter). Yep! Similar even, that a man will offer me a cow to stay in the country with him (What the hell am I supposed to do with a cow? I don't know!).

Yet, there's much that is different, too - good ice cream, driving on the left side of the road, (the wrong side) from English influences, instead of on the right, from French influence. In Africa there are laundromats in the city (yee haw!), jewelry and clothes, good quality clothing stores with different styles than in Madagascar. W.C.s in villages and a capital city not as congested. There are more people here in a smaller space, yet it seems like fewer people, because they're all spread out a bit more. It's not nearly as developed here in Uganda as in Nairobe. Yet, it's still much more developed than Madagascar. There's much more stuff here too, like Guinness and Bailey's, since it's easier to import goods here. I had four Guiness last night (what a glutton!). I'll treat myself to a Bailey's when I return to Kampala.

Right now, Joe, Kirsten and I are in a town called Bitogatoa. We are on our way to Bevinde National Forest, where the mountain gorillas live. There are only about 400 left here. (Caire, and Rewanda and I don't know if it's likely that we'll see any.

I'm still psyched to be here. We hung out with Eric for the past four days. He is a volunteer habituating chimps in Kibale National Park. It was a great time. We went on a forest walk and a swamp walk, which is where we saw the monkeys I listed. We met all the guides, too. The whole program seemed really well organized.

They have a great campground and a tourist information center. The guides were great too, which was probably because the Uganda National Park Service paid for them to have two years of training. So it was good to see an organized park. Eric was a lot of fun. We went to a party for Monica, another volunteer leaving soon. We danced with the guides and had a lot of fun. Before coming here, we were back in Kampala and had beers last night with about seven other volunteers...fun, fun, fun!

There was one guy, Dave, that I hit it off with and talked to a lot (not "hit off" attraction wise, but friend wise). So I'm definitely getting my share of volunteers. We've been having fun together. Yet I don't feel as loose as I did by myself in Nairobe. There's always an underlying wave of tension I feel when we're all together, as if when I express my feelings they'll get shot down instantly. It makes me turn a bit inward. I always feel that there's such a lack of acceptance on all of our parts. I don't know why it's like that. I just know it feels very unnatural being with so many other volunteers. I think it has been good for us all.

Hopefully, the fun will carry through for the whole trip. It's just hard for me because I feel I'm pretty laid back in my friendships with people. I feel, for some reason, like these guys's initial reaction to me is defensive. I'm not sure why that is, but it's definitely there. Joe and I are getting along quite well.

So, enough of that. I'm psyched to go to Bewinde tomorrow. We'll be staying at the campground in a bungalow for three nights, meeting up with Thor. Then we'll go to Eric's house and seven other volunteers and we will go to the guide training. We're in the Rift Valley right now. It's mountainous with banana trees growing everywhere (as in all of Uganda), the forested canyons with mud huts/thatch roof villages. It's really pretty. This is the place that Diane Fosey studied gorillas. (Gorillas of the Mist or something like that was the movie).

Eventually, one (I think) killed her. Kibale National Forest, where we already were, is where Jane Goodall studied chimps (one of the places), so we're in pretty famous territory. I feel quite lucky to have been given such an opportunity.

Well, I think I'll study a bit of French and then crash out!

Write soon, Your PCV, Nancy

July 7, 1995

I love it when the date is the same as the day (7/7). Then I don't have to figure out if I should write the date or the day first! (In Madagascar they write the day first.)

We're here in Bwindi National Park, where we went for a forest walk today. We saw no gorillas, but we saw the border of Zaire. I was quite excited with that. It's $125 a day to go gorilla tracking, and I don't see myself paying that. I'm already so thrilled with the wildlife I've seen between here and Kenya.

We met Thor ("Tor") here, a volunteer working in this area. I fell so in love with him that I dare say I got a bit too excited and made a bit of a fool of myself. Maybe I didn't. I just felt like I did. I came back to our little bungalow feeling a little rejected, because I felt like I had messed it up. When we got back I wanted to cry, but I decided to do sit-ups instead...I sure as hell didn't want to cry in front of Joe and Kirsten. They would have thought I was nuts and they wouldn't have understood. So I did about 70 sit-ups and then went outside to do some yoga, which centered me a bit.

I've been on my own now for so long with so few to interest me, or reminders that I'm lonely, that when I meet someone I truly am attracted to, all my feelings come pouring back with the realization that I'm lonely. Alas, that if I was back in the U.S., I probably wouldn't want to be lonely anymore. It's just that in my environment I don't realize that; because there's nothing to remind me of the style of life I could be having...this other life I'd be craving if I was in a different environment.

Yet now that I went through that evening and feel like I blew Thor having an interest in me, I've decided to just be me from here on in, and not worry about what he thinks of me. Fate is the determinant in my life.

A funny thing happened when I was doing yoga tonight. As I was standing in the form of a warrior, I saw my arm in the moonlight. My peach-colored, boutique shirt covered my arm. I realized it has gotten to be a very skinny arm. I concentrated on it. I never thought I could be that skinny in my whole body and I loved me greatly for having gotten as thin I was. This gave me such high confidence in myself. This is possible. I never thought I could feel so beautiful. I wanted to love myself the way I had at times in my past, but this is beyond those feelings. I feel I'm much more whole than I was at any other time. Yet, I still don't truly love me or feel truly confident in myself. It's not that hard a task. "Mind over matter"; "Mind over body" I'll keep working on it.

July 8, 1995

We went on a forest walk today to the waterfalls. It was fantastic...we saw 13 gorillas! Six feeding, six babies and a silverback (220kg male = 4 Joes). They were crossing our path on our way back. I first saw a black head pop out on the path and then another behind it and I thought it was a couple people. Then two gorillas walked into the path with babies on their backs. I was so surprised. Then, a three-year-old gorilla sat in the path for a while. Next a huge silverback sat in the path. I mean, HUGE! Another group of people came, and all the gorillas went into the woods, but still close enough for us to get pictures.

The gorillas have all been habituated to humans-two groups of gorillas. This was Thor's job. When he started here, along with the other guides, he sat with them six days a week to get them accustomed to people. I have to say I'd consider doing a third year of Peace Corps to take his place here. His home is a dream home of mine- with mud walls, a banana thatched roof and overlooking the rainforest with the river gurgling below. It's what you'd see on TV, a researcher studying gorillas or chimps...a truly neat life.

It's opposite of where I am in a lot of ways...total solitude. It would be a wonderful, self-contemplating year.

There's a volunteer replacing Thor in September. If I go home and still crave to be here, I'll get in touch with Peace Corps when I'm finished in Madagascar to see if the person's still here. Thor said that there's another volunteer in Uganda who lives by Lake Victoria at a National Park with a dream house and a porch overlooking the forest and lake. It has elephants coming through to scratch their backs on the house.

I'm happy in Madagascar and with my placement. To be here to see the rainforests and all the animals of Africa has been a truly special experience. There's something very exotic about the whole thing. I'll have to travel more in Africa sometime later in my life. I still have a great interest in working with massive animals though. So if I do seriously consider doing a third year in Peace Corps, it may be fun (and helpful in the direction, respect) to do something in marine parks or environmental education or habituating humpback whales (ha, ha, ha!). Something to get into scuba diving and studying the marine environment and mammals. Oh ,well...I'll see what comes up.

I don't think I could get a marine job in the states without former experience other than through the Peace Corps. They were willing to put me in Seychelles Marine Environmental Educational Program just having a minor in Marine Biology. I'm so glad I didn't choose that program, 'cause they just closed it down! I think it may be because it's too touristy and they're maybe not third world anymore. I'm glad I followed my gut and went to Madagascar! (If I had chosen Seychelles maybe I'd be put into Thor's shoes here - who know? Things always work out).

It's evening now and we just had dinner at Thor's. It was delicious. We had spaghetti with eggplant, tomatoes, carrots and onion sauce, with an international moment for dessert. And I'm still in love, Ugh! I've never been so miserably infatuated. It's awful cause I don't know if he feels anything at all for me. I think I saw him looking at me a lot while Kirsten was talking to him. He was across the room and I was behind Kirsten sitting to the side. He may have just been looking at me wondering for what reason there was drool coming out of my mouth and why I had a lovesick look on my face. Just kidding...no drool. I'm at the moment trying to figure out how to nonchalantly tell him tomorrow that I'd like to marry him and have his children.

Well...I'm sure I'll at least just get his address tomorrow and leave the next morning from here feeling totally depressed, realizing it was just a crush on my part only. That's life, I guess. Saga to be continued tomorrow.

July 9, 1995

Another nice walk today. We saw the gorillas again in the distance off the path. With the binoculars, I could see the silverback eating through the leaves. He was alone.

We just had dinner at a cantina after having been with Thor. He made a joke over beer. Amy, a girl from the States who's joined us today, asked him if he had any training in habituating gorillas before . He said in a dead pan way, "Yeah, I habituated my parents before here." Oh man, it was hysterical. He's great. We'll have breakfast with him tomorrow before we go, but that may be the last time that I'll see him. Bummer. Oh well.

The training is going really well. I think Kirsten and Joe and I have some good ideas of what to do to train the guides. Just getting started will be the tough parts. The lack of organization with the guides is really severe.

I hope I can focus when I return to my site. It will be hard though with everyone constantly visiting me. I think I need to make myself a private space to make a work atmosphere for myself. Oh well, I'll see. Maybe Mom can give me some ideas when she visits.

July 11, 1995

We are in Mahaginga National Park, here for the guide training with Eric, Craig, Peter, Brad, Kelly, Gavin, and the guides at the park. I was right; I left Bwindi with only Thor's address and a heavy heart. My crush is all done and I'm okay. Such is life.

We're having a lot of fun here...a good bunch of guys. I was going to be staying with Kelly in his tent, but Peter and Kamay, a Ugandan who works with Brad at his site, are staying in a banda and there was an extra bed. I'm up here. It's been warm and comfy though. One of the men is awfully gasy... indigestion problems. Others say it's a normal situation for him. I'm glad I can't smell very well or I may be wishing I'd stayed in the tent.

July 18, 1995 (Mom's journal)

National Express bus has dropped me at Terminal Two in London. It was necessary to get to Terminal Four so again the luggage battle went on. There was a shuttle bus, but for the first time I had to wrestle those darned bags myself. The driver got impatient with me and finally threw the last bag into the middle of the isle and away we went.

We drove through London. There was a railroad strike on, so many had their cars in the city and the traffic was bumper to bumper. It took an hour for a twenty-minute trip. Man, cutting it close!!

Got checked in and had to rush for the plane. So much for last minute shopping - 4:00 on board. My boarding pass said seat 57k.Yeks! I must be sitting in the tail of the plane. I was directed to the left as I entered the plane; then, guess what - up the stairs - 2nd row, window seat. There were about fifteen rows up there with three seats on each side. We had enough room to hold a dance. Talk about royal treatment!

We finally taxied out, that's why air tickets cost so-o-o much, it's the taxi fare that costs. We approached the runway when we heard, "This is your captain speaking". The control tower said it would be one hour before we will get a take off. "We are going to shut off the engines to conserve fuel". Oh well, to my French lessons.

Finally, we were off with the usual, dinner movies - Oh, I don't believe it - "Don Juan". It was so bad I couldn't watch it, so I tried to go to sleep. I flipped through the channels and came to, "You are very relaxed. There is a little opening in the back of your head. A circulating wind came in and is whirling around in your head. Now, it is going round and round in your chest. It fills your whole body _ _ _"

"So, as all this is going on, my brain leaked out." Ok, well let's try Don again.

No! This is more than I can take!"

The entire night went on like this mixed with fear. "What if Nancy didn't get my letter and doesn't meet me? Well, she told me the hotel and telephone number where she'd be tonight. Ok, go to sleep. You'll be OK, God will be there to guide you. God, will you please put me to sleep?-Please!!!"

That should have done it, but it didn't. Not a wink of sleep all night. Fear was where I was!

Eighteen

Mom Arrives

I arrived at the Nairobe, Kenya Airport at 3:30 am and found that my travel agent had neglected to get me a one-day visa to go into Nairobe. This was another fear filled experience because the airport was almost empty when I exited to the public area.

Nancy and I took a safari. It was not a movie. We really did it!

July 19, 1995
3:30 a.m. (Mom's Journal)

At last, we landed, checked through customs and I got a visa. I desperately search all of the faces which revealed - no Nancy! F-E-A-R!

There was a front line of cab drivers to plow through. One got my, "OK." He let me call the Lakeside Hotel that was supposed to be housing my child.

"Nancy C-O-U-T-U, No? Are you sure? Please look again!"

After a long pause...a long pause..."Is she with the Peace Corps?"

"Yes, yes, yes!" I shouted with great relief.

"Yes, she's here. Shall I wake her?" The desk clerk questioned.

"No, this is her mother. I'm at the airport and I'll get a cab and come right over. Let her sleep and I'll surprise her." I responded joyfully.

My heart pounded. It couldn't decide if it wanted to remain

normal because of relief from fear, or take frantic leaps from excitement. "O.K, God, I'm here and my daughter is, too. Joy, relief, and happiness and, "Thank you, dear God. That's all I can say for now. Just enjoy my happiness and excitement as my prayer, Lord."

I made my first attempt at negotiating prices with this cab driver, but he sensed I didn't really care. I just wanted to get to Nancy. I was too happy to be scared of riding alone to the hotel at 4:15 a.m. with this cabby. If I were normal, instead of crazy with excitement, I should have and would have been terrified. $18 took me on a half-hour trip to the Lakeside Hotel. When we arrived there was Nancy out front! She jumped up and down and waved her arms as she shouted "Mom! Mom!!" "Nancy! Nancy!" - Tears-hugs, hugs-tears, lug the suitcase. Then more hugs and tears. We talked three hours non-stop until 8 a.m. There were many happy tears and hugs during this time. Then went to a restaurant for breakfast. (You wouldn't believe that place. It was apparent there was no board of health here.)

"Do you need to sleep or do you want to go to the State Park on a safari?" Nancy asked.

"Are you kidding? I can catch up some other time. To the safari!" I replied. I may never get to Africa again in my remaining life! To the safari!"

July 19, 1995

Mom met me in Nairobe on the morning of July 19th at the hotel where I was staying. We took a safari for the day to Nairobe National Park. It was great! We hired our own car and driver, Daniel. (There are surely a lot of Daniel's in my life). The three of us had a real fun trip together. We saw zebra, giraffe, water buffalo, impalas, and coudas(I think). Another ungulate, and-get this-a family of cheetahs, a mom and 7 babies. It was a great day and Mom got to see a little of Kenya on her way through. I'm glad she caught me at the hotel. I hate to think of how uncomfortable it would have been for her in Nairobe alone for the day!

(The same story - Mom's Journal)

We got to the Nairobe National Park and first saw some giraffe, two of them. As we rode around, we saw water buffalo, ostriches, more giraffes, including a mom nursing her 6-foot tall baby.

There were single, double, and herds of zebras everywhere, lots of them. There was a warthog-or three or four.

When we came to a herd of water buffaloes, I had to get them on video so I stood up with the top part of my body out the window.

"Get in! Get in!" Daniel pleaded. "If they decide to charge, we will move as fast as this car can go." In I went. Daniel seemed quite relieved.

We followed them. The mom just strolled along, not paying us any mind. The seven babies, however, went 10 - 15 feet back to turn around and look at us. These darling babies got quite brave and soon ran right beside the car. Yep! They were only about 6 feet or 7 feet from us. Then they crossed the road and changed sides. As we escorted them for about 15-20 minutes, we experienced excitement beyond words. Then the mom and her seven veered left and headed across the savana. Soon it was over - five hours. What fun!

We headed back to Nairobe. I got a two-hour nap while Nancy went to dinner with her friends.

When she returned she woke me. We assembled our belongings and got a taxi to the airport. I can hardly believe that I spent a whole day in Africa and went on a safari with my beautiful daughter.

Other PCV's were to take the same plane. However, Kirsten and Joe did not call to verify their reservations, as required by Air Madagascar. Their seats were given to 2 new passengers. The PC leader would not let the plane take off until they were allowed to board. All were let on with the stipulation that we had to find seats. There were no assigned seats on these planes.

Nancy had me take a single and disappeared up front. The plane took off so I felt sure we were all seated. It was dark out so I felt I would miss nothing if I slept.

When we landed I asked Nancy where she had sat.

"O~h, I went up to first class." She responded with a grin.

Nineteen

Touring in Madagascar

Nancy did not write much during my visit. There are entries from both my journal and Nancy's. We visited the Periniet Rain Forest. Going to Toamasina, a pous-pous ride made me feel uncomfortable but Nancy changed that. We passed on an overloaded boat to the Isle of Saint Marie.

Nancy wriutes, "My fingers are okay, by the way, as well as my toes. The doctor needed to take off some of the nails because my skin was getting really infected under them, and he gave me penicillin, which seemed to stop the bacterial infection. I've had no more pain since he took the nails off..."

July 20, 1995 *(Mom's journal)

Fortunately, the Peace Corps driver met us, 7 PCV's and me, at the airport. "Thank God!" I thought.

Our first instructions were: "Stay alert, hold onto your things, and try to stay together." All got their luggage and gratefully, got into the large van. Nancy and I sat up front with our driver, Parfait. He is a native of Madagascar, who drove for the Peace Corps in the capital.

The ride into Antananarivo was a shocker. The time was 5:00 am. People were all walking, pulling wagons, and carrying baskets on their heads. All were barefooted. Their clothing looked worse than what I throw away. The shock of what I saw pushed away the desire to sleep. As time went on, more and more people poured into the sometime dirt and sometime paved, but always very bumpy street.

"Are these all street people?" I whispered to Nancy.

"Parfait, who are all these people? Where are they going?" Nancy asked.

"They are natives who walk 8, 6, 4, or 2 miles to take their goods to work at the street market. Some of them have good jobs in banks, post offices, stores, and travel agents. They are the ones with the shoes on." The public buildings where many worked were quite nice - simple but nice.

When we got to our hotel that Nancy had made reservations at, they had given our room away because we were not there on time. They got us a room at another hotel. It was two blocks away. Lug those suit cases!

I didn't care what our hotel room looked like but it was quite nice. Just let me at that bed!!!!! In the past 48 hours I've had one 2-hour nap and one 4-hour nap. Down went the bags and in I climbed into bed. It was now about 6 p.m. To sleep-Z-Z-Z-z-z-z-z. I slept through the night until 10:00 a.m.

July 21, 1995

Hi ya', Donna! Happy Birthday!

Here I am back in Madagascar and Mom's here with me! Mom and I met with three other sets of parents in Tana for breakfast. She rested and I visited with PCV's.

We're on a train now from the capital city to the Periniet, a nature-preserve with many species of lemurs. We'll stay in a little bungalow for a day or two and then take the train to the east-coast.

It's good to have Mom here. I think she's already learned a lot with just the little she's seen in two days. I must admit, I'm surprised she came. I'm so glad she did, though. It'll widen her perspective on life, as it has with me. It'll also give me someone at home who knows where I've been.

I wish you all could come visit. But I must say, having Mom visit me here seems so odd...it's as if she was dropped from another planet into mine. That's actually not too far from the truth!

It's fun watching her reactions. It reminds me of how I was thinking when I first got here... things I've now forgotten about. There are things that I now just take for granted because I'm used to this culture. For example, how to balance on a pit latrine used to be difficult for me...mom's learning the technique now! She's also finding that in comparison to Madagascar's toilet paper, England's is not all that bad!

Here's our itinerary:
July 21st - Train to Periniet
July 22nd - Nature walks in Periniet
July 23rd - Train to Andaside
July 24th - Taxi brousse to Mahamrd
July 25th - Boat to Isle of St. Marie
July 28th - Fly to Tana
July 29th & 30th - Drive to Ranohira with Kirsten
    and her mom, Peggie
July 31st - Camp at Piscine Naturelle
Aug. 1st - Go to Bereketa

I'm so glad to be heading back to my village soon. I miss my hut and my friends and my village lifestyle. I've been away a long time between going to Kenya, (when I was medically evacuated to the head Peace Corps doctor), going to the guide training conference in Uganda, and now traveling with Mom.

My fingers are okay, by the way, as well as my toes. The doctor needed to take off some of the nails because my skin was getting really infected under them, and he gave me penicillin, which seemed to stop the bacterial infection. I've had no more pain since he took the nails off and they're looking better now, as if they may grow back normal. The whole problem was that the doxycycline I was taking for my acne reacted with the sun on my long bike rides to my village and lifted my nails a bit. This left space for an infection to get under them. Weird, huh? But I'm okay now and it seems to have stopped. At least I got a free week in Kenya out of the deal! Well, Donna, we're almost there, so I'm going to sign off for now. Thanks so much for those incredible granola cookies with chocolate on them from the last package you sent. They were heavenly. Thanks for that light, too...a perfect gift that I wouldn't have asked someone to send, because it would have been a pain. I've been going to bed at 9 p.m. in my village because my eyes got so tired of candlelight or lamp light...yet I don't like to go to bed that early. Thanks for the help!

Mom said you gave me more stuff too, but I've yet to open the big blue suitcase, so I don't know what is in there. I'm pacing myself on surprises.

Denise sent me some good stuff like underwear and tank tops. That made me pleasantly surprised and happy. I didn't realize Mom would be seeing all of you before she arrived. I bought stuff for you in Africa to send with her. Since she's not going to see you on her way back through, I may just mail it.

Okay, I'm signing off for now. I love you, Donna! And I miss you and John and the kids. I will probably mail this letter tomorrow in Toamasina since we take the train there. We spent today and yesterday in the Periniet Reserve. I have seen the indu lemur, mouse lemur, wooly lemur, and brown lemur. Mom's quite happy about it. Last night was tough, 'cause we went in the woods at 7 p.m. and it was dark and pouring and slippery. Mom fell down some but laughed. She was in pretty good spirits.

Happy Birthday, Hon.
I love you! Nancy

(Nancy's Journal)

Here we are at the Periniet. We just took a train here from Tana. The trip took from 7 a.m. to 7 p.m. It was beautiful to see some of the country.

We'll take some walks in the reserve to see some lemurs and then try to get on the train again to go to Toamasina. As for now, we're staying in a nice little bungalow and we've just had a great Chinese soup in the hotel across the road. We're just kicking back now reading and writing.

In a couple of hours we'll go on a nature walk with some Germans we just met here. They are touring around too, to the National Parks here. They approached me when they heard me speak the language and we chatted about Madagascar. So we'll all go trucking through the forests tonight. We'll probably do a morning walk, too, to see and hear the Indies (lemurs).

It is nice having Mom here and it's good to be out of Tana now. It was depressing her and I'm not relaxed there, either. It's much more laid back here.

I will be psyched when we get to my home later.

The lemurs we may see at Periniet are: Grey Bamboo Lemur (Mapalemur Gnseus), Red Furred Lemur (Lemur Rubriuemter), Wooly Lemur (Avani Lariger), Indri (Indri Inori), Aye-Aye (Daubertonia Madagas Caribuis).

July 21, 1995 (Same story - Mom's Journal)

Nancy and I got up at six thirty and set out through the army of umbrellas. She moved like a tornado and I did my best to keep up. There were hundreds of people already at their train stations, even though the train was not due for a half-hour. It was my first chance to sit still and observe the people. Such poverty! Of all those people, one mother and her two children were well dressed. It brought tears to my heart. Can they afford tickets? I wonder where they are all going? The train came and Nancy discovered we had first class tickets, so there were only about ten people in our car.

As we traveled, my eyes couldn't believe the sights of huts and people that were so poor. The train rolled past them, then past rice fields, and then we were in the mountains.

160

Tanim-bary (rice fields)

When a mountain was too high, we tunneled through it.

After about eight stops were people with cooked sausage, French breads, bananas, and tangerines. Hunger overtook us. Natives stood outside the train windows and sold to the passengers.

Now, let me give you the correct impression. Running water was not available to most of these people and cleanliness was not part of their lives, it seemed. We didn't buy anything but fruit at first but hunger soon erased our hygiene concern and we gave in. The food was quite good.

On the train a German family named Boon approached us. They were in first class with us. They heard Nancy speaking Malagashe, and asked us to join them. This was a scientist, his adult son and his wife. Professor Boon talked Nancy and me into going into the rain forest for a night hike. Yep, we were booked with a guide to go out into the rain forest in the Parinet Protected Park. Can you imagine? I was going into the rain forest -at night! What magic did my daughter work on me now?

We finally arrived at Andisabe after twelve hours of viewing much beautiful scenery during our trip. Nancy had rented an A-frame cabin that was actually quite nice. As per usual, not all in it worked. The toilet didn't flush. Oh, well, at least there was - that bucket of water trick and there was one supplied.

After Nancy and I had dinner, it was time to go to meet Prof. Boon and his son. I can't believe I'm doing this. I can't believe I'm doing this! I can't-believe-I'm-going-into-the-rain-forest-at night!

Two flashlights and four people...for two hours! Flashlight searching revealed the mouse lemur, which is the smallest primate in the world. With cute little beady eyes looking down at us, he was sitting in a tree about twenty feet up. Then we saw the world's smallest frog.

The forest began to live up to its reputation. It began to rain. The path got slippery and still, more slippery. I slipped and went down on one knee. Well, that wasn't too bad. I laughed and got up. We continued at the men's pace, which was a problem with my short legs. Ten minutes later, down I went again. This time I muddied my left side to my hip. I sat laughing. Nancy, being the good daughter that she is, took my muddy hand and - after uncontrollable laughter - managed to help me up.

The rain increased. You maybe won't believe it, but about fifteen minutes later, I slipped right on my bum. I laughed and laughed as I thought, "I could stay on my feet if they would slow down." Nancy pulled and pulled on my two muddy hands and pulled her mud covered Mom up, for the last time.

At last, our tour ended. The rain continued as my, super tolerant daughter, and I walked a little slower back to our A-frame chalet. This was a laughter filled half-hour.

As we strolled along in the pleasant drizzle, I asked Nancy, "Do you know why I couldn't get up that last time? My bladder was full and with all the laughing, I actually peed my pants."

"Oh, my gosh, Mom. I don't believe you actually did that!" Nancy roared.

"I don't either." We laughed all way home.

I was required to disrobe on our porch. Nancy brought out a pan of water for me to de-mud my hands, feet and anything else that could benefit. A shower for each seemed a fitting end to our memorable evening. We felt like two college kids sitting on our cots and laughing about the whole crazy day and night's activities. Nancy can always get me to do adventurous things that end in immense fun.

When trying to go to sleep, one of us would go off and the other would giggle. This happened again and again. Needless to say it took well over an hour for sleep to set in. What fun!

July 22, 1995 (Mom's journal)

We took an afternoon tour through the rain forest. The forest was quite quiet for the animals had eaten and were inactive. After dinner we inquired, "What time is the next train to Toamasina?" "6:00 a.m.," was the reply.

Nancy and I went to our chalet, packed and retired early. We both wrote to bring on sleep.

At 6:00 a.m. we were in the restaurant, which adjoined the train platform, across the street. We had breakfast - then lunch, and - then dinner. Two young German teachers, Michelle and Annemarie, sat and commiserated with us during this endless time.

I had plenty of time to draw this picture
of the building across the street.

The evening entertainment arrived at 8:00 p.m. and entertained us for three more hours. (Still no train.)

At 11:00 p.m. we were, apologetically, told that the restaurant was closing and that we would have to go out to the train platform.

There were no seats here. More and more natives joined us. Did they know something that we didn't? Why were they out there earlier?

Finally, nineteen hours of "what to do" ended. Our seven-hour train trip started. It was now 1:00 a.m., a far cry from 6:00 p.m. yesterday. Did I tell you that there are no transportation schedules in this country?

In the train we sat with Michelle and Annemarie. Nancy sat sideways with her legs over her suitcase.

The three of them shifted around this way and that until, finally, they got a position that allowed them to go to sleep. I wasn't as lucky so, I kept vigilance. Of about thirty people, only five remained awake. I watched a boy about ten years old, crawled down the isle, got a duffel bag of another passenger, tipped-toed back with it and dropped it in the back seat. What appeared to be his mother, a brother, and another woman kept watch that the "victim" and those around didn't see him. I didn't know the language and I didn't know the customs. It seemed wise to say nothing, even though I really hated to be quiet. I was a white visitor in a foreign country. (This gave me an in depth look at what it feels like to be a minority. Not fun.)

My intentions were to have Nancy tell the victims when she woke up but I dozed off. While we slept, the train must have stopped and the group made off with their loot. This took place four hours into the trip.

I slept through many stops. At 6 a.m., the fifth hour of traveling, I woke up to yells and excitement in the car. A bird had flown in and everyone was trying to kill it. A man whipped a piece of clothing and killed the bird. It pained me to think they would do this, instead of trying to help it to get out!

The trip went on and on and on. We stopped every half-hour for about 10-15 minutes. At each stop, people sold food. There was no such thing as wrapping the food there, since paper and plastic was almost unheard of in most places. The sales people were all quite dirty. But, as hunger grew, the dirt seemed to become a reasonable risk to buy food.

The trip finally ended after thirteen-hours for what was supposed to take seven hours. Did I tell you that there are no transportation schedules in Madagascar? The food stops were unscheduled and very numerous.

We taxied to a hotel. By Malagasy standards, it was quite nice. The room had a shower and toilet.

That day we walked around the marketplace, which is a collection of stands with either a roof above or a table with an umbrella over it. Some of the sales people were just out in the open with their products on the ground. You could buy live chickens or pigs that you could take home on a taxi brousse or a train.

There were vegetables in the open, but my stomach rebelled when we walked through the meat section. There was cut-up meat and ground meat sitting out in the open for God knows how many days. The flies had first choice at it. The desire to avoid inhaling was immense. People seemed cleaner here than in Tana, but poverty was everywhere. Employees in the market sold goods or ran pous-pous (a human drawn carriage). I had a great problem with another human being running us to our hotel.

Nancy explained, "Mom, they would have no income if people didn't hire the pous-pous runners." The explanation softened my feelings, but it still felt wrong.

Nancy and I returned to our room to dress and talk. I had brought only three extra videotapes, for I, mistakenly, thought I could get some more in Madagascar. Wrong!

I had Nancy view the videos I had shot of all her kin. We would tape over them on the rest of the trip for I mistakenly thought I could buy more film for my camcorder in Madagascar. There is a lot to learn when going to a third world country.

Nancy was having a Bailey's that I had gotten on the plane. When she saw Jessie, she started to cry. She had missed much of Jessie's growing. What happened next really, really upset me.

Nancy put the camera down, looked at me very seriously and said, "Mom don't let them forget me! Please, don't let them forget me, Mom!" she pleaded.

"Yes Nancy, I promise, but Honey, you'll be home in a little over a year." I tried to comfort her, but thought, "What is all that about?" Something within me made me think it wise not to explore there.

July 27, 1995 (Nancy's journal)

We took a taxi brousse to Toamasina. As usual, it was crowded with people, chickens and a pig in a cage. Our plans were to take a boat the next day to the Isle of St. Marie.

Mom and I realized our fate is to spend the next two days in Toamasina, not the Isle of St. Marie. I got us a room at the most luxurious hotel in the area.

Pous-pous runners
waiting to run hotel guests to town.

Ocean view from third floor of our hotel.

Our room had two beds, a television with five channels (including CNN), a bathtub, a swimming pool, casino, restaurant, bar, and a balcony overlooking the ocean. It's healing our wounds quite well. All for only $30 per night, since I'm a resident. This is the most enjoyable time we've had yet!

Tomorrow we fly to Tana and then, if things go as planned (yeah, right!), we'll rent a car and drive down to Isalo with Kirsten and her Mom, and then somehow get to my village.

Mom is glad she came. She said it's depressing, but a real eye-opener. My emotions have been all over the place since she's been here - sometimes I enjoy her and sometimes I am snappy with her and can't seem to control it. I think I find it hard sometimes, because she said she wants to see as much as she can. Yet when we travel around at all, she complains about how much her body hurts from carrying her one bag - it's a contradiction that frustrates me. That makes me feel like I often don't know how to please her. How hard can it be with me carrying my backpack and her two?

Being in this luxurious hotel has taken the edge off things. The rest of the trip should be easier, since we'll soon be in my home area. I'll be a lot more light-hearted then, 'cause I'm itching to get home. I should be meditating and doing yoga while on the move, because of the tension I've been feeling while traveling with her. The same was true when I traveled in Africa with Joe and Kirsten and sometimes alone but to a lesser degree. This is uncomfortable and self-destructive. It's not natural and it's not necessary. I lose control of my emotions when it happens and I tell myself I'd control my feelings toward Mom on the trip and make it a pleasant and bonding time.

When the tension comes, it stems only from my feelings and thoughts toward her, not from her to me. I have no right to judge her and become so frustrated by her. I feel she hasn't yet accepted me as an adult and still thinks of me as her little girl. Actually, she probably thinks of me as both, and she has that right as a mother. Maybe I haven't accepted her as an individual and still only see her as my mother. I'll work on it. She deserves to be treated the best.

July 27, 1995 (Mom's journal)

Nancy and I just couldn't get to St Marie. We went to the boat on a run because we were late.

We embarked when we arrived. It was difficult to get through the crowd. Nancy went down to the lower deck while I stayed with the suitcases.

"It's packed," she reported. "All the seats are gone so we will have to stand for the thirteen-hour night trip." This vessel was already over crowded.

When the captain announced, "I'm going to wait a few more hours to fill the boat," that was enough for me. I could visualize the boat sinking for defying the "law of buoyancy."

An hour later, Nancy and I lugged our suitcases up three flights to a very nice hotel room. No elevators, of course. From the terrace, we saw endless waves rolling in for we were at the ocean. It seemed St. Marie could not offer us more. We even got CNN on TV which caught us up on the outside world. Yes, a perfect place to wash our clothes - hot running water and hangers, to boot! Nancy soaked in the bathtub for over an hour while I trimmed the terrace railing with underpants, socks, jeans, and blouses and just about everything we had with us. Nancy's socks turned from river- gray to near white.

This two-day stop was a delightful break from all the poverty and dirt. In Madagascar it rains, in most places, two full months (the rainy season). The rest of the year is almost completely dry. Therefore, when it is breezy, the flying dust evidences the wind. It gets relocated on sidewalks, streets, building and people. This hotel, The Neptune in Toamascina, gave us a temporary break from all this. Nice stop!

July 28, 1995 (Mom's journal)

We flew to Tana next. There I met Kirsten's, Joe's and Gretchen Young's parents for breakfast at a very nice hotel. Later in the day, Nancy and I met up with Kirsten and her mother, Peggy, and set out for Rinohira and Bereketa. We had hired a taxi.

Travel brought us to Kirsten's village, Ranohira. She had

already heard that someone had broken into her hut. She had hired a guard. Great guard...he aided the thieves. Missing were Nancy's $500 bicycle, (she had left it there while attending the African training session and this vacation), lots of personal items, jewelry, clothing, and cassettes. The most incredible thing was taken, her foam rubber mattress. The police station was another experience. There was a prisoner lying on a metal mattress spring and cuffed to the metal bed. It appeared this was his "cell". With the report completed, Nancy and I got a room at a "hotel". Kirsten and Peggie stayed in Kirsten's hut.

Reporting the theft at the police station

I must describe this hotel to you! There was electricity provided by a generator. The light was weaker than this kerosene lamp that Nancy and I are writing by. The room was large with a double bed; when I sat on it, the wooden board, which served as a spring, and the two-inch foam mattress did not give much. The windows were two wooden doors that bolted down to the windowsill. The bolt was stiff and wouldn't budge. I "vasalined" that rascal down in short order. Nancy showed me how the shower worked. She then went off to say "hello" to friends.

I collected things for a cold-water shower and proceeded to lock the door, per instruction. Horrors! When the door was locked, a hand could fit into the opening between the two doors. The lock bit into the wood so even a very little child's hand could have pulled that door open. This was where we were going to sleep. Fear grew like a cyclone.

After speaking to myself, I regained emotional control. "O.K.," I said as I went for that well deserved shower. My mind kept repeating, "You're calm, you're O.K.! You're calm, you're O.K."

I headed for the community shower - a shed. It seemed wise to learn to work the overhead showerhead which was protruded from an overhead barrel that supplied the water. The miniature faucet allowed the handle to turn around and around and around.

"Get out of here", the returning panic said. "It's getting dark. You've seen these people with layers of dirt and they are surviving. You can live with two days of dirt!"

When Nancy returned, I lost the fight, for my face was splattered with tears. Everyone gathered around and reassured me this was a safe place and not to worry. The two nights we were to stay there would be perfectly safe.

That night the four of us set out to dinner at a Madagascy restaurant. In the United States, I would have passed up this place as a "D" rated camping eating spot. But, here we were. By then, I was pretty much a vegetarian. Well, I got through that night.

The next morning in the light of day, I looked around. I was impressed. These people had dug a well for "hotel" water. Kirsten later pointed out that it was twenty feet from the toilets, which drained directly into the soil.

We passed the day with walks through the village, where street stands were run by dirty but happy people.

The pigs, chicken and dogs had as much access to the street as the people did. I saw this on the two short center sections of the village. Cars were almost nonexistent.

Dinner that evening was one of the really delightful experiences of the trip. Nancy had given me a gorgeous silk dress that she had for my birthday. We got dressed in our fineries and were, literally, off to the castle. This place was out of a Cinderella story. It was made of beautiful large stones. There was electricity, and well-clothed waiters with white gloves and all. The owner, a Frenchman, greeted us with the appropriate French kisses on the cheeks.

Guilbere, Nancy, and Kirsten

Guilbere, the owner, plans to buy veggies for the restaurant from Nancy's village.

Nancy was teaching English to the waiters.

We were treated to a drink and delightful conversation in French. Then the four of us were escorted to a table near a cozy fire, which caressed the granite fireplace.

The meal of roast pork and the evening was quite French and delightful. It was a welcomed escape for a few hours.

July 31, 1995

The next day we hung out in town. We met the new park rangers for newly established Park Ranger Service.

Nancy and I went visiting the convent to see if the nuns might need a ride to her village the next day. Here they were, in the middle of extreme poverty. They had electricity and running water. Ma Mere, mother superior, fed us cookies, soda, and homemade peanut brittle, before the grand tour.

Much could be seen from the second floor porch. There was a well-established vegetable garden, two trailer trucks with rice to feed the poor. Off in the distance we saw forest fires, all over the mountains. (This is the method used to clear the land. People burned again as the grass replenished itself. This second burning often rendered the soil useless and erosion would follow during the rainy season).

(from left to ritght: Hery, Mpiandra, Nicolas, Pascal, Rivo, and Xavier)
Newly hired park rangers receive their mountain bikes.

Although we did not prearrange a ride to Nancy's village we had a memorable visit. We could get to that tomorrow.

That night as we dined, the Peace Corps driver, Parfait, poked his head in the doorway. It was wonderful to see him. He raised our spirits by telling us that he could drive us to Nancy's village the next day. This was no small gift, because I still had all that luggage I hauled half way around the globe. I was really worried about how these treasures would get to their final destination. (Not to worry. The Lord will provide.)

Nancy and Kirsten enjoying the moment

Twenty

Off to Bereketa and Final Departure

Nancy and I are greeted by hundreds of villagers. It is obvious that she is loved by many.

During my week in Bereketa I lived the village life carrying my own water about ****? of a mile every day. I wove a mat, ate rice went to a village funeral, a party and, oh yes, we ate rice.

The night sky was so full of stars that I had to constantly look up at them. They were like a well lit Christmas tree. We do not see that many in the Northern Hemisphere.

Nancy writes, "Mom's visiting, has showed me I've put up quite a wall of numbness to the poverty level. Without that wall, I'd constantly be miserable. Yet with it (numbness) has come a lack of ambition to get anything going...

I need to find the balance of the two: my old sensitivity to want to truly make a difference in the people's lives, yet giving myself the space I need to be alone when I need to. I need to keep it all in perspective..."

August 1, 1995 (Mom's journal)

Morning came. Nancy and I went to get a coffee at one of the stands. The coffee was very strong; without milk in it, my stomach rebelled. I decided to pass. The immense dirt on the server and the counter said, "Smart move". My decision was reinforced when someone finished his/her coffee, and put the cup on the shelf. Our server rinsed the cup in a pan of cold water. I knew that was the meager cleaning for the day.

My favorite animal to watch was trying to get his breakfast off the street. This was no simple task, since there were no leftovers or waste here. What was it? A pig that walked around freely in the company of ducks and chickens. Skipping a meal often seemed wise. This seemed like a good day to do this.

To our delight, Parfait in the P.C. van picked us up and we were finally off to Nancy's village, luggage and all. The roads along the 2-hour trip resembled a miniature Grand Canyon. When we arrived in the village, hundreds greeted us.

Jardinier, the village doctor, taught me how to weave. When I looked up there were about 30 people watching me.

Nancy greeted many with the traditional kiss on one cheek, then the other, and back to the first. Fortunately they were receptive to a good old United States handshake from me. We had arrived.

Parfait, our faithful driver, soon departed after a rather comprehensive village tour.

It was time to fetch water. About fifteen children followed us down to the river near the garden. The yellow leaves on the plants were crying, "Water, water, I need water!" Our army of children dug in, (the girls, that is) and we toted pail after pail of water from the river. "Thank you, thank you," the plants seemed to say as they once again stood tall to resume development.

In the next four days I did lots of things villagers do every day. I was surprisingly good at carrying a pail of water on my head and really enjoyed weaving a mat.

Jardinier, the village doctor, taught me how to weave. When I looked up there were about 30 people watching me.

The following night Nancy and I were invited to a dance. We went calling at the host's house about 8:15. There were about fifteen people sitting along three walls in a candle-lit room. Nancy and I took the fourth wall. Just after us, the musicians entered and everyone squished.

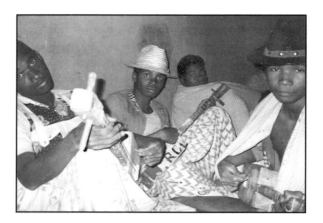

I watched in amazement as they tuned up. There were three homemade, let's call them - guitars; one had two strings and two had three strings. The lovely music that came out of those eight strings astonished me.

This picture was taken two years earlier when the musicians had just created their instruments.

Meanwhile, more and more people entered and gave new meaning to "how many people you can fit into a room." Someone asked permission for us to go outside. Everyone rose, excited and wrapped in lambas, they lined the outside side of two huts. The dancing and music continued for another two hours.

At the dance, Nancy made arrangements to take a charette with bulls to our last stop for us to get a plane to the capital. This involved getting up at midnight and, of course the charette was not ready until two. We sat on large sacks of rice and rode for four hours out to the main street.

Next, we waited another 4 hours for a taxi brousse to come along. Here you just sat and waited until an empty one came along.

This last trip went on, as usual, with hours of delays; a reservations at a hotel that had not been recorded, and rattling around in, I-don't-know-how-they-stayed-together-taxies, and dozens more delays before Nancy got me to the airport. I hated it when people there asked, "How do you like Madagascar?"

"It's different," I'd stumble out with a few kind words.
I'm on my way home now. All I can say is, "Thank God I was born in America!"

Nancy will finish her year in the Peace Corps in Madagascar. I'll try to get "my villagers" to help, too! My colleagues and friends will have to help send basic life supplies to Bereketa, Madagascar. The biggest problem will be the shipping, for it is very expensive for just a small box. Now Nancy's got me setting goals.

"Take care my darling daughter! I love you! You don't know how much I love you." I had to tell my daughter several times on the long trip to the airport.

July 30, 1995

Hi, Bry & Joanne, Jessie and Garrett,
I am sitting with Mom, on the back verandah of a nice restaurant on the beach of the Indian Ocean. This is our last excursion together. I decided to go all the way to the airport with her. There are outside tables here. There's someone in the restaurant singing and playing the valia (a stringed instrument here) and I am drinking a T.H.B. "Tae osh bae" is how it is pronounced, standing for "Three Horses Beer", the only beer in the country. It is quite relaxing. Mom's hacking next to me quite a bit though. She got a bad cold on the 5-hour charrette (bulls

and wagon) ride from my village to the main road. We left at 2:00 a.m. 'cause the bulls can't handle the heat of the day. I couldn't believe she did it actually (not that she had a choice, unless she wanted to stay with me in my village, which I don't think she did!)

She's been quite a trooper. She was okay the time we waited 19 hours for a train, the time we waited 5 hours for a taxi brousse, the time a villager tried to pick her up. He backed off though when I said the price for her was 4 cows, the time we lugged all our luggage and went to get on a cargo boat to the Isle of St. Marie. The cargo" turned out to be hundreds of people. We walked away from that one because she said it reminded her of how the boats were packed to the point of sinking when Haitians came over to Florida...very much the truth! I figured we'd either sink or be robbed!

So now she's preparing to return to the comfort and familiarity of life in the U.S. Yet she is glad she came, and so am I. I think it gave her a new perspective on things. I don't think she "liked" it here, but she is glad she came. It's been good to see her, and to see pictures and videos of all of you, and to find that everyone's well. I sent some stuff home for all of you and she'll probably bring it all up to you for Christmas. So, in a way, I will be there with you guys this year. She said people have been asking what I need, so I sent a list of many little things that I can use any time - no big stuff 'cause I don't really need much big stuff and it's too expensive to send!

Mom has gotten to see quite a lot while she is here, even stuff I hadn't seen yet. She's heard some live Malagasy music on the valias; she saw the east coast and the west coast; she attended a Bara funeral (my region).

I've got to tell you about the funeral. The villagers put the deceased into the homemade caskets, nailed the cover on the casket and then ran it to an area where they set it down. The women chanted and the men drove the herd of cows together and took turns holding on to the bulls' humps and riding them. The cows here are from India, so they have humps like camels. It was like a rodeo. After an hour of this, the casket was carried to a cave in the mountains. Only a few people followed. Others were waiting for a gift of meat from a slaughtered omby (cow). It was getting dark. We hated to be rude but Mom and I had about 2 km. to walk to get back to Bereketa for we were in the next village.

There were men off to the side cutting up cattle they had slaughtered. It is customary to give some meat to all who attended.

"Nancy! Nancy! Wait!" One of the men shouted.

"That's O.K.," I replied. We have to get back to the village." Mom and I walked along and about ten minutes later we heard, once again, "Nancy! Nancy! Wait."

Running to us was a man with about 4 lbs. of meat swinging in the air. I graciously accepted the gift and Mom carried the swinging treasure. We had not eaten meat for three weeks but decided this might be safe to eat since it was truly fresh.

Wrong! Inspite of the fact that it made a delicious stew, Mom got diarrhea. Yes! She has much to remember.

Sorry for the excursion. Let's see, Mom took a long charrette ride, and she stayed in a couple of beautiful hotels that would cost $100's in the states that only cost $30 here. So she's seen a lot, and she has a lot on video for you guys to see, too.

I'll probably do some travelling in Africa this next year by myself or with another volunteer before I leave this area. Uganda and Kenya were beautiful. I heard the countries southern part are even more incredible. English is spoken in many parts of Africa, which makes travelling easy.

I have to explore Madagascar more, too. There are some places harder to get to that I wouldn't take Mom, but I still want to see myself; and my Malagache language is good enough now to make traveling easy.

My French is still pretty unimpressive, though. I am working on it...It's tough, 'cause I think in Malagache before French, so I tend to convert things to Malagache and then to French when I try speaking French, so it often becomes a mix of the two. It is no big problem when I am speaking with Malagache. But when I speak with my French counterparts, they think I am quite an idiot. Ah, well, comes with the territory, I suppose.

So I travel back to my village the day after tomorrow and Mom heads to Tana to head home. My village really enjoyed her. We spent one evening dancing to the kabosies (Malagasy guitars) and drinking tokoa gasy (moonshine)...Mom, of course, passed...I drank her share!). They wanted to kill a chicken for her and give her rice, their custom in welcoming a visitor. All the chicken in the village recently died from some sickness that went around, so they couldn't. Mom understood. She actually pounded some rice and carried water on her head, and wove a mat, too. She fit in a lot.

I'll be glad to get back and get things going though. I have been away a long time. I think we'll work on rebuilding the hospital when I'm back and starting a pharmacy communitaire for when people are sick. I'll also help them garden vegetables to sell to hotels to raise money for a class on environment. I would like to raise money by making products to sell, like rope swings or instruments from bamboo, etc. I am glad to be getting back into it.

Well, you guys, I love you and miss you so much.
                                          Nancy

August 2, 1995

Danny,

You write great letters! I just got your letter from the beginning of your road trip with Lucky Dube, and you were in one of your philosophical moods. I love it when you get in those moods on paper. I'll rewrite your last line to you cause I'm sure you've forgotten it. "This world is only so big and we can only go so far. Some day we will both touch earth in the same place at the same time." Profound aren't you? I really enjoy getting letters like this.

As I sit out in my mud hut reading your letter by candlelight and hearing the breeze outside and the omby (cows) eating the hay by my door, I know how far my experience is, at this point in my life, from your existence. Yet I'm feeling so close to you. I just want to tell you, if you're confused over what to do next at this crossroad of your life, I think you should come to Madagascar for a while...or become a poet.

The novelty of being here hasn't worn off at all for me. It's probably because I've just gotten back from four weeks in Africa and one week in Madagascar with Mom. To some degree, I feel like I've just been given permission to stay put in my village and go nuts on projects here. I only have one year left and I want to accomplish something before I go. I truly feel I can make a beneficial input to these people's lives in many ways while I'm here.

Dan, you asked what the Peace Corps is, anyhow. You thought we were sent here to help the country stop degrading the environment. How does the Peace Corps expect to do that if they drop us way out in a distant village?

I've thought a lot about it to try to figure out how to respond. I think I've got it now. Peace Corps knows it's not going to be solving any big problems in any countries. It's impossible to send 18 people (not even professionals, mind you) to a country as environmentally degraded as this; with a population of 12 million - plus and expect us to make a difference. And Peace Corps doesn't-doesn't expect it I mean.

Peace Corps is just small potatoes. It's just a little United States-help giving, service (civil service?) organization. It takes a little bit of the massive amounts of United States tax dollars to put people in small places to make little differences in a few people's lives. That's all volunteers do and that's all that is expected of us. It helps some people that otherwise wouldn't be helped, and it also gets the United States known in a good manner in many countries. The government, I think, has motives behind our placements. It seems that the government is trying to get its foot in the door. It's like a game of Monopoly where they're trying to put hotels on as much property as they can. Yet, the entire Peace Corps family, so to speak, is made up of volunteers and former volunteers. It's a trip, Dan. Most all the staff in Peace Corps are former volunteers. So therefore all the people who are working in the Peace Corps unit want to help the people in these countries who would otherwise never been offered help probably. It's all small scale, and everyone working within the Peace Corps knows it.

So much of it is just a cultural learning exchange. I learn how to pound rice and then I teach them how to listen to James Brown on my walkman and dance to it. In my village many people had never seen a white person. I've made such a difference in many of their perceptions just by being here.

So Peace Corps is not an organization to make big differences or to solve any country's problems. Yet, the advertisements would make you think so. It's all a bunch of hype. The United

States government would like it, I think, if we were more entrepreneurs and really solving big problems in other countries.

So that's my theory (heh-hmm!) I hope I didn't just fill your ear with tons of stuff you already knew. I must say, I thought Peace Corps was a much bigger deal, accomplishment wise, than when I got here. Then I realized it's all just for publicity's sake.

So I just got your next letter...my coffee's great, thank you. I'm sending you a little bit I cooked for you, but I didn't pound it, 'cause I figured you have the luxury of a machine. It's funny you're lost in a world of Styrofoam, plastic, and rubber, etc. I look at my year's worth of waste here and it consists of one small basket full of trash, all of which can be burned. This is a different world.

Well Dan, Mom's here with me in my mud hut and I'm going to make us some coffee right now, so I'll get back to you later. Mom's faring quite well. I'll write to you about our trip soon.

Love you Dan! ("Do good things")

Thanks for the newspaper article...it's nice to get some news now and then. My short-wave radio isn't overly dependable so close to the huts. I haven't read it -your letter yet. Mom's reading it now.

August 6, 1995

Hi Caleb!

I just got back from a trip to Uganda, Africa and Kenya. I saw monkeys, chimpanzees, and gorillas in Uganda in the rainforest. There were thirteen gorillas -mothers with babies on their backs and 1 silverback, the huge male. (Denise and Lee, show Caleb a Gorilla picture in the encyclopedia.)

I also saw in Kenya, which is mostly open grasslands-zebra, antelope, giraffe, and leopards. I'm back in Madagascar now and Grandma Connie is visiting. I'm sending a couple of things for you with her, and she'll either send them to you or bring them to you when she visits at Christmas. I love you, Caleb! I'll try to send you pictures of me.

Love, Aunt Nancy

August 6, 1995

Hi ya', Denise!

Today is the sixth. Mom will be leaving the country within the week, so you will probably get this letter within a couple weeks - not bad! Thanks so much for the stuff you sent me. I haven't looked through it all yet because I want to do it when I get back to my hut alone. Why? I don't know - I just do. The suspense is fun.

Mom brought a lot of stuff and I wanted to wait and make it special. Donna sent me some things, too. It'll be like an early Christmas!

Peace Corps gives me enough money to buy gifts. The problem is there's nothing to buy in my area. I must wait until I go to Tana (the capital) to shop, and then I often don't have enough time.

I've been here a year now - does it feel that long to you? It doesn't to me, but yet I'm comfortable enough for me here to realize that it probably has been that long.

I'm nowhere near ready to go home yet, though. I've been out of my village for the past couple of months. Before that I went to Ranohira often to help train the park rangers and for my language training and first in-service training, so I've basically gotten nothing started yet. Yet I have the love of the people in my village now. I have the language down pretty well, so I'm really itching to get things going.

I think I'll start with getting the people to build the hospital by going to the different surrounding villages and having meetings. I'll also continue vegetable gardening with my village. So the people will have enough money to start a community pharmacy by selling vegetables to the hotels. I'm also going to start a weekly class (environmental education and just plain ol' havin' fun) with the children. I'll be doing a lot of other things but that's it to start.

It's sometimes paralyzing to be here, Denise...to see the intensity of the poverty, the dirtiness, the sickness, and to keep upbeat enough to get anything going. I think once I get things started though it'll snowball, and the villagers and I will be psyched to do more.

Mom's visiting, has showed me I've put up quite a wall of

numbness to the poverty level. Without that wall, I'd constantly be miserable. Yet with it (numbness) has come a lack of ambition to get anything going...I've just been going though the daily routines, not knowing how to get any more started, simply because I'm always somewhat in a trance from the numbness.

I need to find the balance of the two: my old sensitivity to want to truly make a difference in the people's lives, yet giving myself the space I need to be alone when I need to. I need to keep it all in perspective so that I'm not drowned in the depression that goes along with the sensitivity.

I truly feel I can make a difference for the people around me here, D. I'm just slow at getting it going, 'cause I need to do it delicately so that I don't lose my contentment in the process.

It's such a hard balance. I must say, though, I no longer see myself as naïve. I now understand just how foreign Mom looks in any city (or anywhere, for that matter) with her camera hanging around her neck!

I've had a good time with her visiting. It's a difficult country to travel in. She's been pretty much of a trooper through all the rough parts, which have been many! It's not what I'd call a "relaxing vacation!" She's glad she came, though, and I think she learned some things that have changed her entire perspective on life.

Same goes for me, of course. CARE commercials do nothing for a person's understanding until you're dropped into one. I think Mom will be glad to go home. I'm sure I'll feel a void when she goes. It was nice to feel a connection with all of you and I cried when I saw her videos of Bry's and Donna's kids and saw pictures of all of you. I'm happy here and I have no desire to leave yet, but I also know how much I'm giving up to be here. I miss all you guys so much and I so much want to see your kids grow. I'll be back to see some of it I know, most of it I should say, but you know how it is...I want everything now. Spoiled brat, eh? How's it feel to want? Just ask me! I've been away from my family and friends for a year, ugh! But I'll survive. I've had a lot of incredible self-growth by being so much on my own here.

It's amazing how much you become your own best friend when you're in an environment where no one understands your world and no one speaks your language. I've taken to drawing a lot lately ...it's very soothing. If I take my time at it, my drawings don't come out all that bad. Since I've been here, I've become a much more relaxed person-more laid back. I used to feel depressed and stressed, constantly trying to take care of everyone else and forgetting to take care of myself. I'd often get frustrated with whomever was close to me in my life, my close friend, I'd choose people whom I saw as less talented or ambitious than me so I'd feel better about myself. And the people in my life who I didn't see as less than me, I'd rely on their views of me for my self confidence. At these times, both with my mate and with the people I depended on for my self-approval, I felt yucky and I'd feel like Mom, (or how I thought Mom feels inside) often. Yet, if the people I was dependent on for my self-worth made me feel good about myself and responded well to me, I would feel like I think Dad feels inside. I would feel good about myself. But it was because I was looking at me through other people's eyes. I don't think either tactic is overly healthy. Yet since I've been here, I've gotten to know myself pretty well and I've found out that I'm quite a strong person. I've come to truly like myself. I'm starting to enjoy myself for who I see in me, instead of for what I think other people see in me. I feel very pretty lately.

Since I'm changing and I'm starting to blossom, so to speak, I'm cherishing the part of my personality that's breaking loose that feels like you, because it's a part of you I've always admired. I'm still so different from you in so many other ways that I feel like we truly compliment (complete) each other. I've missed being with you, but I think we'll be so close when I get home, because I finally feel more comfortable in whom I am. I think my doing this will bring us a lot closer. It's been nice to be in a totally new environment and to see things from a different perspective. I think I've become more accepting of everyone, and situations. I feel much lighter here. I hope I can feel that way when I come home. I think it'll be pretty intact after another year and half here.

Well Denise, I love and miss ya'. Take care of Leroy and Caleb.

Love, Nancy, "Rakoto"

August 9, 1995

Hi, Donna!

I sent you a gift, a hat, for Lauren and money to Ryan. It was ages ago. You never wrote and said that you got them. I don't know if my things get to you.

This one should since Mom mailed them from London. She must be so sick of lugging bags! I can't believe how much stuff she brought with her for me! Thanks so much for everything Donna - you gave me a lot of nice gifts. I felt like it was Christmas time here! The barrette is beautiful and I love the card set. Of course, haven't started reading the book yet, but I shall soon.

I saw the video of you guys, too. That was a major tearjerker. Seeing Jessica and Lauren just made me cry...they grow fast without me there to see it.

Mom heads out tomorrow. She takes a plane to Tana, the capital. Another volunteer and her Mom are on the same plane up there and then on the same plane with her to Nairobe the next day, 'cause they're vacationing in Senegal. (This never happened.) So she'll only be alone from Nairobe to the United States.

It's been good to see her, but a bit unreal to have her here. It's as if she was dropped in from another world. It's been hard traveling here, but she's hung in pretty well. I don't think she realized just how poor it is here, and it affected her a lot. It's made me realize how much I've numbed up to survive here. It's incredibly depressing and destructive to internalize it all. Transportation is tough here, cause nothing is dependable except a hired car, which is more expensive than in the states or Europe! You are welcome though if none of that bothers you. There's a lot of soil erosion going on here. You could probably give advice on stopping it!

I'm falling asleep as I write and Mom's flying out in the morning, so I must get this in the box. Sorry so it's short.

Love, Nancy

Nancy's neighbors in the compound

Twenty-One

Back to Business

"Mom is gone. I'm going to get something done!" was Nancy's attitude now.

Nancy poured herself into her work. It helped to mask what she was really feeling. There were things that she wanted to tell me but she held back.Making beautiful necklaces with such poor people might not have been the best thing to do.

Many meetings took place once Nancy decided that her first project was to start the small school.

The villagers traveled before sun up to get supplies because it was the beginning of summer and it is really hot very early in the day. There were many problems getting the wood for the school.

When I had first gotten to Madagascar we went to the district office to meet those in charge. I inquired how Nancy and the others communicated with the office and each other. I was told, "It's not possible." I was furious. They heard a loud and clear response that that must be rectified or I would go to the media. It worked!

August 12, 1995

Ah - I look at the dates in this book, and...mapalahelo! (It makes me sad!) I'm sorry for neglecting you, my little diary! But there is another little blue notebook that I wrote in before this while I was in Africa. But I still missed a lot. I don't think I've written since Mom left, and I've gone through many emotions since then.

At first when I got back here, I was just sad. I think because I wasn't sure how to get things started here after being away two months. I haven't really yet started anything. I've learned a lot of their culture and vice versa, but I haven't yet done anything I see as "worthy" in improving their lives here, which is really what I want to do.

For a few days I took walks to think, and sat around feeling sorry for myself for not knowing how to get things going. As I thought, I started prioritizing the desires of the villagers. And I realized their first priority is the school. But the big school can't get started until the road is done. Then why not repair the little school now?

I spoke to the president (drunk as he was). He and I spoke to the committee and the committee said we'll hold a meeting tonight. They yelled, "Fokonolo,"(Yeah, let's do it!)

Tomorrow I go to Ranohira to radio Peace Corps to help by bringing cement, since they're passing by in one week. That's all it took. If this whole thing really happens, before school starts on Sept. 11, I'll know I can easily make things happen here. I just need to get my butt in gear. So, this is the test.

Today, was a bit of a crazy day. Mom gave me really beautiful beads to make necklaces with the kids, which I did today, but there's more kids here than I had even imagined, so it got totally insane. I was quite upset, but I'm learning. I knew this whole experience wouldn't be easy! I should have known bringing in so many beautiful beads in would make the children (and the adults also) want, want, want. But I guess I didn't think it through first. I'm learning.

I must admit after doing necklaces morning and afternoon, having a meeting with the Reimen Dreny this evening and dancing with Abodo and drinking wine with him and Hoasa, Labaro, Leva and Donald, I'm quite "miadamila" tired,, so I'll sign off now.

Tomorrow morning, Leva and I are going to see the school and decide what we need to buy. Then I'll probably go to Ranohira, so I can radio Tana, and maybe go to Toliar to get some cash. I hope this school project works out...it means my success in the village in future endeavors.

August 15, 1995

Hi ya', Mom,
I've been told we'll have a party to celebrate. They will use any excuse to drink tokoa gasy!

I keep thinking that you should have stayed longer, like another month in my village. It's not like it costs anything in Bereketa! After you spent so much to come, I wish you could have spent more time. But with all the circumstances, it wasn't really possible. I don't feel we had enough deep conversations and there's so much deep stuff in me to talk about...yet I think it's all so fragile right now. I don't know if I can truly tell someone all my emotions now- until I'm in a different environment. I'm happy here, but I don't know how composed I'd stay if I started spewing out my heart's feelings to someone. I have a wall up now, simply as a survival mechanism, 'cause if I didn't have one I may crumble. It's all a bit depressing if I internalize it. Yet if I keep up some sort of shield, I can maybe get something done while I'm here to make these people's lives happier and more meaningful. I went through a long period (basically right up until now) where I didn't do much. There's so much to do, in a sometimes so defeating environment, that I don't know how to start. I end up doing nothing I see as valuable, and time just slips away. I keep turning over all the things I want to do in my head, but feeling so overwhelmed that I start nothing.

Last week I prioritized the needs of the village. Tomorrow the president of the village and I will hold a meeting with the villagers concerning repairing the small school since school starts in one month. I will go next week and buy supplies (Peace Corps will pay me back later) and will start repairing it right after. I was thinking of getting the road repaired as the first project, so we can truck supplies in to repair the big school. Then I decided, since school starts in a month and the road definitely won't be done by then, to get the small class fixed up first. It'll give the kids a nice place to learn for now and will let the villagers know what they can actually accomplish with very little outside support (and that being only supply money). People are already excited about it. It'll get me motivated, too! I'm starting a weekly environmental education class for the kids soon. I will also teach a weekly English class.

I've been wanting to start things for so long but have been away so much-especially the last two months-that's it's been hard. So I'm finally staying put now so I can really start my work. I have 1 1/4 years to get a lot done!

It was wonderful to have you here, Mom. I wish we had talked more, but I honestly don't think I can let my emotions loose 'til I leave here. I need to contain them within myself so I can function well. I think spilling my guts now would be more detrimental than useful to me. I really can make some people's lives happier and better if I stay focused.

I have to say it's probably going to be a wonderful thing for me when I arrive home to have someone who knows what I've seen. Thanks so much for always supporting me, Mom.

I love you dearly! Nancy Rakoto

August 16, 1995 (2nd letter)

P.S. Written ahead of time to totally confuse you...give Aunt Doris a big hug for me!

Yo- What's up babe?

Sorry if I seem a bid odd, but I'm on a sugar high as Joe and I just ate a pack of M & M's and a box of peanut butter Girl Scout Cookies! Wee! Thanks, Mom! I can't imagine how broken out I'd get if I ate all the chocolate in that box right now! I think that'll hold me for a year at least! I'm giving one chocolate bar to my sweet little postman.

I'm in Ranohira now. I had two meetings with the elders and the president of my village this last week and I've motivated them to repair the small school. I'm here to buy cement blocks and stuff like that. I just walked here yesterday, the 36 km to Andonlakaka (that little village on the main road you loved so much!) My feet are sore!

I radioed up to my director. A car's coming down next week and will bring another bike - yeah! It's coming down with the training director for the new volunteers, so she can decide where to place the 4th Isalo volunteer. The car will take me and all my cement (and my bike) to my village. Then I'll go with the villagers and a few charrettes, 12 km away. There we shall buy planks to build desks and doors and windows for the school. Then after, we'll start the hospital...yee, ha - On a roll!

I made your necklaces with the kids and it was an absolute insane fiasco, I must say. Children came out of the woodwork in my house. Parents yelled that they wanted necklaces too. Children cried, the president screamed, people ripped necklaces out of people's hand. But in the end, most everyone was happy.

I was literally exhausted, but I learned a grave lesson...I will never do such a thing again. It was a much too beautiful gift for people who have mostly nothing. But, it was greatly appreciated, I must say that. In the future I will give only one big community gift to prevent the change from villagers into wild, vicious gleaming, bead-drooling animals.

Don't take me wrong, Mom. Thank you. It was a beautiful gift and you gave them all something they've never had. Well, I'm gonna sign off, Honey. I hope school's going well and you've got a good class this year.

I love you, Mom. Thanks for my great package! Although the package of you coming was better!

August 16, 1995

What an exhausting day today was. I had many people coming to my house asking for "ravakas"- (necklaces)... I had many people ask me as I walked outside. Hanta even asked me into her house so she could give me hell for not giving her one. It

191

was pretty defeating altogether. That, along with all the people who asked me to take photos today. I'm glad I'm leaving tomorrow...I need a break!

We went to the school today, Leva, Romose and I, to see what it needed. Then we went to get Sata to measure the tables, to figure out what we needed to buy. In the evening we had another meeting with the Reimen Dreny. They understood that I'd buy the wood and cement and akata, if they do the work. They want to do it, and Nata even offered to cut and give the akata, so P.C. doesn't need to buy it. Then after the meeting Leva got the guy from Ilemby who cuts the wood and ordered 36 planks and 29 bois casse to do the building. The wood's already there, so we'll go when I get back to pick up the wood.

I'm excited that things are happening, but the whole necklace-making thing at the same time was just too much...I'm burnt! -but it's okay, 'cause I'm not feeling useless like I did last week, but things are happening. If the school actually is done by Sept. 11th, I will have gained the people's trust and also realized my own ability and theirs as well; and things will keep happening.

It's funny because I get frustrated with people constantly coming to me asking me for necklaces, especially when the children come. I expect them to know how tired I am of it and how I need some space. Yet, how could they understand that? Space is not something they've ever had in their environment. They'll never know how much I enjoy to be alone a lot...nor could they understand if they did know.

September 1, 1995

Hi Dan!

It's about 8 p.m. here (about 3 am for you, I think), and it's a sweater and legging type breezy evening - a rare occasion here and one I love. The moonlight's spectacular and the stars are as bright and unbelievable as always. It's amazing how brilliant the sky is when there's no electricity for miles upon miles here. No one would believe the sky here in the Southern Hemisphere. You can actually see the shapes of two galaxies, or at least that's what they look like. I haven't felt like writing anyone for a while now, not even in my diary, which I'm quite bad at lately.

I'm listening to your tape with Jamie, "As Birds Fly," and I felt a desire to write to you. I always feel more bonded with you when I listen to one of your tapes. Tonight especially because this is actually the first time I've been able to hear this whole tape. I had fallen off my bike awhile back and got oil in both my tape player and this cassette (the cooking oil bottle busted- I think I've told you about this). The two wouldn't work after that. Mom gave me her small tape player and the cassette works now. There is only a small glitch where it lags, but I think it'll smooth out after a bit.

Dan, I have to tell you, what an utterly gorgeous tape. I was cooking rice and beans while listening and I just ended up sitting and listening for an hour after my cooking was finished. It amazes me how much your music stirs up emotions in me...I feel more connected to home. It makes me a bit "mannve" (homesick), and yet not so all alone.

I sometimes meditate or do yoga to your's and Jamie's tape, and I often wish there was a way I could have let you know then, so we could meditate at the same time.

So many whites or organizations had come through this village saying they'll help with this or that and then never did. They didn't believe I'd do what I said. So they cherish me since I'm true. It's nice to feel like I'm in a community of people who all know my care, my intentions.

In the United States I've never been in an environment where I'm with a large group of people day in and day out, really knowing what each person in a big unit is made of. It can be very exhausting, but sometimes it's really neat. There are some big disadvantages, though, like I can't just have a casual fling with someone here...everyone would know and they'd constantly be telling me we'll marry soon and that I won't be returning to the states.

There's no such thing as casual dating here. I was friends with a Malagasy guy, outside my village. Within a month, he asked me to marry him or he'd be joining the priesthood. A confused man, eh? I wished him happy church going and went on my way. I just wanted someone to cuddle with! I've decided, in this environment, it is best to stay on my own. It's not like I run into people from our culture out here too often! I often get lonely to be with someone, but I'm also enjoying the personal growth I'm having with all my attention focused on me and the people I'm living with. I must admit, I think my time left here will go by much faster than I expect. I think I'll feel ready to go home when it's time to, but not before then.

Well, Dan, your tape just ended. I'm done with dinner and I want to play a bit of guitar before I sack out. So I'll say good night for now. I can't say I've seen past 10 pm too much in my little world here! It's altogether a different life.

I love ya, Bro, Nancy

P.S. I'm doing good things!

September 4, 1995

Here I lie, on the World Book blanket Mom brought me, under a small group of mango trees. The wind is whipping around and my body, in shorts and a tank top is feeling it. I now realize how long it's been since I've taken the time to feel like me. Recently, I've been working so much with Leva (the committee president) and the villagers to get the school construction going, that I've stayed in the village every day. We start building the day after tomorrow. I'm excited about that. We go with charrettes to Mesaby tomorrow to get all the wood.

I've gone through some serious periods of loneliness lately...not so much for my culture or for my family as for my companion. I'm starting to feel like a prettier person as each day goes by, but yet have no one to share any experiences with. It's funny, 'cause sometimes I picture my development as a circle, and I haven't yet come the whole way around. I don't feel where I want to be is very far from me now. I don't feel like my circle is lacking a lot at this point.

Something tells me to be patient when I feel lonely, because things will just happen. I feel like, by the time I've completed my time here, I'll have come close to filling my circle-not to say that my growth will stop at all when the circle's full. It will just be at a different level instead (I'll still be struggling to be a good person level). At that time, maybe I'll be ready to share myself with someone.

September 7, 1995

Rough day yesterday. I went to Ilemby with Leva, Rauly, Georgae, Farana, Dori and Saboto (all villagers) with 2 charrettes at 4 a.m. to get the wood for the school. We travel at 4 a.m. because we are entering summer, so it is best to leave even before the sun is up.

Ramose's charrette met up with us later in the morning. But when we got to Mesaby, Nono wasn't there yet. Also, all our wood wasn't there yet. We ended up hanging out all day waiting. We went visiting (that is, drinking tokoa) from house to house. Nono still wasn't back, so we all went to eat at one of the gendarme family's place. We decided at 3:30 that we should just buy the 2-meter expensive wood that was already in that village and return later for the bois carres. After, the charrettes were loaded up, we would leave.

"Leva, Dori and I shall go ahead on foot while the charrette and the bulls are being hitched up," I said. "The other two charrettes are already on their way."

Leva and a gendarme informed me, "Nancy, it is the custom to buy a bottle of tokoa gasy when doing a project like this," inferring that I should buy it.

I responded. "My money is gone now, except for 1500 fgm (American= $.35)."

"Not to worry, Nancy." Said Leva, "I'll take care of it."

"I'm really tired and I just want to leave" I said. I was tired and they were all drunk.

"I understand, Nancy, but it is the custom and you really need to do it. Farana will hook up the bulls while you buy the bottle."

I agreed if we would leave soon. So I went with Famose, Leva, and 2 Gendarme who were already absolutely smashed. The head gendarme had thrown up in the house. I bought a small bottle of tokoa. I drank some, too, so the bottle would be done faster, because I knew they'd stay and give gosh darned speeches until it was gone.

With every bottle of tokoa, they each gave a speech. The air became all respectful and serious, and each man would say how glad he was to have the others there and "My house is your house." As they would get more drunk, they argued over who was going to give the next speech. Each thought that he could say things better than the others could.

After the speeches, someone would blast the radio to koas, koasha music and everyone would start drinking again and the party went on. - An exhausting but sometimes fun way to spend a day.

A gendarme had told me that the last charrette would wait for us, so I assumed he had told Farana, our driver. Well, he hadn't. All the charrettes had left without us. Maybe, they were thinking we had gone in a charrette before theirs. All these guys, who were grossly drunk put our heads together (not too close). We had no charrette to cross the waterway near Ilemly which, supposedly, had crocodiles. Finally, one of the gendarmes got his family's charrette to take us back. The sister of the gendarme came, too, because she had to go to Bereketa.

When we had crossed the waterway, there was much taba taba (noise) about whether the driver would take us all the way to Bereketa or return home to Ilemby. Ramose and Leva were so drunk that the sister and I just wanted to get out. All the drunks fussed at us. It was at this point that the gendarme decided to return home, so everyone had to get out.

The conversation made it an extra long walk. Ramose and Leva complained about our charrette driver; I defended him. Leva, drunkenly talked about work, "presidenty asa", and I just wanted to take a breather.

Leva was trying to invite himself over for coffee, but I refused. The next day the people were pretty ticked at Leva and Ramose for not looking out for me. Leva was sick as hell, but the work started and the vibes cleared after a couple days. Nono's wife brought the bois carre to us, so I didn't need to return to Ilemby -yah! I must say I don't really enjoy being around tokoa gasy anymore, and the thought of drinking it makes me nauseous to see its effect on people. It was like getting sick on it myself (which I must admit, I did once before).

It's taken me a few days to write this story and things have been going along well since that mission. The cement is all done inside the school, and tomorrow we cement the outside step. The next day we'll start mudding, and later we'll do the roof. Paul and Sata should be starting the door and windows soon.

On our wood mission, I learned a lot about what not to do.

That is, no matter what their fomba (culture) is here (which, come to find out, the gendarme lied to me about their "custom"), I shouldn't sacrifice myself to the point of unhappiness in order to show respect. I know that now.

September 12, 1995

A passing thought after reading Mom's letter. After safely returning to the States but having had to wait in Nairobi an extra day more than expected she stated,"I walked around Nairobi for the day with the "This isn't where I want to be attitude."

I thought, "Stop wasting time being angry at things you can't change. You may even wind up enjoying yourself!"

More thoughts, the same day. After reading "The 7 Habits of Highly Effective People," by Covey, I finally realized just why it is that I feel my environment here in this village of Bereketa is the best opener/path to the person I want to become. It dawned on me what Paul Siegel, one of our trainers, meant when he said, "In the Peace Corps you will find out who you are and what you are." I don't know if other volunteers experience this as much as me-unless they are in a setting such as mine.

I think that our environment might be what makes us more accepting of others and less judgmental. Sure, there are traits in the people we live with that we don't like and we get angry with them from time to time, but very rarely do we ever " throw out" the whole person. We can't exclude them from our lives completely here, 'cause we live with them every day!

Americans are used to choosing whom we have in our lives. There are so many different people we're involved with all the time, we tend to just not associate with those in whom we see traits we dislike. We just pick different friends. And it's not so much that this trait of ours is wrong; it's just why we're different. It's why being dropped into a village of 350 people is a difficult event.

At first, I left my village often, for "sanity" reasons. I needed to do that, and the commonness of shutting my doors, began making my village feel stifling. So I switched tactics. I began staying in my village for longer spurts, but yet taking a walk out of the village every couple or few days, alone; to draw or medi-tate, before I felt like I needed to leave. Otherwise, I would have bust.

I started to leave my doors open and let people watch my lifestyle, although through clenched teeth that wanted to say, "please, let me alone!" If I had this feeling within me often through a day, I'd work hard at controlling the clenched-teeth emotion, and say politely when I could handle no more, "Excuse me, but I just want to read/work alone right now." "No problem!" was the response.

Most times the villagers would leave unhurt, just learning a bit more about how "the American" was different from them. I felt a major pressure release in my chest and a big sigh would exhale. I felt like I conveyed my message, while quite content in my home here.

I've been in my village almost a month now, my longest stretch yet without a break, and I'm truly okay with it. I'm not leaving my village at the end of this month for a break either... because my work needs me in other places at this time. So I feel I've come "full-circle" so to speak. I'm learning who I am.

September 12, 1995

Hi, Mom!
I was so happy to get your letter...I've been waiting for it. I wasn't going in to Ranohira for a few more weeks, but my friend Farana went in, Kirsten gave him my mail...a real treat after being here two weeks without a connection to the rest of the world. After you left, I decided my first project would be the small school, as school starts next week and the big school can't be fixed till the road's rebuilt. So I've been working my butt off, actually.

I went back, after writing a report to Peace Corps and hold-ing meetings with the villagers, to buy all the supplies. I walked to the main road in flip flops, 'cause my Teva's are still lost. My feet were pretty beat up. But a Peace Corps car was here and brought the cement to Bereketa...with another bike. I've been in to Ranohira since and fell off the bike and my leg's a bit scuffed up - I do believe I'll be a walking war-wounded when I return

198

home! I feel it's worth it...we've got the cement floor done in the school, we're now doing a cement step in front and we started remudding, (and finished it all in two days). Then the roof, doors and windows were done (and then a party, of course).

I've lived a lifetime since you left, Mom. This will be the longest I've been out here with no break. It'll be three weeks when I go in to Ranohira - but the fact that I've gotten to this point of being able to stay out here for this long and still being content shows me how much I've grown.

Every time I'm out here for a couple weeks, I feel likeI've lived a long life in another time zone when I go into Ranohira. Get this Ma, the people who work for Isalo came out, last week, and installed a radio in our village-in my house. I can actually call Ranohira or even my director in Tana. I figured that'd make you feel better. Your complaint got action. Thanks. I can call Joe now; Joe in Andriamanero has one, too.

This morning I listened in on Joe talking to Roland Sakana, Linda and Todd in Ft. Dauphin. My radio is not strong yet (solar panel) for people far to hear, but Joe hears Kirsten and me; sometimes he hears me call Ranohira. I'll take the radio in with me for a tune up next week when I go to Rinohira.

I'm well enough (my leg's getting better). My pride's up because I'm contributing to improvements for these people, and time is flying now that I'm working hard. Jardinier and I are done building a new WC (toilet) for us too!

My garden's looking pretty nice. I'll plant flowers and fruit trees and build a couple of swings around the school with the kids when it's finished - they're so excited! They've been lugging all the water up for the work - a bunch of troopers!

Well Mom, thanks for the letter. That's a bummer about your plane deal in Nairobe. But everything happens for a reason, huh? I do believe things like that happen to make us more accepting of the fact that life is unpredictable...you can either get mad at that fact or roll with it and enjoy it.

I've gotten much better at rolling with life since being here, since almost nothing ever works out the way you had expected it to! I must tell you, Mom, I missed you once you left. As I struggled with my tomato plants that the wind knocked down, I wished you were here to help. I thought to myself, "Why did she not come and spend the summer here with me? A month in my village is far from expensive, eh?"

Maybe you felt it was long enough, I don't know. I know with my conference in Uganda and you needing to get back to school, you had no more time. I just wished you had stayed longer. I felt like we got along well, but after our times together, I always wish we could re-do it, 'cause there were things I wanted to talk about but didn't. It's odd. I do feel like we're getting closer. For some reason I feel when I have a child, we'll get a lot closer. Is that silly? I feel like it will bridge a great gap of understanding. Well, we'll see someday! I don't know why I brought that up...I think I'm getting bored with being single!

I love you dearly Mom, Thanks for caring!

Nancy

September 25, 1995

I've been in Bereketa now for 2 weeks and will be here another week or more with no break. This is the longest stretch yet. I've learned a lot about myself by being here for a long time. I think I've come a long way.

I've been really starting to like the way I act and interact with other people. I feel at home with the people. I feel I'm becoming - though keeping my cool. No~I've become.

Twenty-Two

Completing the School

Nancy has learned what she has to do to stay happy while she's in her village for longer periods of time. She's no longer timid of directing people in building the school. The necessity of being a kick-in-the-pants-cheerleader now seems obvious to her. The school was down one year before Nancy arrived.

More of the country's funeral customs are shared as we are told about a faty and a famadiana .

Nancy's letters to my class are like doing a fun social studies lessons. They're real; she's living it; it's painless to learn about a culture that is so foreign to my students.

Nancy found much laughter in the visit from the new PVC's. Her acquired knowledge helped her to see humor the new volunteers learned with this funny experience.

The first major goal had come to completion. Nancy was on an emotional high.

September 30, 1995 (mailed a lot later)

Hi D! (Denise)

Maresaky? (What's shakin?) (Nancy's translation only)

I'm just hangin' in my hut, eating soup and fried dough, and enjoying the coolness of being inside. It's about 85 degrees out and it's getting towards summer time here...October and November are supposedly unbearably hot, with no moisture whatsoever. But the end of November starts the two-month rainy season. I'm already ready for that!

It's so amazing that it never rains here-except then! I often wish for it to rain, so I'm guaranteed privacy to just kick back and read a book. It doesn't happen, though. I suppose it's good the rainy season is short, because with it comes homesickness of wanting to be at your house or a friend's house curled on a couch watching a movie. Yet with homesickness comes the thought that I'm here a year plus, which doesn't seem like a very long time to me. The last year went so fast, and this place is so beautiful that I don't want to go yet. Living by gorgeous mountains with a river on each side of the village and wild mangos and banana trees everywhere is a bit of a paradise. I have a lot I want to do here too before leaving. We still haven't finished building the small school - we'll begin building the roof this afternoon. Tomorrow we're having a meeting with our village and the three nearby villages on the building of the road and the hospital here. If I can see these three projects through, as well as the construction of the big school and some vegetables and tree planting along the way, I'll leave here a very satisfied girl.

I'm doing work on my own, too, for the park, 'cause the rice-planting season here is not a time to work with villagers on projects - food comes first! I'm making a lemur and a bird display for the park information center in Ranohira. I'll also help make park brochures, and help train the guides in Ranohira.
Things happen here at such a slow pace though - I hope I'm not setting myself up for disappointment by striving for too much. Oh well, we'll see.

I'm having fun anyhow. My leg's almost all better. Did I write to you that I had an abscess on it? I've been pretty content. Two of the twenty-seven new volunteers are coming to stay with me in a couple of weeks - it's part of their training program - which should be fun. There are only three men in the whole group, Denise - bummer, huh? It was just chance that it happened that way. I was hoping to have many more American men in this country to hang out with! It's amazing the communication gap when you're not from the same culture. Been starting to get lonely from time to time now, but not too often. It comes with the territory.

Did I tell you that when Mom came we went to a famadiana (funeral) in the next village - a big celebration here where they build the casket and then carry the body into the mountains of Isalo to bury it in a cave in the rocks? They stop half way and herd the cattle together and the men take turns riding them on their humps (the cattle here have humps - India cattle); it's like riding a bull in a rodeo. The women sit by the casket and cheer the men on. It's pretty fantastic.

When we were walking, there were some men across from us. My friend, Dori said, "Nancy, listen to their conversation."

So I did. These men didn't know me and didn't know I knew their language. Their conversation was "Ia tianao? Ny Vazaha antitsy sa my anaky?" i.e. who would you like to have the older white foreigner or her daughter?

I yelled over to them "Manao akory?" which means, "Excuse me, what was that?"

Their mouths dropped in shock and everyone walking along with us died laughing (Everyone else knew me and already knew I understood the Malagasy language). Then I said, "fa tianao iendriko, tsy meintos meinome iakoy efatsy umbe" meaning, "If you want my mother, it'll cost you four cattle!" (The going rate for a wife is only two cattle!)

Everyone was dying laughing now, even the men now that they were over their shock - everyone that is except Mom, who turned to me and said, "What are you saying about me, Nancy?" I explained it all to her. She didn't seem to find it as funny as the rest of us- I don't think she was interested in the man - maybe he wasn't her type, huh?

As for me, I was just offered nine cattle last week to marry a villager in a nearby village - my best offer yet! The omby (cattle) would go to my father, which is why I told him I couldn't accept because the airplane flight to ship the ombi to the U.S. would cost more than Dad would make from selling them. I was still flattered. Here it's not if they wine and dine you, Denise; it's how many cattle they're willing to cough up! Well Denise, I love you and miss you. Give my love to Leroy and Caleb!

Love, Nance

October 7, 1995

Hi ya', Dan!

I'm in good health (finally), running every day. I haven't been running yet in my village. I decided to just start and if the villagers think I'm odd, so be it. I really don't feel like me if I don't run...it's very much of a negative energy release and good thinking time. Here it's so exhilarating, 'cause it's the one time I truly feel American; something that I often am alienated from here, but yet that I often crave. So I'm really starting to feel content, because I've learned how to be me, and still fit in to this not-so-me environment.

Now that I've earned the villagers respect and love, they're very accepting of me for now, I'm not the "vazaha" anymore. I'm Nancy. It took a while, but it happened.

We've been working on rebuilding the small school and everyone's pretty excited about it. Starting that project is basically what let them know what I'm all about, and that my intentions here are all good. I feel pretty lucky for the fact that they've welcomed me in.

I've been dancing and partying a lot lately here. Last night I had a birthday celebration for my friend Abodo in my hut, and tons of people ended up coming and dancing. The night before, one of the elders here, Pauli, brought a charrette."Malagasy tomobile" they call it. (Connie ? Automobile?)

He had a big party to celebrate, with lots of wine made in Fiararaboa (3000FMG/liter=70 cents a liter) and tokoa gasy (moonshine). Everyone danced up a storm.

I entered his house and everyone cheered - that's always how I'm greeted at parties, Dan. It's pretty wild. They definitely like my spirit, and I think I've dissolved a lot of their previous ideas, that vazahas are "stuffy desk people" (pencil pushers).

It's been all play lately, and no work. Today there's a famadiana in our village, which is a celebration of a dead person. The people go into Isalo in the rocks where they've buried their dead (they hike a person's body in a wooden box up to a cave in the mountains of Isalo when someone dies). This famadiana occurs two or three years after the dead person's been in Isalo. They get the coffin and bring it back to the village where a new coffin's been made. The body's taken out, splashed with a spiritual liquid and rewrapped in a new silk lamba. There's singing and celebrating and everyone drinking wine and tokoa gasy, and a bull's killed. It's a happy worshiping event.

I've yet to see one of these, so I'm psyched for it, but the idea of seeing a body after it's sat in a box in the mountains for three years is a bit...different.

I've seen the funeral celebration here, which is incredible, too. Mom was actually lucky enough to be here when there was one. The men take turns grabbing onto the back of a bull, their hump. The cows here are from India with huge muscular back humps and are ridden like in a rodeo. The women stand together and teasingly chant to them, "Sakaforareo Iahal" which means, "We're your food." I didn't understand the rest of the chant. I just knew a lot of hormones are flying during this event. Well Dan, I'm out of space so I'll sign off.

I love you! Nancy

October 1995

Hi, Denise. Hi, Leroy.

Your work situation sounds good. I'm glad you're still doing art and only doing the post part time. As for your class at school, it sounds great, too. I've been getting into drawing a lot myself here. I'm not overly good at it, but getting better! I've been playing the guitar a lot, too. I don't seem to ever really improve with that. I seem to need another person to teach me - I just can't grasp it learning from a book. I'm hoping Dan can explain some music theory to me. I know a lot of chords, but I don't know why they go together the way they do, or what inventive things I can do with them. I'm definitely looking forward to some guitar lessons when I'm back. And I also want to get into a health club for the first month or two while I'm going through the "Oh, my God, look at all these choices in food!" phase.

Next week I go up to the capital for our mid-service training (two months late) with my group of volunteers. It should be fun to see everyone again. After, I'm going on vacation to Fort Dauphin, on the southeast beach of the island with my friend, Linda, another volunteer here. Then, I'll get back to my village and get the building of the hospital started. I'll feel good if Bereketa has a new hospital before I go. I pretty much have all my work planned out until it's time to go. It's a good feeling. Well, D. I love you and miss you guys. I can't wait to see how Caleb looks now.

Take it easy girl! Nancy

October 11, 1995

Hi, Mom,

I'm wondering how you are cause I just heard about Hurricane Opal on my short wave and it sounds like it was right on top of you. I'm sure everything's okay with you, because if you had called Tana, they would have radioed down to Ranohira by now, and someone would have driven to me by now.

I'm in great health now. I just got back to my village this last week after being in Tana for the week - the doctor drained my leg and gave me penicillin and I'm back to my old self now.

I started running in my village, Mom. I was timid to before 'cause I figured they'd all think I was strange. But now I think I've earned everyone's respect and love from fixing up the school.

I figured it was time to start fully being myself. I had no idea how much running is a part of me. I've run for twelve years now and it really bothered me not doing it this past year. So it's made me feel wonderful to start again...it's such a massive release of energy for me (tension releaser), and it's really beneficial here to take it as a meditation time for myself and a time to feel fully American. So all in all, I'm feeling quite content and natural here; leaving the village daily gives me the space I need, before I need it!

The repairing of the school's been a very rewarding, although a slow moving (of course) project.

We've done the cement and have built the doors and windows. Tomorrow (maybe!) we start building the roof. Next, we'll need the walls.

I bought paint for the doors, windows and desks, and I got flower seeds for the kids to plant around the school. We're also starting to build the road next week with ANGAP, another organization working in the area. It will be a long hard project, but it will open up many other avenues for the villagers. Hotels will have someone drive out here to buy vegetables and rice. The doctor will visit now and then (once we build the hospital-after the road's done). Tourists will come out to visit and buy crafts. We'll see if it all happens. I'm still feeling like I'm not doing enough.

There are other things that I want to get started but haven't, because I want to get the school done first. I think, for me to feel like I'm doing enough (and to be able to fully relax when I'm not working, and not having any guilt when not working), I need to do a few projects at once. For example, I may go to the next village and start a tree-planting program. Soon, I want to start a weekly environment education class with the kids here. I'd still have more than enough time to draw, read, play the guitar, run, etc. I'm glad I still have most of a year left though 'cause I have a lot I want to do before I go home.

Mom, I love and miss you and hope you're well. I am.

Love, Nancy

P.S. Mom, please don't send any money to me here for that gift you asked me to get. I have enough money here and I doubt yours wouldn't get stolen on the way.

October 14, 1995

Hi ya, Denise,

How are ya? How are Lee and Caleb? I'm doing okay myself, though having major ice cream and mall shopping cravings. Oh well, I'll get more than my fill soon enough. As for the ice cream, there is some on the coast here - I just have to bike five and half hours and then taxi brousse five-and-half hours to get it. So both cravings will have to wait.

I've been very busy here lately, 'cause we've been working on rebuilding the school almost everyday. Different people work each day, and only about six or seven people daily, so it's slow moving.

Yet it's happening. I'm kind of the kick-in-the-pants cheerleader. It seems that if I'm not here, no one does anything (if I leave the village for a bit). But if I'm here and get people motivated, it all happens. So I plan not to leave the village until the school is done, because the kids have no class while we're rebuilding the roof. Yet, I've been really craving to just be alone for a bit - bad timing.

I think when the school is done, I'll take a few days vacation on the coast and just kick back. Hopefully that'll do the trick.

New day - Hi D! Well, we're not working on the school today cause there's a "faty" or funeral. A villager's mother died last

207

night in her village 2 km from here, so some of the villagers went to get the body. That's the program for today and tomorrow. There's a famadiana in the next village that we'll go to, so I'm doing both ceremonies in two days. Then there are two volunteers visiting me here. They will visit all the volunteers already working here. So things will stay busy for me. Maybe somewhere within all this, we'll get the roof done on the school. Well, Denise, I'm happy but missing you guys. I'll likely stop through England next year (November) before returning to the states. If you want to, you can join me.

I love you! Nancy

November 10, 1995

Dear Mom's Class,

My name's Nancy and I'm your teacher's youngest daughter. I'm 28 years old. I'm writing to you from the country of Madagascar where I'm a Peace Corps Volunteer. If you don't yet know about Peace Corps, it's an organization of the U.S. government that sends Americans who request it, and who are eligible, to work in third world countries for two years. Peace Corps pays for our plane ticket to and from the country, and gives us enough money for food and travel and a place to live, which is basically nothing in American dollars. Third world countries are very poor countries, so the money here is very weak in comparison to our very strong dollar. For example, I pay $7 in rent each month, which is outrageously high here. The going price for a nice and neat dinner at a hotel is 2500 Malagasy Francs, which is the equivalent of $.50; that's with tea included. So that's why we're called "volunteers" because we have enough money to live here for the two years but we obviously don't take home an income when we're through! Yet we're given a bit of American money when we've arrived back in the States to get us on our feet, and we get first crack at government jobs, and non-government organizations are quick to hire a returned volunteer. And since I'm learning a whole new way of life by being here, I feel I'm getting back a lot more than I'm giving.

As far as what I'm giving, I work and live in a village of about 350 people and it's on the edge of a national park. I have a

Bachelor's Degree in wildlife management that I earned at the Unversity of New Hampshire. So that's my work here. I work to help train the tour guides and park rangers and to make environmental education displays for the park information center.

Even more so, I'm helping the village where I live in with stuff like rebuilding the school and hospital that got hit by cyclones last year, and planting trees and vegetables. The village is called Bereketa, which means "Big Cactus" and it's 47 km (1.6 km=1 mile) from the nearest town, which I bike to every other week for flour and sugar and to see the other volunteers. (The bike ride takes about 5 hours, as the road is all dirt.) There is no electricity or running water in the village and the houses are mud huts with thatched roofs. Mine is an extravagant three-room hut, which is actually huge here.

We go down to the river to get water, and see at night with kerosene lamps. We grow rice and vegetables by the river for our food.

There are a couple of little stands in the village that sell coffee and soap and things that they've bought from the big town on the coast. It's a five-hour bull and carriage ride to the main road, and then five more hours in a bus called a "taxi brousse" to get there.

This is my life for two years. No English spoken here whatsoever. The language, being "Malagache," is an Oriental like language. French is also spoken in the bigger towns.

Life is totally different from the states. I've learned an incredible amount being here and I'm enjoying myself, although it's nothing like what I'm used to. I'm finding it fun living in another land and living off the earth. I've always disliked the amount of waste in the United States.

You're probably wondering, why is this chick writing to us? Well, Peace Corps has what's called the "World Wise School Program", where volunteers write to a class in the states, so you guys can take advantage of our being here and learn about another country and it's people. The people here want to learn about you too. If you write, I'll translate your letters into Malagache and read them to my villagers. I'm also psyched to get mail. I did this with Mom's last year's class and it was a lot of fun for me and for them, too. Maybe my mother already showed you the slides of my village that I sent her.

As for the country, Madagascar's an island country off the east coast of Africa - it supposedly broke off from Africa millions of years ago (you'll have to look it up in the encyclopedia to find out how many millions of years because I've forgotten!). Get out a map and take a look. It's one of the four largest islands in the world.

If you've ever heard of it, it's likely you heard of it due to the population of lemurs here, which is an animal that's a relative of the monkey. It's found nowhere else in the world, except on a couple small islands close to Madagascar, where they were introduced. (Their original home is Madagascar and someone brought them to these little islands.)

There are 30 plus species of lemur. One left the protection of the national park last week and leaped from tree to tree in my village with the villagers chasing it. They finally caught it and tied it up and were deciding if they should eat it. (Mind you, there are no Demoulas Market Baskets here and meat is a major luxury here), or who should keep it as a pet.

I explained to them why they shouldn't do either, and why they should protect this animal. I took the lemur and put him in my backpack and biked him back into the mountains and forest of Isalo National Park. The idea of having an animal similar to a monkey in your backpack is pretty comical. I laughed when I looked back as I biked along to see his face sticking out of the pack looking over my shoulder with the wind blowing his fur and his eyes wide opened... I felt like the little boy in the movie biking E.T.through the air! But I got it safely back in the park. Well, I seemed to get off the track with that story.

Anyhow, you guys, I just wanted to introduce myself to you and to let you know I'll be writing to you now and then, so you will know and then get to have a break from what you are usually learning in class. So the more you write to me and ask me questions, the longer my letters will be, the longer it will take my Mom to read them to you, and the less work you'll have to do in class. So please write! Ask away! If I don't hear from any of you first, I'll probably write again in November. Well, take it easy.

Yours sincerely, Nancy "Rakoto"   Velumo! (i.e. goodbye)

Hi ya', Mom!

How ya doin', hon? I hope this "book" finds you well and happy. I'm sorry my letter to your class was so long. I'm sure it took up at least a class to read it. But they had a lot of initial good questions that needed answering. I know you were probably psyched to get a long letter anyhow.

Mom, that letter from them totally made my day! I'm so glad we're doing this. I think your class will get a lot out of it. .
P.S. They are very Christian here by the way - there are two little churches in my village alone (Protestant and Catholic). I actually go sometimes. Although I understand nothing, the singing is gorgeous. The children sing and it's so sweet and beautiful. I get tear jerked! I feel unified with the people and God when I go.

Love, Nancy

November 10, 1995

Hi, Bry and Jo!

How are your guys over there? How are the little guys? I'm doing okay. I'm feeling a bit lonely. It's only because I just had a couple of the new volunteers visit me for three days. It was so nice having company who speaks my language and can understand my background. But now, there's something lacking here that they are gone. Not much new for me here. Putting the roof on the school at the moment and will re-mend it next week. Two new volunteers will start working here and in two other villages near the park in December. They are coming for a site visit in two weeks for a five-day visit before their final swear-in, so I am psyched to meet them. One is a 21-year-old woman, and one's a 29-year-old guy; in parks wildlife like myself, supposedly a really nice guy - yeah! He is supposedly good looking, too. That's good. I could use seeing some good looking American men in these parts!

Bum luck! Another girl came in his place.

The two volunteers who visited me here last week won't be working here, though. It was just a visit where all the volunteers came to visit us "veterans" to get a taste of the country and our jobs.

We went to picnic on the river when they first arrived. I could get to know them before the villagers totally bombarded them. I asked them if they had brought bathing suits.

They said, "No."

"No problem, cause I always just skinny dip here" I informed them."It's what we have to do and villagers respect this area is reserved for women only."

Right when we got to the river I stripped and jumped in. Later, when I got out and Maryann was in, an omby came around the river bend. She jumped out of the water, in fear that a cattle guard could come next. She ran toward her clothes yelling, "I am naked! I'm naked!"

Christine and I laughed hysterically and yelled,"No kidding!"

The bull started running after her! As she was putting her shirt on, he had lowered his head, with his horns aimed straight for her butt! She was still worried about her darn clothes.

I ran across the river to distract him. When the second of danger was over, I started laughing hysterically again, especially since I knew there would be no cattle guard passing until many bulls and cows had passed us. (The guards are always in the back.)

She was still screaming, "I'm naked!"

I don't think I have laughed so hard since I got here. So needless to say, I had to say a great visit with them.

I asked our embarrassed trainee if I could do a comic strip of her to put in the P.C. newsletters, but she said only if I drew a bikini on her... doesn't that take all the fun out of it? That's what was so hysterical. I wanted to caption it, "New trainee, taking her Peace Corps experience by the bull's horns." Oh well, it was great fun.

Well you guys, hope you are all well. Sorry, I didn't write an in-depth message on what I am doing, here, but I didn't feel like it... I didn't want to bore you, ha, ha! (My life hasn't exactly been boring lately.)

Love you guy, Rakoto
(pronounced "Racoutu")

November 26, 1995

Hi Mom,

I just decorated my pinecone yesterday. Mom, thanks so much. Dad sent me a Christmas present (new sturdy sandals). Your box will probably be waiting for me at the post office. I'll put all my gifts beside my pinecone tree. I made a Christmas tree decorating party for myself. I cooked popcorn and fried some peanuts and sweetened them. Then I had the shot of Tia Maria in coffee (the one you brought from the airplane) and made a little angel for the top. So my hut is somewhat Christmas-y (although it doesn't feel Christmas-y at all here). Thanks for sending it though, Mom. It was a well-appreciated gesture.

I'm going to make angels with the kids from straw (like what you made your mat with) and use the glitter decorating the halos. I'll wait 'til December though, as it is November 26th today.

I totally forgot to celebrate Thanksgiving, until I heard it on Voice of America at 7 p.m. I think I've adapted to their holidays instead!

We'll have a party Saturday, 'cause the school's done - Yeah! Travaux Publique's here now to start the work on the road. I'm planting flowers with the kids tomorrow by the school. We'll plant papaya trees next week and other species of trees with the villagers next week.

Work and things are moving along.

Emotional wise -I'm hangin' in there, but that's about it at the moment. I've been really homesick and depressed this last week. I think it has something to do with hitting the one-year point. A year sounds like a long time to me right now, although I know it won't be. I've been running to help to reduce my exhaustion and it seems to be helping. I've been a little more upbeat the past couple days.

If I get down again, though, I'm going to the ocean for a few days. I'm getting together with Joe and Kirsten and the new volunteers to the area (who will arrive in two weeks) for Christmas. We may do the "Grand Tour" (six plus days) hiking in Isalo.

Hi, Mom! I left you there for days, actually, to go work at final touches on the school. Hey, by the way the pictures are great! Thanks so much. You made not only me, but many other people, happy. Dori was asking about the picture of her and me, though. Jardinier asked about his photo in his store and Mama and Kirsten in the charrette.

Well, I finished the school today - YEAH! A major high for me!! I got three guys to mud the last wall with me this morning. Then I painted the windows and doors and trim around each. It's downright beautiful. I was thinking as I was working, that everywhere I've been I leave a pretty scene behind. Every apartment I've been in is freshly painted or stenciled, and every relative/friend of mine has a stained glass or macramé...it's a neat feeling. The villagers will call the school "Souvenirs de Nancy" when I'm gone, which is so true. It's nice to know a mark of my beauty will be left here, too.

Anyhow, I'm feeling good today, very "up" from my feelings of two days ago when I wrote...ah yes, that good ol' Peace Corps roller coaster. I've always loved roller coasters, but I must admit the idea of getting off and having an ice-cold beer and a hot dog, sounds very appealing. (It will be soon enough, eh?)

Tomorrow I may bike to Ranohira and then to Joe's to do a waterfall hike with him (a belated Thanksgiving weekend)...I've earned it.

I love you dearly, Mom.
Nancy

The Building of the School

Men hewning beams

Shaving the boards with a hand tool

Boys collecting sand for the school floor

Women and girls carrying water for the cement

Pouring the cement floor

Framing for the roof supports

Time to lay the roof supports

Final preparations for thatching

Gathering grass for the roof

The school is finished!

A souvenir of Nancy

Nancy's halo is showing!

Many children ready for school.

Twenty-Three

Hotel de la Reine

I was always trying to find things that would be pleasing to Nancy and luckily I found a simple gift that meant so much. Who ever would have thought. The rainy season offers relief from the heat and is a welcome break.

November 28, 1995

Hi ya', Donna!

How ya doin' girl? How's family life treating you? I'm doing all right and single life's treating me well enough for now. I'm just kicking back by the river for the moment with a friend's dog, named "Big Dog," sitting next to me. He likes hanging around with me, because I'm one of the few (if not the only person) in the village who doesn't kick him.

I'm relaxing today. The school's finished. This last week I planted flowers with the kids by the school, and we made Christmas angels for the church from grass. Tomorrow I'll go to Ranohira, because the new volunteers to the area will be coming.

I'll go with Carrie to her village. I've been organizing her house for her. She's in a village about a 45 km bike ride from me - I rode it last week and it's a nice back road (not all sand). I'll probably visit her now and then. I've met her and she's very young ... I like her. We'll see if we click.

David will be living in Ranohira, based on the other side of the mountains. I met him, too, and I think he is someone I'll hit it off with. There are also two volunteers at the protected area about 90 km from here, and one more (an English teacher) who will live in Toliar on the coast. It'll be nice to have more Americans close by. We'll likely all spend Christmas together.

I have been doing okay, although a couple of weeks ago I experienced my worst homesickness yet. It was only for about five days. I found if I stayed busy and also kept telling myself how someday this will all feel like a dream and I'll wish I had it back, then it wasn't so bad. Sometimes I'm just lonely in the respect that I wish someone were sharing this with me.It's so beautiful here and my life is so simple (although confusing and aggravating). I have so much time to relax and contemplate life and me.

An average day for me is getting up at 5:30 (can you believe it?), having a coffee, and then doing some yoga. Then, I go for a three or four km run, then go down to the river to bathe, water my garden, and get some water. I come home to have a banana and mango breakfast salad. Next I do something with the villagers (plant trees or vegetables, work on the school, or just socialize). After, it's time for a fried rice and vegetable lunch. I read a book or write or study some French or Malagache, or continue whatever project I was doing with the villagers in the a.m.Then I take an evening walk, and draw or write.It's time to make a rice and vegetable dinner and practice my guitar. Maybe I shall meditate and read again before sleeping at about 9 p.m.

Some days I go to the mango tree to pig out or I'll take a

walk to the waterfall and pick fiddleheads for dinner. Although it's often a difficult life here, because their way of life is so different from what I'm used to, there are still many good aspects to being here. I've become pretty strong, physically and mentally. I get better each day at looking positively on some really uncomfortable situations. Why did this letter turn into an autobiography on my life, anyhow? Oh well. Maybe you already knew this stuff from past letters, but that's okay. I'm sure you like to hear I'm well!

Love you, Donna, Nancy

December 2, 1995

Dear Mom,

I love you! I love you! I love you! You can't guess where I am right now. I'm at the Hotel de la Reine, the gorgeous Hotel of Isalo where Kirsten and I took you and Peggy to dinner. The owner offered me a room for the evening, 'cause I was biking back to Bereketa in a downpour. I just took the most exquisite hot shower and now I'm wrapped in a towel and I just opened your package from the post with the raisins and popcorn. I was so thrilled about the raisins that I ate almost all of them right now. They are so good. Thanks, Mom. It's a great gift.

Now's a good time for the popcorn, too. The rainy season's started, so I can pop it in my hut without everyone hearing and running into my kitchen to get some. So thanks, Mom...you and Orville Redenbacher made my day.

I feel like quite the little queen here. I was definitely due for some special treatment. I think I may have offended Gilberte in the past by not accepting his offer of a relaxing room and shower - I'm so darn proud - so it felt good to finally simply say, "Yes, thank you."

Why am I so stubborn and resist letting people help me or do things for me, Mom? It's a trait I don't like in myself. I do so much for so many other people, but yet when someone offers to do something for me, I always instinctively say, "No." I'm so independent. Yet I'm becoming aware of it and I'm also becoming aware that I'm actually starting to crave having someone to take care of me. I really can't get used to the way there's no touching here...no hand holding, no hugs, no kissing, no back-rubs. It's such a different culture and it's difficult for me, being such a touchy person.

I went to a dance last night with Kirsten in Ranohira and one song I danced slow with my friend, Rivo, and I just clung to him. It was so nice to be held. I realized I haven't really been held in more than a year! It'll be nice to get home to some huggy, feely family and friends.

Hey, my "pen pal" returned a letter to me, Mom. Remember? The one I wrote to and let him know I was jealous when he mentioned "missing his baby" on his vacation, and I was relieved to find out it was his dog! He wrote back with a picture of his dog enclosed and said "No, it's just my dog...I'm very single and have been for a long time, and you are very special to me." Underlined even, Mom! So, yes, I have a crush on my now three-year pen pal, and it seems like it may be mutual. Crushes are fun. I haven't had one in a long while. So I've been writing to him more, 'cause I want to get to know him better...hopefully he'll do the same.

The idea of getting home and meeting the right person to settle into a life with sounds very appealing to me now. I really don't want to be single much longer, but I also don't want to date people with whom I know there's no future with. I'll be 30 a few months after getting home...getting to be time for some family extensions, eh? You're probably saying "Yep, I knew it - I knew she'd get to this point while she's over there, and then there's no one around for her to meet." But that's good, 'cause it gives me a year to do some fine tuning on myself (always easier to do while alone, I've found!). Although lonely from time to time, I'm still content being single. You know how it goes.

Anyhow, tomorrow a.m. I'll bike home. This coming week I'll plant some trees and vegetables with the villagers and then I'll be biking back here Friday, (which is when I'll mail this out), to meet the new volunteers who will come here on that day. I will meet them to take them to their villages. That should be fun.

Well, Mom, I love you dearly and thanks for constantly letting me know you love me dearly. I can't wait to come down to Florida to see you when I get home. I wonder how it'll feel going to Disney World after a Peace Corps experience? Culture shock at it's best, most likely!

Mom, stay well and happy and at peace with yourself. Give Aunt Doris my love.

Love, Nancy

Twenty-Four

Back to Bush Life

Nancy bikes 130km to help a new Peace Corps Volunteer get established in her village. This woman has more strength than I could ever imagine.

Christmas celebration is like none that most have experienced. It was complete with a flood. This caused Nancy another very serious medical condition. It brought on extended rest and relaxation, some forced and some voluntary.

December 3, 1995

Hi ya', Dan!

I'm sitting in the doorway to my hut sipping a cup of Earl Grey-compliments of Donna, of course...their tea here's about as bad as the coffee). I'm enjoying the breeze and smell of rain. I love this season (end of summer and rainy season's setting in...actually summer lasts 'til January, but the frequency of the rain now makes it more bearable. Other people in the village aren't too thrilled with the rain, 'cause they made bricks today to finish building their hut and they'll melt, or because they don't have the grass roof on their house yet. It was pretty comical...about five weeks before the start of the rainy season everyone started building new huts and now it's starting to downpour every other day and only one of them is near finished. No, they're definitely not a people who plan for the future! But anyhow, I love the rain. Although it sometimes makes me homesick for a good afternoon movie on the couch with a bowl of popcorn and a man wrapped around me. How's it feel to want? Well let me tell ya...!

225

Actually, I've been really appreciating life here lately. Afakomaly (the day before yesterday) I got back from Ranohira and Ilaka, where one of the two new volunteers will be. I had to check on the progress of the worker on the new PVS's house. So I went to Ilaka Be, then to Ranohira to visit Kirsten, then home the following day, (130 km total by bike). I felt exhausted and fantastic, in shape and tan. (Although still not glamorous!)

On the way home, I got caught in a thunderstorm, so I stopped at the Hotel de la Reine, (that utterly gorgeous hotel in the rock mountains that I must have told you about,) for coffee. The French owner, who always spoils me when I pass by, offered me a room for the night, so I accepted happily. I've never enjoyed a hot shower so much in my life, I don't think. It was the first one since Mom visited. I had dinner with Gilberte, the owner, and his son and the manager, also my good friends, and I had breakfast with him the next morning before my bike ride home. It was exquisite. It's maybe the nicest hotel in the country.

Gilberte built this "castle" after his military service here because he loves Isalo (the park) and the environment of the place. The hotel is totally opposite to anything I've seen in my life. That makes this an incredible treat. I'm starting to teach the employees English next week so I'll get spoiled on a regular basis soon-yeah!

On my way home, I stopped at one of the many trees. I sat in one and pigged out on mangos and then biked to the waterfall, (12 km before my home) and took a shower. I picked a bunch of fiddleheads in the forest for dinner before coming home. Have you eaten those yet? They're in the States, too...the fern with the head that curls...delicious!

So my life's good. Yesterday was a holiday here for the men in the military, so we had a party. Today I walked to Manda Be, a village 3 km from here, to talk to them about planting some trees next week. Then this afternoon I made Christmas angels with the kids out of the dry grass. Tomorrow I may plant papaya trees with the kids. The next day I'll plant forest tree species here with my village and then the next day I bike back to Ranohira to get to meet the new group of Peace Corps volunteers. When I get back here we'll have a big party 'cause the schools finished (and beautiful too, I must say!).

So life's good for me, although I'm learning what homesickness is lately. This last week hasn't been bad, since I've been so busy. I think I've gotten to a point where I'd rather be with someone than spending my life alone, and it's not like there's a lot of options around here! I have to tell you though, Dan, as silly as it sounds; I have a semi-crush on my pen pal. I've been writing to this guy four years now, someone I met at the Army Corps Park Ranger Training for a weekend. We've been writing ever since and the more he writes the more I like him. So we actually have plans to get together when I'm back. Silly, huh? Oh well, it keeps me going way out here!

Hey, Dan, write to me a bit about your girlfriend. I don't know if you realized it, but you didn't write to me that you had a girlfriend before this letter. Let me know a bit about her. Well Dan, I love you dearly and hope you're content. You sound good in your letters, and no I don't get aggravated at your not writing even though I write to you a lot. I write more to express myself than to get a response. I was happy to hear you're okay though, 'cause I was wondering. I miss you way too much bro!

Love ya, Dan! Nancy

January 5, 1995

Hi Diane! [friend from back in elementary school]

I just got a package full of letters from you! Thanks, hon. I know you wrote, "Don't laugh," but I had to. So anyway, how are you and how was your New Year? I had a very un-festive holiday season, but that's okay. I'll make it up when I'm home with all of you for Christmas next year! But this year I spent Christmas hiking through the park with Joe (a volunteer at the park) and three of the new volunteers. We went for six days!

Joe and Kristen hiking through the park

It was during the rainy season, so it was a wet week. Christmas day we were caught in a flash flood! Amazing and scary! I never have seen such a thing. I got my camera out to take pictures. Joe yelled, "Nancy, you dodo, get up in a tree."

I yelled back, "I have to get this for our future historical record."

I got in a tree, none too soon. The water came up a meter plus in about 30 minutes. We had to put all our tents up on blow-down snags. After five minutes that wasn't enough, so we had to break down all the tents, and stuff them and everything else in our packs. We had to climb up in the trees to wait for the river to go down.

We thought we could forge it. We did forge the water after it dropped a couple feet. It was getting dark and starting to rain again. Man, was the current strong!

We locked arms and managed to cross. That was hard work. Next we set up our sopping wet tents on higher ground. In spite of all these nerve-shaking experiences, we managed to have our Christmas turkey. Our camp is under water! Good thing we moved!

"Nancy, you Dodo, get up in a tree screamed Joe. I yelled back, "I have to get this for our future, our historical record."

Yeah! We survived!
from l. to r. Carrie, Nancy, Sarah, Joe, and David

We hiked out on the next day and we laid everything out to dry. It was a wild trip... a lot of fun, although a bit wet and tough going. It was a bit tougher for me, as I had an amoeba inside me, so I was constantly running to the woods. When I got back I called the doctor, 'cause I had dysentery and he told me to take a flight up to Tana. He actually ended up putting me in the hospital for a couple days because I had lost so much blood. Now I'm fine.

I've been staying at the U.S. Ambassador's house for four days since the hospital stay. She opens her back room up to PC volunteers when we're up here in town. She lives here with her husband and their 18-year-old daughter, Alexandria (who's wise enough to be 40!)], a great laid-back family. [Ambassador Vickie Huddleston] used to be a volunteer herself. So I've been spoiled rotten...good food and desserts, American movies, a pool, tennis courts, a grand piano, and good company.

Today I take the 20-hour taxi brousse back to Ranohira and, needless to say, I don't want to go! I'll be back up here in February for our mid-service training (late), so I'll stay here 2 nights before the training. I feel like I've adopted a family!

I go home today, but only to my village for a couple days. I'm going to the beach with another volunteer .

My village likely doesn't think I'm coming back! I must admit, I haven't minded being away so much. I only have about ten months left and I'm quite sure I'll be ready to return home when it's time. I will travel with my U.S. friend Andrea in Africa before going back and will visit Donna in England. After that, home to New Hampshire in time for Christmas. Well, girl, I love ya'! Give my love to your family!

Love, Nancy

February 25, 1996

Hi, Mom!

How are you? I'm bored with being single. I know, you told me this would happen one day. Well, here it is.

Just not enough Americans in my life right now. I'm craving a close friend, someone from our country, but not many Americans travel here. They go to Africa, instead, where they can see more. My languages, French and Malagasy, aren't good enough to have close relationships with the locals or with French or other tourists.

When you get right down to it Mom, I want a deep and meaningful relationship with a man. Yes, you were right, I'm craving it while I'm still in this country. At least it's during the last lap.

There is a Canadian guy who's building windmills here and who's a total sweetheart. I had a major crush on him last year. I think I wrote to you about him, but he had a girlfriend at the time. I just saw him last week in Tana and he's single now. I again was totally attracted to him and it may be mutual, but I don't know. He's a friend with many of the other Peace Corps volunteers; he speaks English, not French, so he spent a lot of time with us. We were in Tana for our mid-service training. I can't tell if he's attracted to me 'cause he's so sweet to everyone! I think I'd fall in love with him in the States, too, even if I weren't so desperate! Oh well, time will tell, right? I unfortunately don't spend enough time in Tana for us to get to know each other well.

I'll be going back in a taxi-brousse next week. Maybe fate will send him down my way to work. Pathetic thought, huh? I've been here almost two years and I've had a crush on only one guy! I wouldn't mind that, if I knew I could take this one home with me! So anyhow Mum, that's about the biggest news in my life at the moment.

At the moment I'm sitting on a beach in Mahajanga at my friend Gretchen's beach house. I sent you a post card. I don't know if you've gotten it yet...they tend to take longer, 'cause everyone and anyone reads them along the way.

I decided to take a week's vacation up here before going back for the last lap. It's been nice and relaxing. I'm very moody. I seem to have a lot on my mind. It seems like during the last 1/3 of service, my thoughts spend as much time on the future as on the present. School? Work? Travel? Live where? You know how it goes. Back into the American mode of "planning for the future." I don't mean it's a bad thing, but I need to get it in control, so I leave some of my time for enjoying the present moment...something we often forget to do in the States.

I'm sure when I get back in my village I'll get my mind on

the present. I'll feel better when it's time to go if I get a bit more done before I leave. I must admit, if I could do nothing for my last 8+ months here except plant vegetables, pick peanuts and socialize with the villagers, I would. But I know I couldn't do it guiltlessly. I'll get a little something done on the side, to make it seem like I'm working. Maybe that should be the definition of Peace Corps, "the toughest job you'll ever have at making it seem like your doing something."

There! That was written so badly. People would think it was profound just 'cause it sounds so complex!

Mom, I'm hanging in and, yes, I want to come home soon, 'cause I miss you guys! I'll be psyched to see all of you and also to eat good ice cream! I'll be glad to do and have all those other American things over there.

I wrote a letter to your students, too. You hang in there too! Remember that the toughest jobs in life are often the ones we learn most at. I love y'a, Mom! I'll send Doris' tablecloth soon (don't send money it was cheap about $15 only! Good bargainer, I am!)

Love, Nancy

P.S. Mom, I may just mail this out tomorrow and write your class this week. I suppose you'll know by now if there's a letter in here to your class or not, eh?

March 5, 1996

Hi, Mom!

I just went on a ten-day cruise in one of these boats on the Indian Ocean. I almost got eaten by sharks! Ha, Ha, just kidding.

Actually, I'm hangin' out on a beach drinking punch out of a coconut shell with my friend, Gretchen, watching two boats pull in a third that just capsized. I'll stay beach bound, thanks.
I'm up here at Gretchen's house on the beach on the Northwest Coast.

We just finished our mid-service training. As we only have eight or nine months left, I needed a vacation to gather my thoughts together before the last stretch. Kely Sisa. Just a little left.

It was very healing to see everyone...it will be even more so to see all you guys; I got Doris' present, Mom, and will send it soon (before the end of March). I'm trying to find something nice for you, too, before sending it.

Well, Mom, I love you dearly. I miss you. Love, Nancy

March 7, 1996

Hi, Kids! Hi Alex, Ryan and Lauren, too!

Things are going good for me. I've been away from my village a lot, because I've had a lot of meetings lately with the other volunteers and then others with ANGAP, because they just wrote the new management plan for the park. But now I'm back to spending most of my time in the village, and I'm glad for it. I only have about seven or eight months left and I want to spend most of it in the village.

Last month I went through a real low, where I didn't want to be here, or even be in this country; but I'm back to feeling good being here. I'm trying to savor being here. I know the remaining time will fly by and someday I'll crave this experience again.

I've considered transferring to another country, but I'm leaning toward going home, to the Northwest to do a Masters' Degree somewhere. I'll start writing for schools soon. As for now, I'm starting to get the money to get the hospital and the big school built. (They both got knocked down in the cyclone in '93.) I'll soon start painting a world map on the inside wall of the small school with the kids (a program many PCV's have done in many countries, and I have a guide on how to do it).

So I'm busy, happy, healthy and not painfully lonely like last month. So life is good for me. Well guys, I love you all!

Love, Aunt Nancy

March 14, 1996

Hi, Doll! (As you'd say) [Mom]

How are all my building and my projects going? Well, I'm basically just getting started on many things. This week I go with a villager to research funding for the hospital and the big school. I've already started people vegetable gardening. And I bought paint to start painting the world map on the wall inside the little school. Things are going well. I've been in and out of my village lately for meetings. It's been tough to start anything, but I think I'm over that now...back to two-week-at-a-time stretches in my village, the way I like it.

I'm sorry things aren't going well for you right now, Mom. I wish I were making enough money (or even some money) so I could support you! I hate to think for all that you've given me I can't even help you when you need it. Maybe sometime soon I'll be in a position where I can help you. That'd make me real happy. You'd think having five adult kids, we'd all be well off enough that we could help you but it seems that in these times, well off is hard to come by. Why don't you ditch it all and join the Peace Corps? I heard it's a difficult job, but good for the heart!

The wildlife class you did sounds great. Did it happen to be a "project wild" course? That's a class I plan to take when I get home. The canoe trip sounded good, too, but I can't believe the men got out and walked you through the water with alligators in it! Daring guys! Were any of them single? Ha, Ha, just kidding! (Well, sort of!)

Love, your kid, Nancy

March 17, 1996

Akoy Daniel! Maresaky Aminao Aridahirko?
Thanks for the letter, Dan. You sound busy. Hopefully happy though and feeling full of direction. How's life in your new apartment?

Mom wrote that your apartment's gorgeous. I didn't know the name of the band that you wrote you're playing with now. Are your playing with a new band now? Are you liking school? I think I may do the same when I get home, Dan.

I'll write to some colleges in the Northwest soon. I can probably get good grants or even free admission, with this experience. I can extend a year here, but I think two year's of village life is enough for me, as much as I love it now.

As I write to you, three kids are sitting by me on the floor going though my National Geographics and Newsweeks (for probably the 80th time). Another kid is chasing a chicken out of my house ~ for the 4th time today. I think it wants to lay an egg in here, which is fine with me! My friend Abodo is sitting beside me playing a Malagasy tune on my guitar. Another kid,, about 6 years old, just yelled "Sarabavy!" as he points to a pretty blonde with a mini skirt. Sarabavy meaning "Holy Cow." They learn young here. I'm flattered though, 'cause after saying this, he looks at me, smiles and says "Nancy a ti" =" It's Nancy. I'd be psyched to have her legs, I must say!"

Some of my roof just fell beside me. (It comes with the rainy season territory.) There's a pig squealing like crazy out side as a neighbor slices his throat. (Oaky Zay! i.e. rice topping) The church bell's chiming in the background, along with the singing of the villagers. It's Sunday today.

That's my present environment. Nothing like the States. I went through a major low last month where I felt out of sync and not at home here. But I'm back to feeling good again. I've learned that emotional swings are unavoidable here, especially when I go to the capital and get a taste of life similar to the U.S., and especially after spending time with all the other volunteers here. It's tough to get back into the swing of village life. There is a lack of understanding due to differences in language ability and understanding of each other's ways. Our backgrounds are 180 degrees different.

I miss you guys, but I keep remembering how much I'm going to crave this place and the people here when I'm home. It is doubtful that I'll come back here and it keeps me on track to living in the moment here. Eight months is not much time, so I'm savoring it! I hope you're happy, Bro.

Love you, Nancy

P.S. Excuse my writing paper but we can only use so much scrap paper for toilet paper needs here, so it is my stationary instead.

March 19, 1996

Dear Dad,

I'm happy here, though I have lots of homesick pangs. The program's growing, and there are fifty volunteers in the country now, so I can always hop on my bike and visit another American if I want to. There are about eight within 300 km, and it's actually cheap to fly to visit any of the others.

It surprises me how much I crave company of people who speak my language and know my American lifestyle. I think it's just that being in an environment where I'm only speaking an unnatural (to me) language day in and day out, I need intervening spurts of English so I don't constantly feel like an idiot! You can only feel so intelligent talking like a five-year-old. I also really crave in-depth conversations which I can't get with my level of speaking the Malagasy language.

I've grown stronger in myself, though, only having myself to confide in and work through my feelings towards the culture here. I do a lot of writing and drawing, as you saw, and take a walk each evening and go for a run each morning. It seems to keep the balance of living in such a different environment.

It's a nice place to live. The villagers seem to really care for me since the school is completed..so much that I'd be scared for anyone who tried to hurt me.

I do a lot of kabosy (guitar) playing and dancing, too, which always keeps me happy. It keeps the villagers happy watching the vazaha dance!

I'm content for now and am excited to do some travelling in Africa before coming home. My friend Andrea (remember her?) is going to fly over and meet me there to travel until Christmas time. We may go to Scotland, Ireland, and then to England to see Donna after. Well, give my love to Paula and the family. I need to get some shut eye.

Love ya! Nancy

March 25, 1996

Maybe it's all just an illusion.
Hi, Dan,

How are you? No, I mean how are you? I've been trying to figure it all out lately. I came back yesterday from Ihosy, going from bureau to bureau with one of the elders from my village. We were researching how to go about building the hospital, how to get a doctor. We were also researching how the funding is coming along for our bigger school, and why our two military men have left the village and not returned, since 21 cattle thieves with guns recently passed close to our village and robbed some people walking on the road to our village.

Last night I returned to Bereketa, with the Peace Corps doctor who was in town to do site visits. I rode in the Peace Corps car, a rare treat. My landlord, who is the village doctor, asked for medicines. I told him, "He can't."

Later Jardinier asked me where the doctor was from. I said, 'He's American but works in Africa as the Peace Corps regional doctor."

Jardinier's response to this shocked me. For some reason his remarks hurt me or seemed to angered me. He said, "Why doesn't the United States just give me the money instead of spending it all on sending him over for a few days? I need a lot of money. You all have a lot of money."

Why did it bother me? I thought maybe it's because I have the attitude that you have to work to get somewhere; it doesn't just come to you.

Yet, Jardinier is not at all lazy. I find many villagers to be. I'm not blaming them. It's hard to be motivated when you're used to working with nothing but what nature gives you. Jardinier is always building something, or farming rice or vegetables, or helping a woman give birth, or helping a sick person.

After I thought about it for a long time, I realized my anger is due to guilt. I just realized that my attitude of having to work at getting something, that it doesn't just come to us, is so wrong in respects to what he was requesting. The only reason that the doctor is being flown around and Jardinier isn't is because of luck. He was born in Madagascar and we were born in the States. I got upset because he was right and there's not a darn thing I can do about it. I felt defenseless and helpless in that I could not change this truth. What I wish I could convey to him and to all Malagasy (and other people living this similar reality) is that this does not mean our existence is better. Money does not make for a better existence, just different. Yet I got up and walked away from his question (after a long enough hesitation as to not seem like leaving was related to his comment, but excusing myself to make dinner). There was no way I could ever explain this truth to Jardinier. It's the type of learning which can only come through experience. Therefore, it is a realism, which Jardinier will never learn.

I've learned it because I've craved to live only with nature, as many Americans have (craving the opposite of our reality, i.e. craving Jardinier's reality), and because I'm American (i.e. lucky-to some degree) I've been given an opportunity to try it. Now that I've tried it, I realize neither existence is better. No matter which existence you have, you'll want to try the other, since we're dreamers to some degree.

The people here crave to have what we have because world society has taught us (or brain-washed us, I should say) that development (i.e., the U.S.) is the ultimate goal. Those of us who realize this teaching is not true, crave to live on nature alone (i.e., Madagascar) as much as people like Jardinier crave our existence.

Dan, you fall into this latter category with me and many others. The bottom line is that I have the truth in the palm of my hand, yet I can't teach it to anyone. They must each experience it themselves. It's so difficult, because I'm often walking away from comments like Jardinier's. I feel helpless and frustrated because I can't let them know. As much as I tell them how wonderful their way of living is, they'll never believe me 'til they've actually experienced something different.

I was farming rice with some friends last week. The men were cutting the rice; the women were piling it together, tying it in a bunch, and carrying the huge load on their heads out of the field. The parents were whacking the rice on the charrette, the wagon we'd later fill with rice in large bags for the cattle to pull to the village. They were trying to make all the rice fall off the stalks. Sata, the elder of the family, asked me, as I was dropping my huge bundle of rice beside him, "How do they do this where you're from?"

I said, "They have machines to cut the rice and then to sift it from the stalks."

He said, "Makay raha henareo," "You guys know how to do everything." He followed it by the usual, "That's so much better than our way, our way is so hard."

I said loudly and sincerely, "That's so untrue! It's not better! It's faster, yes, it's not better!"

People were sitting around now watching the interaction. They got a kick out of watching me get so excited about things, especially while talking this way to a Reimen Dreny (elder). It's not their custom.

I continued, though he didn't believe me (and even though I knew in my heart he never would), "Just look at this place! It's beautiful! The fields are all shades of yellow and green, the mountains are overlooking us, the river's flowing down below, the breeze is refreshing, we're all here together with enough rice for a long time and no worries - it's wonderful."

Everyone, of course, cracked up at me and the elder stabbed a response at me with a huge grin, "But I'm old and my back aches!" as he was whaling the rice against the charrette again to make the rice fall loose. That was his job in this production line.

I tossed back at him (all this being a very friendly interaction, but very heated and sincere on both our parts), "Good. It's good for you! And admit it; you love it! You joke about vazahas (white foreigners) as office- working pencil pushers with no respect at all, because you know they've missed the point! They come driving into Bereketa, (the big whigs who oversee the National Park and work in the capital and just do quick fly by's to the park, so they can say they know what's going on here,) and are in such a rush. Do you think they really see the beauty here? No way! Sanabavy! Their way is not better - they're so busy that they miss what's the most important!"

Everyone got a good laugh from this because I'm so excited, and I realize that I can never actually make them understand - that's what I mean. But yet, by the look on the Reimen Dreny's face, I was content. At least he knew I truly meant what I said. He's learned that there is truly one vazaha, at least, who appreciates his reality as much as (if not more than) their own. It's a frustrating existence here, because I'm constantly faced with this belief of theirs, which becomes a wall in my own experience here...not just from their words but from their actions.

The endnote, Dan, is this: I'm thoroughly content here,- until I'm faced with the interaction of two worlds, which is of course everyday and often! Although I wouldn't go home yet even if I could, I would take a bunch of these people with me when I do, just so they can learn how much they truly have. Yet, in America we have no less.

Peace and love, Nancy

March 27, 1996

Hi, Dan,

It's a couple of days later and I just had to jot you a note. Setting: I was starting to paint my world map as a guide for the huge one I'll make for the school wall with the kids and adults in my village. Dan, they think the other planets in the world are in the earth. No kidding! They don't understand that there are other planets in the sky other than us. No, that's not right. They think the sky and all the planets exist within our earth. Some thought in the oceans, but the overall consensus is in the earth, the land! Amazing! I think this painting of the world map on the wall will be my most worthy project here yet, 'cause they'll not only learn about the earth, but they'll learn about the solar system. They will learn because so many questions will arise while we are doing the painting. Dan, most here don't know that there are more than one planet and they think there's only one moon, and they think the sun moves around us! They've heard the solar system story from Malagasy professors but people way out on their own (i.e., my village) think it's just that...a story! So, I'm psyched to do this world map and maybe after that, a solar system map on the other wall of the school.

March 29, 1996

Hi Dad, Hi all,

Dad, fantastic letter. You wrote it on your birthday and it arrived on my birthday. Can't beat that! Thanks for thinking about me so much. I feel loved from the opposite end of the earth... a lucky girl! But a pre-warning... you may regret the comment for pina coladas, mud slides, or whatever I want when I return! I may go into fast food, exotic drink mania when I return. But my feeling now is that that won't happen, because I can't handle all the preservatives and artificial everything probably after one and a half years of all natural. I think it'll be more along the lines of a nice thick Bass ale, corn on the cob, and a cheese steak sandwich (i.e., fulfilling substances other than rice). But Pizza Hut is definitely part of the program, even if it does make me throw up... and a raisin bran muffin from Dunkin Donuts (but no donuts), and a lobster and shrimp cookout at Bry's... ooh ooh... okay, I'll stop now before I start drooling on your letter. But actually, today being my birthday, I broke out the cheese mom sent me and cooked up some beans and tortillas, and will have it with my bottle of Bailey's that Aunt Doris sent me- HO! I love Madagascar customs, they are not too good at their job- very beneficial for me.

Diane Holt actually sent me little bottles of vodka and Kahlua, too- the size they serve on airplanes. (I couldn't wait for my birthday to drink it...much as I tried.) So I'm doing fine in the nutrition section with a special treat here and there.

Aunt Lorraine sent me a "greengos", a little man's head (not real, mind you) filled with grass seeds; when I water it, it grows hair. That's a kick in a village in a third world country. I never knew a head of grass could bring so much happiness.

Hey you guys, I have to tell you thanks for the soccer ball. I can't tell you how happy you have made the young men in my village.

I'm off to Fort Dauphin today, on the southeast tip of the island. Kirsten and I got verified by the Peace Corps to go see the national park down there (all work related, mind you) to get ideas to put our own ecomuseum together. The Peace Corps car is taking us, so we'll get to see the road from here down, which'll mean I've seen almost the whole island stretch. (I'm glad we're not flying.) So it'll be fun, and we'll likely see some of our other PCV buddies while we're there.

Well all, I love you. I'll write again soon.

Love, Nance

March 29, 1996

Hi ya', Mom!

Get this. It's my birthday today, and I was hangin' out in my village drinking a bit of Aunt Doris' Bailey's and indulging in the cheese you sent a while back, when the Peace Corps van arrived in my village to get me. Marc, the chauffeur said he came to get me 'cause our director, Therese, verified my trip to go to Fort Dauphin in the south to see Berenty Nat'l Parc (all work related you understand) with Kirsten. When I got to town, there's a birthday card from Denise and also a box from you! It took a while to get to me, 'cause it got stuck in Tana for a bit, but what awesome timing! I just got back from dinner with Roland and Kirsten and Marc. I then opened my box from you to find incredible chocolate-covered peanuts and cookies and other snacks, which I may restrain myself from 'til tomorrow to open. I think I'm going to be on a major sugar high from the chocolate. It may be enough to keep me awake to see the comet that is in the sky here. (People have seen it at about 3 a.m.) So thanks, Mom. You made my birthday. I was going to do a camp-fire party with all the people from the park office. But we're all tired, so we decided to do it tomorrow. Anyway, one-half of my birthday is tomorrow since the U.S. is eight-hours behind Madagascar time. Happy girl! So, Mom thanks for loving me so much. It's nice because sometimes I feel like your arms are reaching out to hold me from half way around the world. I never really feel totally alone here. I never dreamed I'd have so much support.

By the way, awesome timing on the world map...in a couple weeks we're starting to do a world map painting (the kids in Bereketa) on the wall in the school. I think they and I will learn so much from it.

Some older people watched me color a small version of the map yesterday. They started asking many questions, (come to find out, they never realized there are other planets, and other moons and that we revolve around the sun. They thought the sun revolved around us. They had thought that was all just a story, Mom!) I'm so glad I have my star field guide here. It made it all real for them to see photos. Everyone was so fascinated when I explained how the bright star by the moon each night is Venus.

That night three of the six people I had talked to came to me and said, "Hey Nance, there's Venus." It was thrilling to teach them something so important. I'm sure it will happen many times over as we paint our map. I guess there is a lot I can teach them, after all!

Well, Mom, I'm off to Fort Dauphin. Know that I love you. I'll be looking for the two more tablecloths for Aunt Doris.

Love, Nancy

Twenty-Five

No! No! No!

April 9, 1996

5:25 p.m. the telephone rang.

"Mrs. Coutu, this is Mark Gearon, Director of Peace Corps in Washington D.C."

"Mrs. Coutu, I regret to inform you that your daughter Nancy is dead."

I flew to New Hampshire the next morning and U.S. Air was kind enough to put me in first class. Donna arrived the following day from England.

Roger and Paula opened their home for all our family to gather to receive and make calls to Washington. We gathered there because we could all hear their speakerphone at the same time. Roger also had two lines, which made it possible to call out while also talking on the phone with Pam (our Washington mediator).

The calls from Washington were only a few a day at first. The family gathered around the phone each time a call came in.

Twenty-Six

The Murder of Nancy Coutu

The details of Nancy's murder slowly unfolded. Bob Freedmen, the Madagascar Director, informed Pam Palmer that it appeared that Nancy was murdered and then raped. It looked like she was dead before she was raped, for there was no sign of a struggle on the ground. It also looked like there were three at the scene.

Information was painfully slow in coming. We were told that the villagers stayed with Nancy all night that first night, which is their custom and it was greatly appreciated. It also took more than twenty-four hours to arrange to transport her to another village where a plane could land to transport her to the

244

capital city. Arrangements were also being made to send Nancy home to New Hampshire.

On the fourth day, again, Bob reported the three murderers had been captured. Two of them were villagers (one thought to be her friend). The actual murderer was a cattle trader who had gone into the village for the after-Easter celebration. The cattle trader was maybe one of the gunman from last month. Not much more was known at that time.

Another message from Bob and Pam announced that the cattle traders sent the two villagers to ask Nancy to have sex with him and he would pay her. She, of course, said "No".

It was learned later that, during the night while everyone was celebrating Jesus's resurrection, the three had borrowed two axes and one spear. They were needed for hunting, they told the neighbors.

Nancy, who now felt safe in her village, must have been telling the villagers that she had to leave at 4 a.m. to go on her bike to a meeting with Joe and Kirsten. She got a little sleep and got up and on her way at 4:00, as she had planned.

2 km. from her village, she was hit with a hard blow to the back of the head with an axe, which appeared to have killed her instantly. This took place about at a spot where the road was all sand and it was apparent where she would have had to get off her bike to walk in the sand for a bit.

This was an unbearable report for the family to listen to. Tears flowed in abundance from everyone.

Twenty-Seven

Kirsten' s and Joe's Letters

Nancy's friends, Peace Corps Volunteers Joe and Kirsten, learned what had happened to Nancy. These letters answered many of our questions and filled in many gaps. It was much easier knowing what happened than wondering and imagining what took place. Although they were hard to write, they were more than welcomed by the family.

June 29, 1996

Dear Connie,

This will be the first letter of any length I have written since Nancy's death. I recently received a letter from my mother explaining that you would like me to write and tell you what happened...I hope in writing to you now that I will not be reopening the wounds, but rather helping them to heal more permanently. I think the only way to tell you anything is to tell my story, what I went through, everything I remember. It is an event which I will never forget for the rest of my life.

Nancy and Kirsten and the driver, Marc, had just returned from Ft. Dauphin, where Kirsten told me they had had a wonderful time. Strangely enough, I had not seen Nancy in almost a month and I didn t see her then, either. We had been missing each other on our respective trips into Ranohira, and I was greatly looking forward to seeing her, as she was supposed to come to my village on Tuesday with the Development Team to set up a village association. So Tuesday, April 9th, Kirsten arrived with the Development Team sometime in the late morning and said Nancy had decided to ride out to her village to celebrate Easter Monday, which is our Easter Sunday here, and that she was supposed to arrive early on Tuesday morning, but had not. Kirsten and Marc drove out of Ranohira seeing if she was perhaps running a little late. They eventually decided that she had probably been too tired to make the trip so early in the morning and was just running late. I would like to add at this point that riding out of our village at early morning and not showing up on the right day were not unusual for Nancy and me. We kept our own schedules and rode into town early in the morning to avoid the heat of the day.

So Kirsten and the Development Team were getting ready to leave my village at about 3 p.m. when one of the park motorcycles arrived and asked us to step inside for a moment. He told us that Nancy had been killed by someone in the forest south of her village. We had to get him to repeat this three or four times as we couldn't believe what was happening- we thought we must be missing something in the translation. We called Peace Corps on the radio in my house, and they told us to get to Ranohira quickly. When we arrived in Ranohira, Peace Corps told us that we needed to identify the body 100% before notifying you and Nancy's father. Kirsten and I suggested that one of us should go to identify and one of us should stay in Ranohira to keep radio communication open. Kirsten left town at about 5 p.m. to go to Nancy while I took information which would tell me what to do in any contingency. I also asked around and found out that word had reached the office around 1 p.m. The park director, Charles, had gathered the doctor, the mayor, and the police, and had driven out toward Bereketa immediately and had sent the motorcycle to get us. They also made the original report to Peace Corps by radio.

Kirsten arrived back in Ranohira and made her report to Peace Corps at about 9 p.m. That about 2 km. south of Bereketa, three people approached Nancy, she had gotten off her bike and walked for a short while, at which point she had dropped her bike, there seemed to have been a short scuffle, and that she had been raped and killed. But even at that point I did not hear a firm statement on whether or not she was already unconscious before the rape had occurred. I'm not sure, in fact, I'm certain, that we'll never know for sure. I can tell you from the expression on her face, it appeared that she had been unconscious when she died - her face looked rather peaceful, as if she was sleeping.

So back in Ranohira, we made arrangements to hold a wake. Strangely enough, Kirsten and Nancy had talked the week before about what they wanted when they died. Nancy loved the Malagasy tradition of singing all night and Nancy told Kirsten that she wanted this done for her - and so we did. We went to talk to a friend of hers who had lived in Bereketa as a Protestant catachyst and he agreed to help with a service. A bunch of young people from Ranohira and most of the park staff stayed up all night with us. I cried when one of the park staff read the 23rd Psalm in Malagache and then in English. It was really an incredibly moving and spiritual experience for me.Everything was as it should have been. A bunch of guys played cards off to one side. People drank coffee and rum served by some of the women. A drunk guy showed up who had once been a representative of the church but who had been kicked out of the clergy for drinking. But he knew every hymn and sang at the top of his lungs. Meanwhile one of the park staff tied things onto his belt loops as a joke and everyone laughed as he got up and dragged sticks etc. with him tied to his belt loops. It provided the much needed comic relief. The rest of us sang and wept, and listened to the words of Joelson, the young catachyst as he comforted us with his strong and steady voice.

The next morning at about 4:30, we left Ranohira for Ihosy in order to pick up Rory, Dr. Peter, and some American and Malagasy officials from the airport. We then picked up several people in Ranohira and dropped by the Relais de la Reine Hotel. The owner, Gilberte Columbie, was a friend of Nancy's, and had come by the night before to offer any assistance he could give, so we asked to use his car. Marc, his son, drove out to Bereketa with us. Finally we passed through a small forest and came out on the other side, about 2 km. south of Nancy's village, and I saw an incredible and sad familiar scene. A couple hundred people, the population of Bereketa, was huddled to one side of a small canopy of lamba, the colorful skirt material people use here, which covered the place where Nancy lay. I noticed an enormous pot of rice over smouldering fires nearby. Everyone's faces were wet with tears. I want to express somehow what this scene means to the Malagasy. They were treating the situation exactly as they would have had it been someone of the village who had been killed. It is difficult to express what a tremendous compliment this is and the accomplishment it represents. Volunteers like Nancy and myself strove to integrate ourselves into our communities, to be a part of their daily lives. It was so incredibly touching seeing everyone there. I walked over to the crowd and sat down with them. An older man who had once visited my village, who was a good friend of Nancy's, came over and sat next to me. He was weeping, and he said, "Oh Joe, something terrible has happened here." I looked around and saw people I knew, like Jardinier, Nancy's landlord, and her young friends who I had met only briefly in my trips to Bereketa. An elder then approached Kirsten and gave her an envelope with money in it - it is customary for the attendees of a funeral to give the family small gifts of money, as it is tradition for the family to pay for funeral expenses such as food and coffee, etc. which the village had provided.

At one point, Dr.Peter, who had been working with Nancy's body, asked us to get some flowers.It so happened that five young girls had come and sat around me with beautiful bouquets of incredible purple-blue flowers. I asked them to give them to Dr. Peter. They got up and stood in a line and presented their flowers. It was so cute and touching. Finally, the village leader stood up and said that it was finally time to say goodbye to Nancy and that all who wished could form a line and pass by Nancy's body. I got up with Joelson and Kirsten, and the three of us walked arm in arm in line with the entire village. I felt my body almost too weak to walk. I couldn't stop saying Nancy's name as I passed by her. Dr. Peter had placed her in a silver-grey body bag with her head visible. He had cleaned up her face and had arranged the blue flowers all around her face. It was beautiful and terrible all at the same time. We sat back down with the villagers. I'd like to also note that before we had walked around Nancy, I had tried to get people to sing to fill the silence, but after two lines of song, everyone was crying so hard they couldn't sing. Once we had sat back down, I addressed the people. I said that volunteers like Nancy are incredibly lucky because they have two families, one in the U.S. and one here in Madagascar. I said that the people of Bereketa had been her brothers and sisters for 1 1/2 years. Now we had to take her back to her other family so that burial customs could be carried out there. I thanked them for taking care of her and said goodbye. There was a brief response from an elder, then we carried the stretcher into the Peace Corps car and drove back to Ranohira.

At Ranohira, we held a brief wake at the city hall. I think most of Ranohira showed up. So many friends. There were so many people your daughter touched in such a meaningful and special way. Soon afterward, they drove Nancy's body back to Ihosy to fly up to Tana. Kirsten, Marc (the driver), and I drove to Toliar and met up with Roland. We flew to Tana the next day. I was so relieved to be out of the Isalo area. It was good to see all the other volunteers. Peace Corps had set up a bunkhouse for all of us to stay in. We talked, told stories about Nancy, we mourned, we cried a lot. I can really remember everyone's face for the first time I saw each one of them. So sad, so lost. The next couple of days seemed to blur into one for me now. Friday the twelfth was the service at the airport. This was probably the most therapeutic for me of all the services. I cried hard. It was the first time that I had not had to deal with any of the logistics of the ceremony. The ambassador spoke- then the foreign minister, who presented the Ordre National, and so Nancy became a KNIGHT. I held Linda Lyon and Theresa Gloacki and Kirsten Leong, and we all had group hugs in the midst of our incredible sobbing. We all stayed long after the service was over. We each went forward and said goodbye in person. Then Bob said goodbye and boarded the plane to go to the United States with Nancy. Somehow I felt a great weight lifted for me at this point. I had finally released all the incredible grief that had been bottled up inside of me for the last few days. I think it was Saturday night that I finally crashed hard. We had had dinner at Theresa's house. The next night after dinner, Anna Prow brought everyone around a camp fire saying that we would tell Nancy stories. "So join around, and if you knew Nancy, share a story with all of us, if you didn't know her, get to know her. And the stories began. All so funny, so full of life. During the stories, I can remember Anna saying, "This is such a neat life". I think she felt what I did- she felt Nancy. Nancy was with us strongly that evening, as tangibly as if she had been there in person. Another volunteer, Paige Panzner, later said, "There was so much love going around that campfire." And it was so true. It was Nancy's love. Volunteers who had not known Nancy left that evening feeling as if they now knew her. We finished off the evening with guitar playing and s'mores with real marshmallows. It was truly one of the most special evenings of my life. A real celebration of life and an undying spirit.

The final service was the next day at the Ambassador's residence. Kirsten and I spoke, and David played a beautiful song that he had written in memory of Nancy. Several other people spoke, songs were sung, and Karen Black read a poem about Nancy. It was finished with the planting of a tree in her memory. It was a beautiful service on a beautiful day. A Malagasy person attending the funeral asked later if this beautiful service was normal for American funerals, and we responded, "No, this was a very special ceremony for a very special person."

From there, the rest seems logistical. We began the process of moving on and trying to reconstruct our lives. Some of the volunteers decided to go home, others changed sites, others returned to their sites from before. I was happy to hear the criminals had been caught and that they have now been convicted.

I know there is probably nothing I can do to ease your pain. Believe me, that Nancy was like a sister to me and that not a day goes by that I don't think of her. I often get a tear in my eye and sometimes start crying and I get very confused, wondering how such a terrible thing could happen to such a wonderful person. If it will help you any, I know in my heart that nothing could have prevented this. There was no way any of us could have fore-seen what would happen, myself, anyone, the Peace Corps staff members. The only ones to blame are the evil men who did this.

I hope that this letter can somehow help to ease your pain.

With all my love, Joe
May 13, 1997

July 23, 1996

Dear Connie,

My dad is visiting now and we are passing through the Isalo region. We moved out of the villages here in May and it is strange to be back. I have been recounting stories to Dad and, of course, many of them included Nancy.

Anything I could write to you about Nancy would be total-ly inadequate. You knew her better than I could have in only a year, but there are some things about her time here in Madagascar that I thought would be important for you to know, aside from the usual.

She loved her village and was glad she had chosen Madagascar over the Seychelles. She had made the right deci-sion to go into the Peace Corps.

I feel like, so often many of these statements get idealized after the fact. Yes, she did love her village, but it wasn't always easy. There were many nights that we would sit in my hut and talk for hours about what we were doing here, how sometimes things were frustrating. There were many days that were hard to face.

The week before Easter, Nancy, my counterpart, Mamy, and myself went to Fort Dauphin to look at the museum at Berenty as a model example for our interpretive Center. It was technical-ly my project, but we got the o.k. for Nancy to go along because she said she'd help with exhibits.

It was probably the best week we ever spent together and things just seemed to click into place. She seemed very at peace with herself and really happy to be in Madagascar. I think all of us on the trip felt it, not from just her, but as a group. I guess it was one of those road trip experiences that is not easily replaced. I thought it would be important for you to know that one of her last times here was one of her best times.

The post-Easter celebrations here are very big. Nancy went to Bereketa because she really missed being there. She wanted to celebrate the joy she felt in her village, where she felt she belonged.

There was also a celebration in Ranohira where I was.

Strangely enough, on our trip to Ft. Dauphin, Nancy and I discussed funerals. There are a lot of tombs of various types. Some had elaborate carvings of stonework. This caused us to start talking of burial rituals and how in the states it is so depressing. She said she really preferred the Malagashe tradition where everyone stays up all night and sings and drinks coffee and toaka gasy. She also mentioned that she thought this would be an effective way to help grieving people deal. Your body gets so messed up that your head gets distracted from the grief.

Well, she was right. Joe and I held a traditional wake, Malagasy style, in Ranohira even though she was still in Bereketa. We were sure the villagers in Bereketa were doing the same. The hymns and the harmony were really beautiful and the whole experience became somewhat timeless and other worldly.

I don t know if this helps but I wanted you to be able to see that people here do care and to know the degree to which Nancy touched our lives.

Love, Kirsten

Twenty-Eight

Coming Home

In Madagascar five services were held for Nancy. It was apparent that she was well loved.

Excerpts from articles in the Midi Newspaper in Madagascar:

April 13, 1996

Yesterday a touching ceremony took place at Ivato Airport, Madagascar before Nancy was repatriated.

Dignitarie attend ceremony in honor of Nancy.

A private room accommodated a gathering of President of Madagascar, Richard Andrianmanjato, Secretary General, Copertino Razafindrabe, American Ambassador Vicki Huddleston, Peace Corps Director Robert Freedman the country's Peace Corps Volunteer, ANGAP volunteers and American and Malagashe dignitaries. At that time, Nancy was Knighted posthumously. She was decorated as Chevalier de l'Ordre National to be known as Lady Nancy.

Presentation of Knight medal for Lady Nancy

On day five, Bob Friedman (the Peace Corps director in Madagascar) and Nancy were on a plane. With the changes it took three days to reach New Hampshire. (Thank you, Bob, for all you did.)

There was a one-night wake that was done as Nancy had talked about to just about everyone. Per Nancy's will, the only ones to see her were Mom and Dad. There was a twelve-inch door that allowed viewing of her face. Each of her parents viewed her privately.

I wanted to-had to do this but spent much thought and fear the night before of what I would see. As I stood in front of the coffin, said a prayer, took a deep breath and I slowly opened the viewing door. She was wrapped in a sheet, which I promised I would not move.

What a pleasant surprise! Her face wore a look of tranquility and, of course, love. She looked like Cinderella waiting for her handsome price to kiss and awaken her. Oh God! That he could!

I whispered, "I love you my beautiful child. I'll hold you in my heart until we meet in heaven where you will be jumping up and down yelling, Mom! Mom! I thank God I was chosen to be your mom."

Friends of all seven Coutu's were beginning to arrive with great Nancy stories to tell. There was much laughter and a sad kind of fun.

Dan had set up a slide show of Nancy and her Coutu family life. Connie had an album of Madagascar pictures which was intended as a gift to Nancy when she came home.

The funeral was held April 16, 1999, and was attended by over two hundred dignitaries, friends and relatives. Pierrot Rajaonarivelo the Madagascar ambassador to the United States offered condolences. He placed a proclamation and medal on her rosewood coffin that was draped with an American flag and named her Knight of Madagascar National Order, thus Lady Nancy. This was the highest honor ever bestowed by that government on a foreigner or a woman. In that country, women are not held in very high esteem so this was an especially great honor.

That night family and friends gathered around the piano for a singalong. Dan played. Nancy was certainly with us.

The name Nancy Coutu will forever be remembered in my country, The Ambassador said. Marc Gearan, director of the Peace Corps in Washington D.C., praised and gave tribute to Nancy's many accomplishments in her short time in Madagascar.

The family was together for three weeks. It was time for Connie to return to Florida and mourn with her "pen pals". It was also time for Donna to return to England to mourn with her family.

May, 1996

Nancy was cremated per order of her will. Some time later the family and a few close friends went to the Pemigewasset River. Some swam in the rain for a while.

Bryan finally said, "It's time to let Nancy go". He gave a wonderful, loving talk about his sister and passed the urn around for anyone who wished to say a final goodbye to Nancy. When the urn was given to Connie, she said goodbye to her loving daughter and then she and Roger released her ashes into he river. Ironically, this was done at the foot of Mt. Nancy.

Group getting ready to venture to the Pemigewasset
River in New Hampshire.

We had to use a rope to cross this strong river.

Roger and Connie release Nancy's ashes.

Dan and Andrea after we realeased Nancy's ashes.

Twenty-Nine

A Murderer Escapes and is Recaptured

August 5, 1997

I received a call from Pam Palmer in Washington, DC. "Connie, I've got very disturbing news for you. Sombila, Nancy's murderer, has escaped from prison."

"How did he get out?" My body went stiff.

"We don't know yet. A hunt is being organized, but we don't have much information yet. You know how long it takes for word to come through," replied Pam.

"We'll have to offer a reward for information that leads to his recapture. I guess having cows in Madagascar can buy you almost anything. Since $1.00 is worth 4303 francs and since most are so poor, a reward should help to get that @#!&@ back into jail. He should have been shot. I'm so mad at their government for changing his sentence," I fumed.

"I know," Pam replied, "I will get back to you as soon as I have more word on what is happening. Information is in short supply right now.

July 23, 1997

A report from The American Embassy contained the following information: The daily Malagasy newspaper Midi ran a headline story on Monday, August 4, 1997 reporting that one of the three men convicted of the murder of PCV Nancy Coutu had escaped from the prison at Nosy Lava.

The escapee, Sombila, was the individual who paid the other assailants for the attack against Ms. Coutu. Sombila escaped with another inmate who was imprisoned for reasons unrelated to the Coutu murder. Sombila and Charles Raharison, known for the latters previous evasion, fled from the prison. It is worth mentioning that he was the only prisoner whose two legs were permanently imprisoned in a bench of wood.

This served as a reminder of his previous escape. The reporter had seen him in this bench wood when visiting the prison for another story in 1995.

The three reporters who visited the prison to do a story on the condition of the prison were surprised that the two escapees took advantage of the absenteeism of the warden.

Nosy Lava Prison is situated approximately 10 klms. from the Malagasy coast. Although not the harshest of Madagascar's notoriously overcrowded and poorly run penal institutions, its distance from the coast had given it the reputation of being the Alcatraz of Madagascar.

According to the midi story, the three reporters had been in the prison to interview prisoners on July 26th. The reporters spoke to the three individuals convicted of Ms. Coutu's murder. However, when preparing to leave the island on July 28th, they were advised by villagers to avoid traveling through an area near the prison for fear that the escaped criminals were in the immediate area.

(Many thanks go to the reporter, Nary, and his companions. Sombila might still be free if it were not for you. Thank you. Thank you. It is unclear if the embassy learned of the escape by this article, or if they were notified. In any event they had no knowledge of this until August 4, 1997 - one week late.)

Many meetings took place with top Malagashe and American officials. Peace Corps offered a 1,000,000 fmg reward ($500). 1000+ posters were put up throughout the country. There were TV interviews and one-fourth page ads in the three Madagascar newspapers.

October 20, 1997

From John Reddy to Pam Palmer.

Here's a Sombila update. Charles, the prisoner who escaped with Sombila, was recaptured some 3-4 weeks ago. The two gendarmes, who have been assigned to work with the Embassy and PC, went with two PC vehicles and a couple of gendarme guards to Antsohihy, where Charles was being held. They took him to Nosy Lava prison and started retracing the escape. They found out some rather disturbing things in their three days in Nosy Lava and then on their trip down to Tana.

From talking to Charles, the other prisoner, prison officials and guards, they learned: Sombila was not wearing chains on his arms and legs, as he should have been. He was given free reign of the island during the day and was only confined to the courtyard at night - he was not kept in his cell. He also appeared to have armed himself with some kind of baton and rock instrument that he used to threaten others. Charles was in stocks and was kept in the cell he was supposed to share with Sombila. Charles had harsher treatment because of his seven previous escapes from prisons.

Free to roam the island during the day, Sombila scouted around and found the pirogue (dugout canoe) he wanted to steal. On the night of July 27, he was not confined to his cell. He helped Charles get out of the cell, broke the shackles off Charles, and with a third guy, jumped on an outhouse, swung onto a tree and dropped down outside the courtyard.

After walking a couple of kilometers, the third escapee turned back. Charles and Sombila stole the pirogue, paddled to the mainland and smashed the pirogue so that it would sink.

They walked north to the town of Ambolobozo where they robbed a house of 400,000 franc and some jewelry. They now had money to travel to the southwest coast. Here Charles left Sombila.

The gendarmes learned that, contrary to the account given to James Knight of the Embassy and contrary to the Ministry of Justice report, no one started looking for the pirogue for two days and no bulletin of the escape was put out for at least one week. In other words, when the alert was given, it was about the same day the first newspaper article appeared. The alert was not given out until August 4, the same day that the article came out in the paper. It appeared that we have been lied to by the prison bureau and low levels of the Ministry of Justice from day one.

The good news is that this gendarme team seems to be uncovering the truth and that Charles is cooperating with them, because they have been able to collaborate his story. Also, the prison director and the chef du poste have been thrown in jail, so now there are four Nosy Lava officials and guards in jail. When the gendarmes were in Nosy Lava, they did a head count of all prisoners. There are 180 prisoners on the books of the prison, but only 130 could be found for the count: fifty prisoners are missing from the island prison.

November, 1997

The state departments received this report from Ambassador Huddleston and forwarded it to the family:

We are now nearly four months from the escape from Nosy Lava Prison of Sombila. During this period, we and the Malagasy authorities have mounted an intensified effort ranging from the extreme northern City of Diego Suarez to the near desert regions of the far south. Part of this report deals with results of gendarme's operations conducted in the south, based on the information provided by Sombila's fellow escapee, Charles Raharison. Charles subsequently admitted that his story to the gendarmes was largely fabricated. He and Sombila split up while still in the far north shortly after the escape.

Charles never had specific information on Sombila's whereabouts. He hoped that the gendarmes might get lucky if he urged them to Sombila's home area - and that he might be able to avoid being sent back to Nosy Lava Prison, where he expected exceptionally harsh treatment for escaping. However, there might be a silver lining in Raharison's fairy tale: gendarmes in the south discovered a letter in the possession of Sombila's family indicating that he was seeking contact with a military officer he knew in Diego Suarez. The gendarme team from Tana has departed for Diego in a Peace Corps vehicles to follow up on this lead.

January 1, 1998

Report from John Reddy relayed by Pam:

We are running out of leads on the Sombila investigation. The last sighting of Sombila was in the Snakarana Reserve in nothern Madagascar. He was thought, at that time, to be digging for sapphires illegally, along with about 15,000 others, in the fature reserve. The gendarmes questioned Commandant

Zeze in Diego about his knowledge of Sombila's whereabouts. He lied that he knew nothing and then disappeared for several days, during which time he could have tipped off Sombila.

Zeze is now being charged as a criminal, which is good news, but he seems in no hurry to inform on his friend Sombila.

We have two ideas:

1) double the reward from 5,000,000 FMG to 10,000,000 FMG and
2) redo the poster, highlighting the photo that Art Rehkemper, inspector general in Washington, sent us.

We would send in a vehicle to the entire area around Ankarana and plaster the new reward poster all over. This would also show the Coutu family that we have not forgotten the escape as 1998 begins.

That same day, John received authorization to go ahead with this plan.

February, 1998

Pam received a report from Howard Perlow and Ambassador Huddleston. This was passed on to the family.

"On the evening of January 31, the embassy duty officer received a telephone call from the office of the prefecture, in the northeastern city of Maroantsetra, informing her that Sombila had been captured in a well-executed operation outside the city. The information was subsequently confirmed late that evening by a telephone call to the charge from General Bory, the secretary of state for the gendarmerie."

Sombila was captured.

Graditude Has No Limits

This is the exact report that came via Pam in Washington, D.C.

February 6, 1998

From: John A Reddy, CD/Madagascar (the new director)
Subject: Sombila update

On February 5th, RSO Bob Murray, Embassy Administrator Sam Rubino, APCD/Admin Nancy Gehron and I had a two-hour debriefing with Commandant Rasolofo, our main gendarmes contact these last six months, on the interrogation of Sombila by the gendarmes. He began by saying that the gendarmes have now transferred Sombila to Tsiafahy prison, about 20 kilometers outside contact of Tana. Sombila has his own cell with toilet, so there is no need for him to mix with the general prison population. The new director of the prison is reportedly very good. Despite the fact that there have been escapes from Tsiafahy in years past, we are guardedly optimistic that Sombila will be better watched over than he was at Nosy Lava, if for no other reason, so that the authorities never have to deal with the American government again.

Sombila verified the general details of his escape with Charles in July. He added the fact that he had bought alcohol for the chef du poste of the prison (now in jail) who got drunk, abandoned his post and went home to bed, allowing Sombila to open the main gate, spring Charles and jump the fence. They did not leave through the open gate for fear of being seen. They stole the piroque, made it to the mainland and to the town of Ambolobozo, where Charles left Sombila to go rob a house, promising to return. That was the last time Sombila saw Charles, who did rob the house and then took off for Port Berge, abandoning Sombila. He still carries a grudge. 90% of the story that Charles told the gendarmes when he was captured was fiction.

Sombila then went alone to Analalava and hopped a truck up North towards Diego. About an hour's drive from Diego he got a job working in sugar cane fields and stayed there for a month or so to earn money. Sometime in late September-early October he left the sugar cane fields for the town of Diego, where he looked up his old acquaintance Commandant Zeze, who owed him money from their time in prison together in Tana. He stayed two nights at Zeze's house, during which time he dictated the letter to Zeze that the authorities found in the South during their big sweep last October-November. Zeze lied to Sombila that he had given the money to someone else, but Zeze did lend Sombila 20,000 francs and then took him to the house of Mme. LaRomaine, who rented him a room.

Sombila remained in Diego for the next few months selling charcoal around town, unrecognized by anybody. Sombila was in Diego during the time of Commandant Rasolofo's first expedition there (November 8-19) and would have been arrested then, if Zeze had not lied to the investigators.

On January 7th, 1998, for reasons we don't know, Sombila left Diego and walked and took a bush taxi to Maroantsetra. He arrived there by January 13th, because on that day he sent a coded radio message from the port of Maroantsetra to the port of Morombe (near his home). The message read:

From Roger of the Nirisoa Bar in Maroantsetra to Mr. Honore, son of Raso. I inform you that the son of Roger has died in Maroantsetra. Send 1,500,000 Fmg. Also Honore, please come to the Morombe radio to talk to Roger. The same day, Sombila sent a registered letter to Honore in Morombe asking for money, and he kept the receipt.

The radio message was delivered to Honore's house. He was not home, so his wife read it, found it suspicious, and went to the gendarmes. Rasolofo says that this was one of the payoffs of the expedition to the South when the gendarmes had talked to Honore, a friend and neighbor of Sombila and his wife, all of Sombila's family and many others, and told them that Sombila was going to be captured and that they should cooperate with the gendarmes. They all, family members included, said that Sombila had shamed them with his murderous act and that he was now a lost son whom they would not protect. The gendarmes questioned Honore, his wife and Sombila's cousin, Roger. They told the gendarmes that they knew no one in Maroantsetra and thought that the message was from Sombila, because Nirisoa is the name of Sombila's son and Sombila owns a Bar Nirisoa in his home town. The gendarmes in Morombe radioed the information to Tana on January 19 and, on January 21, Tana radioed the information and instructions to the gendarmerie in Maroantsetra. The gendarmes in Maroantsetra began a search for Sombila, starting with all the companies that had radios.

Meanwhile, on January 13th, Sombila showed up at the house of a farmer named Velantsoa Bazary, in the woods on the outskirts of Maroantsetra. He said that his name was Roger and that he came from Diego and wanted to settle in Maroantsetra and he asked if Velantsoa could put him up for awhile. He agreed. On the 15th, Sombila left for Ambolamena, the site of gold digging in the forest-about 25 kilometers from Maroantsetra. He wanted to start mining for gold. He returned to Velantsoa's from January 21-24 and then returned to Ambolamena to mine again. Before leaving, however, he threatened Velantsoa that he must never tell anyone that he had a visitor. Velantsoa was nervous, rifled through Sombila's bag and found identity photos and the receipt for the registered letter. He took them to his friend, Cyprien Pledor, a retired gendarme from the area and told him that this weird stranger was staying at his house and he was scared. Cyprien took the photo and receipt to the gendarmes, who were searching the town for Sombila. They recognized him from the photo and made a plan to capture Sombila.

Because Sombila was mining in a very remote, forested area, they were very afraid of him slipping away from them. So, they made up a phony registered letter form and told Velantsoa to take it to Sombila in Ambolamena. He was to tell him that a registered letter had arrived for him from Morombe with money and that Sombila had to come to Maroantsetra, get an ID card and go claim the money. As Velantsoa, Cyprien and the gendarmes walked the 25 kilometers to Ambolamena, crossing three rivers by pirogue. They informed the villagers along the way of what was happening and told them to be vigilant and to watch for the stranger. Then, Velantsoa went by himself to see Sombila, who was very excited about the money and they both started walking back to town. Each time they crossed a river, the pirogue owners hid their pirogues, so that Sombila would not be able to escape back towards Ambolamena.

When Velantsoa and Sombila got close to Maroantsetra, Velantsoa said he was thirsty and suggested they stop for a drink in a bar where the gendarmes were hiding in the back. They sat down in the bar and the villagers, including the women, jumped Sombila.

One villager broke a bottle and stabbed Sombila in the neck while the others pummeled him, until the gendarmes pulled them off and arrested him at 3:30 pm. on Saturday, January 31. We believe that the reward should be divided between Honores wife, Velantsoa Bazary and Cyprien Pledor. We are also debating the idea that some money should be given to Nary, the journalist who broke the story on August 4th, 1997. In my mind, we might never have found out from the prison officials on Nosy Lava that Sombila had escaped, because of the embarrassment, and prison time, it would have, and has, caused them.

The gendarmes are going to go after Commandant Zeze with vigor and the Embassy will be letting the government know that we want to see justice done to Zeze. Let me know if you have any questions. I believe that the Embassy will get a cable out on this by Monday.

Warm regards to all.

All abetting, the escapees were arrested and imprisoned and life went on-without Nancy.

We at home could do nothing more than wait for news and pray. All of you, on the other hand, did incredible investigating throughout the country. We can never express the gratitude we feel.

Thirty
Honoring Nancy

The story and follow up of the murder was on the front page of the Nashua New Hampshire Telegraph for eleven days and was in other papers through the country, on TV and on the internet. There was too much pain to read clearly and hear all the reports during that time. Time has passed and it is now very disturbing to reread some of these stories and find that the spokes person for the Peace Corps in Washington had released for the media that from 1961-1996 only four-teen had been killed in the Peace Corps. I assume that by killed it meant murdered. At a later date I was in Washington and viewed a plaque that had Nancy's name at number 253. I was told that an aver-age of five or six die in services EVERY year. Why isn't this informa-tion given to every new trainee? These are the lives of our loved ones. Maybe they would think, "It could happen to me", and would be con-stantly cautious and not drop their guard, as Nancy did.

May 13, 1997

Dear Coutu's, (from Washington, basically as written.)

Bob Freedman called me this morning and said, "You know that there are a lot of people in Madagascar who loved and admired Nancy and who continue to think of her daily". Bob said the people want to erect monuments for Nancy's memory, one in Ranohira and one in Bereketa.

Bob traveled to Bereketa and visited the school Nancy built. He presented the world map to them, which they loved. When I visited the Peace Corps in Washington, there was a very large world map right outside his office. I told the director he had to take that down and send it to Bereketa to put on the wall of the school. That will make the school complete.

At the park in Ranohira a new Interpretive Center is being built.

A year ago when Ambassador Huddleston had Nancy's Memorial service at her residence, there was a tree planted in Nancy's honor.

A truck load of clothes from an anonymous donor in

Florida had arrived for distribution to the villagers.

We are now seeing how every community Nancy touched has come forth with a meaningful way to honor her. We talked about how far reaching her community is: that it stretches from New Hampshire to Florida to Madagascar.

I hope you are all well. I think of you often.

Fondly, Pam

June 6, 1996

My name is Denise Thompson. I am Nancy Coutu's older sister. I am not sure if you are aware of the situation with Nancy, but I have recently gotten her address book and am reaching out to everyone in it. (Denise went on to tell about the murder.) I will be holding a tree-planting ceremony at my home and a barb-b-q for all those who would like to participate, especially if you are just finding out about this and need to be with us to remember Nancy. We will plant the tree and then anyone can speak or say prayers. She wanted us to celebrate her death as the Malagasy people do, which we'll do.

(In the next 9 months, lawyers prepared the case. In Madagascar, all three were seen as being equally guilty. The three murderers were sentenced to death by a firing squad. It never happened. The sentence was changed to life in prison.)

Everyone helped with this special memorial.

We successfully planted a Japanese Maple
in memory of Nancy.

June 13, 1996
University of Michigan, Ann Arbor, Michigan
Division of Hepetology

This letter appears in most of its entirety:

Dear Roger,

I got to know Nancy over a period of two weeks, when she, Kirsten, and Joe, joined me and my Malagasy students (in the field of zoology) at Isalo National Park. The enclosed photo shows Nancy and my Malagasy students together at the end of the research. I study reptiles and amphibians, and we were making a survey of the Park. We all had a great time together, camping in forests and exploring the canyons.

The research was extremely successful. On one particular day, when Nancy was with me during a climb of Bevato Mountain, she helped collect an especially attractive skink (lizard) with a red tail, and black and white striped head. After further examination back in Michigan, it is clear this specimen is a new undescribed species. We now have three specimens in total, all from Isalo, where it appears to be restricted.

Dr. Raxworthy, his college students, including Nancy

If you and the family agree, I would like to name this species after Nancy, because she helped to catch the first specimen, and also to record her contribution to the island of Madagascar, which she loved so much.

I am writing to ask if the family would like Nancy's name in the classification for it had not yet been classified.

I heard about Nancy's murder while I was still in Madagascar, and was at the Antananarivo Airport during the ceremony held there before she left.

Sincerely, Dr. Christopher J. Raxworthy

Caption: Mabuya, Nancycoutuae (named after Nancy) (Reptilia:squamata:scincidae) from the high plateau (Isalo National Park) of south-central Madagascar.

Thirty-One

More Honors

June 15, 1997

Nancy's brothers, Dan and Bryan set the plaque on a granite stone that was put in place with the help of the park rangers at ElmBrook State Park, West Hopkinton, N.H. The inscription reads:

- Graduated from University of New Hampshire, Wildlife Management
- Park Ranger, Elm Brook Park 1992-93
- Peace Corps Volunteer Awarded Knighthood by the Government of Madagascar for her work 1994-96
- Killed April 9, 1996 helping the people in the village of Bereketa, and the country of Madagascar
- She celebrated life with enthusiasm, gave of herself to all those she met, and brought joy to the lives of all those she knew and loved.

Dan and Bryan setting the plaque which rests on an imposing granite rock.

Immense thanks to David Shepardson, Park Director, along with the rangers, the Army Corps of Engineers, Bryan, Daniel, Denise, all the helpers for the site and the beautiful service, complete with bagpipes. The Memorial was a beautiful tribute to a fallen former Ranger.

July 23, 1997

A Fund-Raising Sky-Diving Event:

"Cheers to those who jumped and will jump.

Led by Roger Coutu, several state legislators and a judge were involved in the Jump for the Nancy Coutu Scholarship Fund at the Pepperell, Ma. Skydiving Center. The event was organized by Representative Loren Jean from N.H.

Together, they've raised about $5,000 at $300 per sponsored pledge for a scholarship, which will be awarded each spring to a graduating Alvirne High School senior in Hudson, NH who has the traits of Nancy Coutu-dedication, helpfulness, and a sense of adventure.

A golf tournament to benefit the scholarship fund was also held.

There is now a perpetual scholarship fund for Alvirne High School and donations are welcome. Send to:

The Nancy Coutu Memorial Fund
C/O Bryan Coutu
P.O. Box1582
Center Harbor, NH 03326

Thirty-Two

The Queen

This Message was received from Department of State:

1. On April 9, 1998 - The second anniversary of Peace Corps/Madagascar volunteer Nancy Coutu's death - her life and work were honored by a daylong round of ceremonies and dedications in Ranohira and Bereketa; the villages where she worked. There events followed, the recapture of her murderer, Sombila, and brought with it a close to this tragedy for both the Peace Corps and the Malagasy Park service.

2. Peace Corps Director, John Reddy (who took Bob Freedman's place,) and the Programmer, Xavier Louis, went to Isalo Park to represent the U.S. mission on April 9th where there were ceremonies honoring Nancy's life and work. There they joined numerous Malagasy officials, including the Secretary-General of the province of Fianarantsoa, the Prefet of Ihorombe, the Director of the National Park of Isalo and other ranking officials of the National Park Service, the Commandant of the Gendarmerie Brigade of Ranohira, the President of the Committee for the development of Isalo, and the Mayor of Ranohira.

3. The day began with the inauguration of a stele at Androtsibe, the site where Nancy was murdered. The stele was carved and erected by the villagers of Bereketa themselves. Malagasy people erect simple stone steles to honor those among their dead whose bodies cannot be buried in a family tomb. During the dedication two flower wreaths were placed at the stele's base.

4. The delegation then went on to Bereketa, the village where Nancy lived for nearly two years. Several hundred villagers were waiting in Bereketa. After the Malagasy flag was raised and the Malagasy National Anthem was sung by all, many individuals spoke to praise Nancy and her work. Each speaker also asked that Peace Corps send another volunteer to Bereketa to continue

Nancy's work. Peace Corps programmer Louis presented the village with sweatshirts - donated by an anonymous Florida company.

5. While school children sang and danced and two groups of traditional musicians played, director Reddy cut the ribbon to inaugurate the four room clinic-now dedicated to Nancy. She initiated the clinic's rehabilitation and convinced ANGAP to provide necessary funds through the committee for the development of Isalo. A zebu bull was sacrificed to honor the dedication. (Malagasy sacrifice zebu on important occasions when they wish to communicate with God and the ancestors). The Bereketa community prayed that God and the ancestors ask Nancy's spirit, now among them, to protect and bless the people of Bereketa and their lands.

6. After the Bereketa ceremonies, the delegation drove on to Ranohira, near the entrance to Isalo National Park. There, hundreds more townspeople stood at attention as the Malagasy and American flags were raised and National Anthems of both countries played. Again there were speeches to honor Nancy and more requests that Peace Corps volunteers return to Isalo. PC director Reddy, The Secretary-General of Fiaanarantsoa Province, The Prefet of Ihorombe, and the Mayor of Ranohira unveiled a monument to Nancy. The marble plaque read:

Nancy Coutu, PC Volunteer, deceased April 9, 1996
Like a Queen Bee, you died and left honey.
The residents of Ranohira and Isalo
Ranohira Faha, 9 April 1998

The delegation then placed two flower wreaths and a traditional priest sprinkled water on the monument while praying that Nancy and God bless the People of the area. Another zebu was sacrificed to conclude the ceremony - and a very moving day.

July 16, 2000

The United States Post Office created a collection of 100 stamps which was entitled, Celebrating Our Country. There was one for each decade from 1900 to 2000. Each stamp was dedicated to an American who gave much to their country.

In the 1960's, President Kennedy created the Peace Corps. The Peace Corps stamp was dedicated to Nancy at a ceremony at Elm Brook Park, Hopkinton, NH.

Peace Corps Stamp

Nancy wrote not long before her death:

Well, I finished the school today - YEAH! A major high for me!! I got three guys to mud the last wall with me this morning and then I painted the windows, doors and trim around each. It's downright beautiful. I was thinking as I was working, how everywhere I've been I leave a pretty scene behind. Every apartment I've been in is freshly painted or stenciled, and every relative/friend of mine has a stained glass or macrame...it's a neat feeling. The villagers will call the school "Souvenirs de Nancy" when I'm gone from here. It's nice to know a mark of my beauty will be left here, too.

The Nancy Coutu Scholarship Fund

The Wild life faculty, Professors John Livaitis, Peter Pekins, and David Olsen, at the University of New Hampshire felt that a student like Nancy did not come along very often and future classes should have the opportunity to hear about her. With the help of a special secretary, Linda Isaacson, the Wildlife alumni were asked to contribute to the development of the Nancy Coutu Scholarship Fund. Also, Mary Ellen Bellhower, in the alumni office has been working with the above professors to procure $10,000 to establish a perpetual scholarship of $450.

Professor John Litviatis hosted a meeting that brought in $5,000. These funds usually go to the Department of Natural Resources to cover miscellaneous expenses. The involved faculty decided to put it into Nancy's scholarship fund. The goal has finally been reached, thanks to so many.

The criteria for the recipient is:

The student must exemplify the character and spirit of Nancy. Students cannot apply for this scholarship, the awardee will be selected based on the opinion of the Wildlife faculty and forwarded to the department chair.

It is nice to know that so many people loved and appreciated this great American as we, her family, do. All that you have done is received with immense gratitude. Thanks to all that have done so much to establish this scholarship and all who contributed. We, the family are so grateful.

Donations can be made to either pertetual scholarship fund.

If you care to make a donation to the University of New Hamshire, donations may be sent to:

The Nancy Coutu Scholarship Fund
UNH Foundation, Inc.
Elliott Alumni Center
9 Edgewood Drive
Durham, NH 03824

Nancy's family and friends have the same desire to perpetuate Nancy's name and her good works. You can send donations for Alvirn High School to:

The Nancy Coutu Memorial Fund
c/o Brian Coutu
P.O.Box 1582
Center Harbor, NH 03226

Donna's (Nancy's sister) rendition of Nancy's village scene depicted into a quilt Donna made.

Francis wrote the recipe for Nancy's life:

A Prayer of Saint Francis of Assisi

Lord, Make me an instrument of Your peace
Where there is hatred, let me sow love,
Where there is injury, pardon,
Where there is doubt, faith,
Where there is dispair, hope,
Where there is darkness, light,
and where there is sadness, joy.
O Divine Master, grant that I may
not so much seek to be consoled,
as to console;
To be understood, as to understand;
To be loved as to love;
For it is in giving that we receive
It is in pardoning that we are pardoned;
And it is in dying that we are born
to eternal life.

John Powell, Nancy's brother-in-law, was not able to come to the United States when Nancy was killed. Like all of us, he loved her very much and wrote this very special poem.

Departure

I didn't want to go, but it started
At the moment of my birth, my departure;
It was arrival and departure
And you had to finish what you started,
You let me go.

I didn't want to go this way
Remembering your pride at those first steps,
Taken in the right direction, but then
You took the hardest step, and let me free
To make my own selection, you let me go.

I didn't want to leave you yet.
I really wasn't ready,
But you never held me back

And you showed through love and kindness

No matter how far I get,

There's always something that binds us.

I didn't want to go this far

To where I cannot hold you;

But now this path's been started

Send me on my way with the love

That's never going to part us,

And let me go.

by John Powell

Lexicon

Places

Ala Lava – forest reserve

Ambuimangg – City where the queen's castle is

Andreamanero – Joe's village

Antananarivo – Capital city of Madagascar

Bereketa – Big Cactus" Nancy's village

Fenetre d'Isalo – rock formation that looked like a window

Fort Dauphin – city for some training and R & R

Hotel de le Reine – Castle like hotel in Ranohira

Ihosy – town

Isalo National Park – where Nancy, Kirsten, & Joe cut trails

Jerama – town

Jhirama – town

Kibale Nat'l Park, Uganda – advanced park training

Lake Naivasha, Kenya – nature preserve

Nosy Be – town near the murderer's prison

Perinier Reserve – a rain forest reserve

Ranohira – Kirsten's village-bordering Isalo Nat'l Park

Ranomafana – camping during training of PCVs

River Fitalana – near Nancy's village

Tana – short for Antnananarivo

Toliar – south west coastal city

Zuma – shopping market

People

Family

Connie Coutu – mom
Roger Coutu – dad
Donna Powell – sister
John – brother-in-law
Alex – nephew
Ryan – nephew
Lauren – Neice
Bryan Coutu – brother
Joanne – sister-in-law
Garrett – nephew
Jesse – neice
Denise Thompson – sister
Leroy – brother-in-law
Caleb – nephew
Dan Coutu – brother
Life long friends – Diane Holt, Andrea Libby, Donna Brown
Dee, What is her last name
Aunts Lorraine and Doris

Government officials

President of Madagascar – Richard Andrianmanjato; (US) Mr. Ambassador to Madagascar
wife – Rose
(US) Ambassador – Vickie Huddleston
Alexandria – daughter
Embassy Administrator – Sam Rubino; (Mad.)
Ambassador to the US – Pierrot Rajaonarivelo; (Mad.)
Secretary General – Copertino Razafindrabe
Attorney General – Charles Raharison
Washington DC Director PC – Mark Gearon
Washington murder corresponent – Pam Palmer
US Attorney General – Howard Perlow

PC Staff and instructors in Madagascar

PC Director In Mad. – Bob Freidman; replaced by Dir. John Reddy

ACPD/Administrator – Nancy Gehron
ROS – Bob Murray

Instructor – Thresa Gloacki, Monsieur Jocelyn, Linda Lyon

Physician--Dr. Boda, Karen Black, Helen, Larry Blake

PC drivers – Parfait and Mr. Marc

Madagascar police – Commandant Rasolofo and Commandant Zeze

Peace Corps Volunteers

Nancy Coutu
Gavin
Kirsten Leong
Gretchen Young
Joe Schaeffer
Jeremy
Anna Prow
Kelly
Benjamin
Linda
Bill
Maryann
Brad
Michelle
Carrie
Mike
Charlie & Bonnie
Mupemba
Chris
Peter
Christine
Rachel
Craig
Roland
Dave
Thor
David
Todd
Eric
Yardei

Villagers

Abodo
Leva
Bota
Narei
Donald
Nata
Dori
Paul
Farana
Rivo
Georgae
Roger
Gredy
Romose
Hoasa
Rosoa
Jardinier
Saban Bota
Jenny
Sabato
Jillian
Sota
Labaro
Xavier

French

aujourd'hui – today
avec – with
Bon annei – Happy New Year

bonjour – good day
charette – towmobile; wagon pulled by bulls
faux pas – social mistake
petite – little
salle de bain – bathroom
taxi brousse – bus
toilette – toilet
tres bien – very good
tres chic – nice looking

Kinds of Lemurs

mouse
indries
brown
oloo
diademed safaka
golden bamboo

Malagashe Vocabulary

afakomaly – the day before yesterday
ANGAP – National Park Service
Bada – dialect spoken in Nancy's village
famadiana – funeral--celebration of the dead
fara fara Fevrier – end of February
fokonolo – yeah! Let's do it!
fomba – culture
godro godro – rice bread
kabosy – Madagascar guitar
kely sisa – just a lttle left
lamba – rectangular cloth--wrap dead in.

mandesa – pilering rice; pounding to remove the husk
mangalatasy – to steal
mannve – homesick
manome – to give
masoandroe – sun-eye of the day
meanatsy – to learn
mehola rice – shaking in a pan to remove husk
miadamila – tired
mofo gasy – rice bread
omby – cow
pangalatsy – thief
pianatsy – student
rareko aho – good night
Reimen Dreny – village elder, president
Rokoto – Nancy's nicname given by villagers
sarabavy – no way--holy cow
taba taba – noise
tiako ravotsy – I like the wind. It's hot here.
tihi – woven mat
tokoa gasy – native made liquor--moonshine
Travaux Publique – highway dept. to repair the road
troka – legumes
valia – string instrument
vazaha – white foreigner
velumo – good bye
zebu – bull